Paint Shop Pro® 9
FOR
DUMMIES®

by David Kay, William "The Ferrett" Steinmetz

WILEY

Wiley Publishing, Inc.

Paint Shop Pro® 9 For Dummies®

Published by
Wiley Publishing, Inc.
111 River Street
Hoboken, NJ 07030-5774

WILEY

About the Authors

David Kay is a writer, an engineer, an artist, and a naturalist who combines professions with the same effectiveness as his favorite business establishment, Acton Muffler, Brake, and Ice Cream (now defunct). Dave has written more than a dozen computer books, by himself or with friends. His other titles include various editions of *Microsoft Works For Windows For Dummies, WordPerfect For Windows For Dummies, Graphics File Formats,* and *The Internet: Complete Reference.*

In his other life, as the Poo-bah of Brightleaf, Dave is a conservation biologist. He and his wife, Katy, and golden retriever, Alex, live in the wilds of Massachusetts. In his spare time, Dave studies animal and human tracking and munches edible wild plants. He also has been known to make strange blobs from molten glass, sing Gilbert and Sullivan choruses in public, and hike in whatever mountains he can get to. He longs to return to New Zealand and track kiwis and hedgehogs in Wanaka. He finds writing about himself in the third person like this quite peculiar and will stop now.

William "The Ferrett" Steinmetz is a freelance Webmaster and editor who helms StarCityGames.com, one of the premier strategy sites for the collectible card game *Magic: The Gathering.* He wrote most of *Internet: The Complete Reference* and has written computer book reviews for Amazon.com and TechSoc.com. The Ferrett lives in Cleveland and is geeky.

Dedication

To the restoration of reason, conscience, and good will in the United States of America and the world. — D.K.

To my wife, Gini. I promised forever. And I mean to keep that, I do. — T.F.

Publisher's Acknowledgments

We're proud of this book; please send us your comments through our online registration form located at www.dummies.com/register/.

Some of the people who helped bring this book to market include the following:

Acquisitions, Editorial, and Media Development

Project Editor: Rebecca Whitney

Acquisitions Editor: Gregory Croy

Technical Editor: Lee Musick

Editorial Manager: Carol Sheehan

Editorial Assistant: Amanda Foxworth

Cartoons: Rich Tennant
 (www.the5thwave.com)

Composition

Project Coordinator: Emily Wichlinski

Layout and Graphics: Carl Byers, Andrea Dahl, Lauren Goddard, Joyce Haughey, Barry Offringa, Heather Ryan

Proofreaders: Laura Albert, Leeann Harney, Jessica Kramer, TECHBOOKS Production Services

Indexer: TECHBOOKS Production Services

Publishing and Editorial for Technology Dummies

Richard Swadley, Vice President and Executive Group Publisher

Andy Cummings, Vice President and Publisher

Mary Bednarek, Executive Acquisitions Director

Mary C. Corder, Editorial Director

Publishing for Consumer Dummies

Diane Graves Steele, Vice President and Publisher

Joyce Pepple, Acquisitions Director

Composition Services

Gerry Fahey, Vice President of Production Services

Debbie Stailey, Director of Composition Services

Contents at a Glance

Table of Contents

Introduction

Congratulations! Brilliant person that you are, you use Paint Shop Pro! Thousands of other brilliant people also use Paint Shop Pro, and for one intelligent reason: It does darned near anything you could want it to do, from fixing photographs to animating Web graphics, and — unlike certain more famous programs — it doesn't set you back a week's salary.

Guided by that same intelligence, you're probably asking yourself "Is a book available that gives me what I want, quickly, without dragging me through a tutorial? One with an attractive yellow-and-black cover so that it doesn't get lost in the clutter on my desk? Preferably cheap?"

Welcome to *Paint Shop Pro 9 For Dummies,* the attractive, inexpensive, yellow-and-black book that lets you get great graphics out of Paint Shop Pro without making you feel like you're going back to school in an attractive, yellow-and-black school bus.

What Can You Do with This Book?

Books are useful, elevating things. Many people use them to elevate their PC monitors, for example. With that fate in mind, *this* book has been created to serve an even higher purpose: to enable you to do the kind of graphics stuff you really want to do. Here's a smattering of what you can do with the help of this book:

- Download photos from a digital camera.
- Fix up fuzzy, poorly exposed, or icky-colored photos.
- Print album pages or other collections of photos.
- Paint, draw, or letter-in all kinds of colors, patterns, and textures.
- Paint like you're using oil paints and canvas.
- Draw using lines and shapes that you can go back and change later.
- Apply cool special effects to photos and drawings.
- Change colors of objects.
- Combine photos with other images.
- Alter the content of photos and other images.
- Remove unwanted relatives from family photos.

✔ Add wanted relatives to Wanted posters.

✔ Retouch unsightly relatives on Wanted posters.

✔ Create transparent and other Web page graphics.

Is This the Book for You?

Is this the Paint Shop Pro book for you? It depends. If, like us, you tend to leave chocolate fingerprints from your bookstore *biscotti* on the books you're browsing, it's definitely yours now.

In addition, this book is for you if

✔ You find most computer books boring or useless

✔ You need solutions rather than lessons

✔ You find parts of Paint Shop Pro 9 confusing

✔ You haven't ever done much with graphics programs

✔ You have used other Windows programs

✔ You need Paint Shop Pro for business or home use

✔ You really like bulleted lists

How Is This Book Organized?

Computer software manuals document features because that's the easiest way to write one: "The File menu presents the following choices. . . ." If features on the File menu exactly matched what you had in mind, that would be great — but how are you to know to use the Clone Brush tool when what you're really looking for is the "Fix Uncle Dave's hair transplant scars" tool?

Some computer books are organized into lessons and teach you how features work. They give you examples of basic tasks and then more complicated ones. Along the way — hopefully, before too long — you find an example that resembles what you had in mind.

This book is organized by different kinds of tasks, like working with photos or painting pictures or adding text. Wherever possible, this book tells you exactly what to do in numbered steps. Wherever that's not possible, it gives you explanations of how things work in nontechnical language.

You don't have to read the book in any order. Just skip to the section or chapter you need. Go right to the index, if you like — or the Rich Tennant cartoons! In detail, this book is organized as described in this section.

Part I: The Basics

This part puts you in the picture and puts your picture in Paint Shop Pro. Chapter 1 puts you in the picture, by explaining how to efficiently find, open, and manage all your graphics files, deal with the peculiarities of different graphics file types, and even convert file types *en masse*. Chapter 2 shows you how to get things oriented and sized they way you want. Chapter 3 shows you all the Paint Shop Pro tricks for selecting exactly the area of interest you want to work on, copy, move, or otherwise enhance. Chapter 4 gives you basic editing tricks: how to copy, move, bend, and resize portions of your image.

Part II: Prettying Up Photographs

When you have an image that needs some sprucing up, Part II is the place to turn. Chapter 5 shows you how to get the image you want into Paint Shop Pro in the first place, whether it's a photograph, a print, or on your PC screen. Chapter 6 shows you how to use the Paint Shop Pro hand tools to brush away wrinkles from portraits, fix scratches, and remove red-eye. Chapter 7 gives you nearly instant ways to correct overall photo-exposure problems, such as bad exposure, poor color, or dim grayish images. Chapter 8 gets into serious adjustment of image quality and content. This part *is* your *Extreme Makeover* part (not to be confused with the part Dave uses for his comb-over).

Part III: Painting Pictures

Part III is for anyone who plans to paint, draw, or otherwise doodle in Paint Shop Pro. Chapter 9 gets you painting, spraying, erasing, and otherwise doing all those basic things that everyday folks have been trying to do with graphics software for years. Chapter 10 is for those who long for some serious support for the digital artist, by giving you ways to get precisely the color, texture, or pattern you need. Chapter 10 also introduces the new Paint Shop Pro Art Media tools, the closest thing to paint and canvas this side of the digital divide. Chapter 11 shows you how to divide images into layers or use layers to combine images. Layers are a powerful tool that make later editing much easier and produce stunning image overlays. Chapter 12 lets you add layers of easily edited text and shapes to your image, by using the Paint Shop Pro vector graphics tools. Chapter 13 shows you how to add artsy effects to your work.

Part IV: Taking It to the Street

All this fooling around in Paint Shop Pro is great, but in the end you probably want your image to appear somewhere else: on a piece of paper, on the Web, or as part of an animation. Chapter 14 shows you how to best fit your image on paper. It also tells you how to print multi-image pages for photo albums, collages, or portfolios. Chapter 15 tells you how to get exactly the image file you want for the Web and gives you tips for getting the fastest-downloading images with the least sacrifice in quality.

Part V: The Part of Tens

Problems often come in threes, so this book tackles them by the tens, just to be sure. Part V has fixes for the ten most-wanted issues that people run into when they try to use Paint Shop Pro. Chapter 16 untangles the ten most common confusions and perplexing problems of Paint Shop Pro, Chapter 17 gives you ten quick fixes for photography problems, and Chapter 18 is an existential conundrum. It tells you about ten topics too advanced to be in this book.

Icons Used in This Book

This icon points out important issues or tidbits of information that you want to be sure to remember. Just remember to look for the Remember icon.

An all-purpose workhorse, this icon offers advice or shortcuts that can make your life a whole lot easier.

Skip over this one if you want. This icon marks geekfest stuff that you don't really need to know, but may find interesting.

Tread lightly when you see this icon because something unpleasant could happen if you proceed without following this cautionary note.

Read on!

(Oh, yes, and please buy the book now. Thanks.)

(If you feel inclined, drop us some e-mail. Dave's at psp@brightleaf.com, and William's at theferrett@theferrett.com. We're just two guys with no special connections to Jasc and no helpers, so we may not be able to answer your questions — but we can try.)

Part I
The Basics

The 5th Wave   By Rich Tennant

SINCE INSTALLING PAINT SHOP PRO 9 THE 4th PRECINCT BECAME NOTED FOR ITS CREATIVE WANTED POSTERS

WANTED   WA   WANTED

"Ooo – look! Sgt. Rodriguez has the felon's head floating in a teacup!"

In this part . . .

When it comes to computer software, nothing is basic. So, it is with some trepidation that we call Part I "The Basics," but, heck — we had to call it something. Here's where to turn when you need more efficient ways (or, for that matter, any way) of finding, opening, and managing image files, viewing images, and making them bigger, smaller, or just plain right side up.

Also fundamental to making any changes to your image is the ability to select certain parts of an image, move it, copy it, and resize or reshape it.

Chapter 1

Opening, Viewing, Managing, and Saving Image Files

Most of the time, images exist as files. Those files may be on a disk, on a digital camera connected to your computer, or on a storage device that looks and acts just like a disk in Windows. This chapter makes you Lord of the Files. It tells you how to open image files, organize those files, and save images as various kinds of files. It also helps you view them in whatever size is convenient for you.

(If you want to open an image that does *not* appear to be stored as a file, see Chapter 5. For example, you may want a picture that appears on your computer screen in a document or a snapshot that needs to be downloaded from your digital camera.)

Images are easy to deal with in small quantities. In large quantities, however, they're challenging to manage. (They're sort of like kids, in that regard.) This chapter tells you about the clever Paint Shop Pro features for keeping an eye on all your graphical progeny, including browsing, previewing, and organizing files in different orders and in different folders.

Image files come in an amazing variety of file types because many software geeks over the years have each decided that they know a much better way of storing an image as a file (a file type). Image files of different types have different multiletter extensions at the end, like .jpg, .png, or .tif. People refer to them by those extensions, saying "jay-peg" or "jay pee gee" for .jpg or "ping file" for .png. These file types sometimes behave differently in Paint Shop Pro, so see the section "Using native and foreign file types," later in this chapter, if someone gives you a file that behaves oddly. Fortunately, although you need to be aware that images come in a variety of file types, most of the time you don't have to give a hoot. Paint Shop Pro can crack open most popular types of image file.

Three Ways to Open Image Files

Paint Shop Pro gives you three ways to open a file:

- **Browsing ("I'll know it when I see it"):** Choose File⇨Browse or press Ctrl+B. The browser window opens, as shown in the following section, in Figure 1-1. You open folders in the left panel and double-click tiny pictures in the right panel to open them.

- **Opening ("I know its name and where it lives"):** Choose File⇨Open; or, click the Open button on the toolbar or press Ctrl+O. The Open dialog box appears, as shown a couple of sections from here, in Figure 1-2.

- **Double-clicking ("There it is — open it"):** If you see a file listed and it displays a Paint Shop Pro icon (a tiny artist's palette), double-click that puppy and Paint Shop Pro should start up and display the image.

That's all you need to know — well, at least most of the time, that's all. The following sections give you some additional tricks and tips for opening files in those three ways.

If you can see the image on your screen, but aren't sure where the image file is, see the section in Chapter 5 about capturing images from your PC screen. Images that appear in a document (a Web page, a Microsoft Word document, or an Adobe Acrobat document, for example) may not be stored as files on your computer. (Or, if they are, they may be very hard to find.) You may need to capture the image off your screen.

For some files, Paint Shop Pro has to translate the image file into a form it can use. Translation may especially be necessary for *vector* image files, such as DXF and WPG. To translate, Paint Shop Pro needs additional information from you: specifically, how many pixels wide and high you want the image to be. See the section "Using Vector File Types (Drawing Files)," later in this chapter, for more information.

Opening, Managing, and Sorting Files with the Browser

We like the Paint Shop Pro browser best for opening files because it also lets you manage them visually. Do one of the following to open the browser:

- ✔ Press Ctrl+B.
- ✔ Click the Browse icon, as shown in the margin. (It's on the Standard toolbar, which runs along the top of the Paint Shop Pro window.)
- ✔ Choose File➪Browse.
- ✔ If the Open dialog box is open already, click the Browse button.

Figure 1-1 shows you the Browse window. To close the window when you're done, choose File➪Close or press Ctrl+F4.

The left side of the Browse window looks and works like Windows Explorer. The right side displays, and helps you manage, image files.

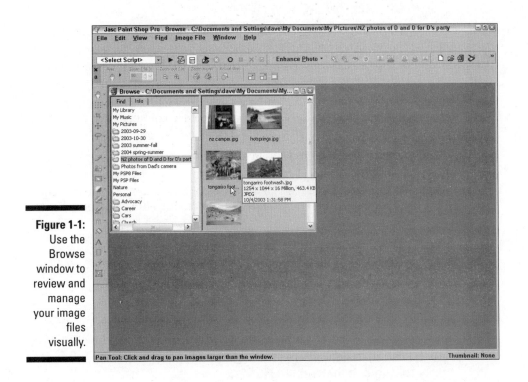

Figure 1-1: Use the Browse window to review and manage your image files visually.

The following list shows you the details for using the folders on the left side (if the Find tab shown in Figure 1-1 isn't displayed, click that tab):

- To see what images a folder holds, click the folder. *Thumbnail* (small) images appear on the right.

- If the folder contains more folders (or *subfolders*), a + sign appears to its left. To see those subfolders, click the + sign.

- To hide those subfolders again, click the – sign that now appears where the + sign did.

Here's how to open and manage files by using the thumbnails on the right side:

- **Open:** Double-click the image.

- **Get image information:** Pause your cursor over any thumbnail, as we did in Figure 1-1. Paint Shop Pro displays basic information near your cursor. For more detail, click the Info tab in the browser's left pane.

- **Rearrange the order that's displayed:** Drag thumbnails where you want them. You can also sort files by name, date, or other criteria. Follow the numbered steps that appear after this list.

- **Move to a different folder:** Drag the thumbnail from the right pane to your destination folder in the left pane.

- **Copy to a different folder:** Drag the thumbnail to another folder while holding the Ctrl key down.

- **Create a new folder:** In the left panel, click the folder in which you want to create a new folder. Choose File⇨Create New Folder, and in the Create New Folder dialog box that appears, type your new folder's name.

- **Delete:** Right-click the file's thumbnail and choose Delete from the menu that appears.

- **Rename:** Right-click the file's thumbnail, choose Rename from the drop-down menu, and enter a new name in the Rename File dialog box that appears.

- **Select several files for opening, moving, copying, or deleting:** Hold down the Ctrl key and click their thumbnail images. To select a series, left-click the first (or last) image; then hold down the Shift key and click the last (or first) image. Follow the instructions in the preceding bullets for opening, moving, copying, or deleting files.

To sort your thumbnails in different ways, follow these steps:

1. **Right-click the blank area to the right of the pictures and choose Sort from the context menu that appears.**

   The Sorting dialog box appears.

2. **Choose A<u>s</u>cending or <u>D</u>escending sort order in the Primary sort order area of the dialog box.**

3. **Choose what to sort by in the Sort Condition selection box: file attributes, such as date, or image attributes, such as dimensions (size).**

4. **To sort within a sort (such as sorting filenames alphabetically within each file date), choose your secondary sort criterion by using the Secondary sort order area of the dialog box. (It works just like the Primary sort order area.)**

5. **Click OK to sort.**

Files from some cameras now contain EXIF data: detailed and technical information for professional photographers about how and when that photograph was taken. The Paint Shop Pro 9 browser now lets you choose to sort on that information in the Sort Conditions selection boxes.

Opening the right file with File⇨Open

If you know the folder where your file lives, the fastest route to opening the file is to use the familiar old File⇨Open command. (Every program has one.) As with most programs, you can alternatively press Ctrl+O or click the File Open button on the toolbar (as shown in the margin of this paragraph).

Figure 1-2 shows you the Open dialog box that appears. As in any program, you click a filename listed in the Open dialog box and then click Open to open a file. Paint Shop Pro, however, adds a few special features for working with images.

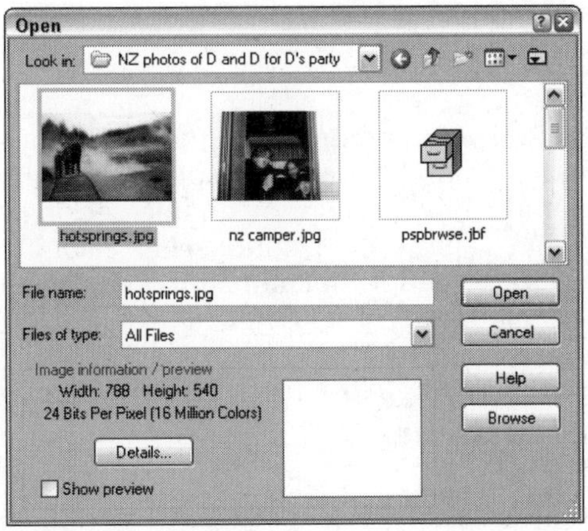

Figure 1-2:
The Open
dialog box.

If your file isn't listed

If the file you want isn't listed in the File Open dialog box, make sure that the wrong file type isn't chosen in the Files of Type selection box. File type choices are "sticky." That is, if you chose last time to display only GIF files, this time the Open dialog box still displays only GIF files. If you're looking for a JPG file now, you don't see it! Choose All Files in the Files of Type selection box to see all files again.

- ✔ **To open more than one file at a time:** Hold down the Ctrl button while clicking filenames, and then click the Open button. Or, to open a bunch of image files listed sequentially in the Open dialog box, click the first file, hold down the Shift button, click the last file, and then click the Open button.

- ✔ **To trim down the list of files to show just one type (if you're looking for a GIF file, for example):** Click the Files of Type selection box and choose that type from the many file types Paint Shop Pro can read.

- ✔ **To see information on the image width, height, and color depth:** Click your file and then read the Image Information area of the Open dialog box.

- ✔ **To see more information about an image you have clicked, such as date or file size:** Click the Details button.

Secrets of opening a file by double-clicking

If you see an image file listed on your computer — in a My Computer or Windows Explorer window, for example — and it displays the Paint Shop Pro palette icon, you can open it in Paint Shop Pro by double-clicking that icon. If you have several images you want to open, double-click each of them separately, and they all get a separate window in Paint Shop Pro. You don't end up with multiple copies of Paint Shop Pro running.

If you have an image file that Paint Shop Pro doesn't open when you double-click it, three things could be responsible:

- ✔ **The file doesn't have an extension, like .jpg or .gif.** This problem often happens when someone sends you a file from a Macintosh computer. Use the browsing or File➪Open technique described in the preceding sections. Or, if you know what kind of file it is (JPEG, for example), right-click the file and choose Rename from the context menu that appears. Then type the correct file extension (.jpg for JPEG, for example).

✓ **Paint Shop Pro can't open the file.** Paint Shop Pro can open many different types of file, but not all of them.

✓ **Paint Shop Pro may not be configured to open that file type.** See the nearby sidebar, "Making Paint Shop Pro open the right file types when you double-click."

Making Paint Shop Pro open the right file types when you double-click

Two problems can occur with double-clicking as a way of opening image files:

✓ Paint Shop Pro may open files that you would prefer to be opened by some other program. For example, if you're running AutoCAD or another AutoDesk program, you may prefer that the AutoDesk program open DXF files because they're one of AutoDesk's own file types.

✓ Paint Shop Pro may fail to open image files that you want it to open. For example, you may install new software for a new digital camera, and, suddenly, when you double-click JPG files, some program other than Paint Shop Pro opens the file.

These problems usually occur when you have more than one graphics program. The latest one installed may grab all the file types for itself. Both problems can be solved the same way. Follow these steps to specify which files are to be opened (or not) by Paint Shop Pro:

1. **Choose File➪Preferences➪File Format Associations.**

   The File Format Associations dialog box appears. This box directs Windows to open certain file types by using Paint Shop Pro.

2. **Click the check boxes to enable or disable the file types you want opened by Paint Shop Pro.**

   To disable all check boxes, click Remove All. To enable all check boxes, click Select All. (After that, you can enable or disable check boxes manually, if you like.) To have Paint Shop Pro open only the file types that aren't opened by any other program, click Select Unused.

3. **Click OK.**

At this point, Paint Shop Pro is properly set up to open just the file types you want it to and leave the others alone. The *other* program you use, however, may still not be properly set up to open the files you want *it* to open. We can't give you much help with that, but we can tell you one place to get help: Choose Start➪Help from the Windows taskbar. In the Help window that appears, click the Index tab at the top of the Help window and then, in the text box in the upper-left corner of the window, type **associating file**. Below that text box, a line appears that reads Associating file extensions *(or types)* with programs. Double-click that line to get help with associating file extensions with your other program.

Viewing and Zooming an Image

Working with images involves a great deal of *zooming,* or changing the magnification of your view. Sometimes you need to work close up, to take that nasty gleam out of Uncle Charley's eye, for example (something Aunt Mabel has been trying to do for years). At other times, you really need to see the whole picture, but Uncle Charley's gleaming eye rather scarily fills the whole window.

Zooming doesn't change the size of an image (in pixels or in inches). It only changes how big Paint Shop Pro displays the image onscreen.

Zooming and moving an image in the window

The basic way to zoom in (enlarge the view) or zoom out (see more of the picture) is to use the *Zoom* tool. The Zoom tool and its sidekick, the Pan tool, live in the same position (which we call a *tool group*) at the top of the Tools toolbar.

Follow these steps to zoom:

1. Click the tiny down-arrow on the top tool group on the Tools toolbar.

Two tools spring out to the right of this button: the Pan tool (the hand) and the Zoom tool (the magnifying glass).

2. Click the Zoom tool, as shown in the margin.

Your cursor changes to a magnifying glass icon.

3. Click with the zoom tool on the image in this way:

- Click (left-click) to zoom in.
- Right-click to zoom out.

You can choose the Zoom or Pan tool quickly by pressing a single key. Press the Z key for Zoom. Press the A key for Pan.

If the image gets bigger than the window, use the Pan tool to move the image around (pan it) in the window. Click the top button on the Tools toolbar, as you did in Step 1, but this time choose the Pan tool (the hand icon) — or just press the A key. Drag the cursor (it's now displaying a hand icon) on the image to move the image.

To see the image at its actual size (100 percent), choose View⇨Zoom⇨ Zoom to 100% or click the button labeled Actual Size on the Tool Options palette. (The Tool Options palette runs horizontally near the top of the Paint Shop Pro window and changes depending on the tool you choose. See the following sidebar about the Tool Options palette.)

The Tool Options palette — the toolbar-ish thing that changes a lot

Every time you choose a new tool (from the tool buttons that run down the left side of the Paint Shop Pro window), a toolbar changes just above the image window. (If you're not sure which toolbar it is, press the F4 key repeatedly to flash the toolbar on or off.) This toolbar, the Tool Options palette, contains all the various fiddly bits you may want to change on a tool. For example, with a paintbrush, you set the brush width here. With the Zoom or Pan tool, you can choose shortcuts named Zoom more rather than click repeatedly to zoom a lot. Each tool has too many fiddly bits to cover in detail, so we alert you to any important ones and let you, well, fiddle with the rest.

Paint Shop Pro also lets you magnify a portion of the image rather than have to enlarge the whole thing to see a detail. With either the Pan or Zoom tool selected, choose View➪Magnifier or press Ctrl+Alt+M. Move your cursor over an area of the image, and a special 5x Zoom window shows you a close-up view of that area. Repeat the command to remove the magnifier.

Working on several images at a time

You can open several images at a time in Paint Shop Pro. Each one gets its own window. Having several images open is useful for tasks such as cutting and pasting between images. To help manage those windows, use the commands on the Paint Shop Pro Window menu. That menu contains the usual suspects of nearly all Windows programs: Cascade, Tile (Horizontally or Vertically), or Close All to close all image files.

Remember that Paint Shop Pro tools and commands apply to only the image window that's *active* (the one with the colored title bar). Click an image window's title bar to make that window active and bring it to the front. Alternatively, you can choose a window by the name of the file it's displaying, as listed on the Window menu.

Getting Information about an Image

Simply looking at an image doesn't tell you the whole story. You may be asking yourself, "What exactly am I looking at, here? I mean, how big is this image, really? How many colors? What folder is it from? Is this really Uncle Fred in Cancun?"

To get information, choose Image⇨Image Information from the menu bar or press Shift+I. The Current Image Information dialog box appears and displays all available information about this image file.

Saving an Image File

After you're done working on an image in Paint Shop Pro, you need to save it. Saving an image in Paint Shop Pro is just as easy as saving a Microsoft Word document, for example. Choose File⇨Save or click the Save button on the standard toolbar (the floppy disk icon) or press Ctrl+S.

Paint Shop Pro saves (without complaint, in most instances) an image as the same type (format) of file (JPG, for example) that it was when you opened it. It may, however, raise a warning, depending on what changes you have made — see the nearby sidebar, "When Paint Shop Pro notes your limitations."

If you have added text or shapes or overlaid images on your original image, saving the modified image as a Paint Shop Pro file is a good idea; see the following section.

When Paint Shop Pro notes your limitations

Paint Shop Pro images are sophisticated! They can have layers, selections, and as many as 16 million colors. Many common image types (like JPEG or GIF) cannot handle layers, selections, or that many colors. If you try to save such a sophisticated image as one of these more limited file types, Paint Shop Pro displays the following query box:

For example, if you start with a JPEG image and put text on it, Paint Shop Pro normally puts that text on a separate layer. If you save the image as a JPEG file, Paint Shop Pro has to combine all layers into one single layer.

Go ahead and click OK on the query box. The file you create is limited, but the image you have open in Paint Shop Pro is unaffected. It still has its advanced features until you close it. We recommend that you take this opportunity to also save the image as a Paint Shop Pro file so that you can access those layers.

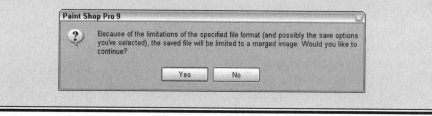

Saving an Image As a Paint Shop Pro File

Saving your image as a Paint Shop Pro (pspimage) type of file is a good idea, even if the image started life as a different type or even if you ultimately want to save the image as a different type.

Paint Shop Pro files are a good choice because, among other things, they save layers and any current selection you may have made during the editing process. Most common file types (except the common Photoshop type) don't save that stuff. Some file types are *lossy* (like most JPG varieties), which means that they may even lose quality.

After you have taken the precaution of making a Paint Shop Pro file, if you also need a different type of file, save a *copy of the image* as that other type of file. If you make subsequent changes to the image, always make the changes to the Paint Shop Pro file and then make copies of that file in the various file types you may need.

Follow these steps to save your image as a Paint Shop Pro file:

1. **Choose File⇨Save As.**

   The Save As dialog box appears.

2. **Click the Save as Type box and select the Paint Shop Pro Image option.**

3. **Select a folder and type a name for the file.**

   Do this exactly as you would to save a file in any other Windows program.

4. **Click the Save button.**

The image is now safely stored as the best file type possible for a Paint Shop Pro user, with nothing lost.

Saving a Copy of Your File As Another File Type

After saving an image as a Paint Shop Pro file (refer to the preceding section), if you also need the image in a different file type, save a *copy* in that different file type. Follow these steps to save a copy as another file type:

1. **Choose File⇨Save Copy As.**

   The Save Copy As dialog box appears.

2. **Select the file type you want from the Save as Type box.**

   If an Option button appears and isn't grayed out, it provides access to variations on your chosen format that can sometimes be useful, like reducing the file size (compression) or putting the file in a particular form that somebody needs. This section provides a few examples of options.

3. **Click the Save button.**

Keep the following pointers in mind to avoid confusion, disappointment, and bad hair days:

  ✔ We recommend that you keep your ongoing work in Paint Shop Pro files (.pspimage) to avoid losing features like layers. If you need the image as another file type, use the File⇨Save Copy As command and avoid using File⇨Save As.

  ✔ When you save a copy in a different file type, the open file isn't affected. It remains whatever file type it was. For example, if the open file is a Paint Shop Pro file type and you save a copy as JPEG, the open file remains a Paint Shop Pro file type. (You can tell by the pspimage extension on the filename, on the title bar in the image window.)

  ✔ If you have used layers (or floating selections) and save a copy as something other than a Paint Shop Pro file, Paint Shop Pro may have to merge (combine) those layers into a single image. The program displays a dialog box to warn you if it needs to merge layers into a single image. (See the nearby sidebar, "When Paint Shop Pro notes your limitations.") That merge *doesn't* happen to the Paint Shop Pro image you're working on — only to the file copy you're creating. Don't worry about the message — just click Yes to proceed.

Saving the Whole Enchilada, Your Workspace

Got a hot and spicy date? Need to wrap up one Paint Shop Pro project and start chewing on another?

You can close Paint Shop Pro at any time and go back later to exactly the way things were: what file you had open, what palettes and tool options you had chosen — the whole enchilada. This process is called *saving the workspace*. It's also a good feature if you're finicky about exactly how the various Paint

Shop Pro controls (palettes and toolbars, for example) are arranged. It's a nice way to save different image projects by name.

Follow these steps to save a workspace:

1. **Choose File⇨Workspace⇨Save.**

   The Save Workspace dialog box makes the scene and lists any workspaces you have previously created.

2. **Type a name for this workspace in the New Workspace Name text box.**

   If you want your workspace to include any images you have open, click to enable the Include Open Images check box.

3. **Click the Save button.**

If any images are open, Paint Shop Pro prompts you to save them now. If you're going out and your PC may crash or your cat may dance on the keyboard, consider clicking Yes.

To restore a previously saved workspace, follow these steps:

1. **Choose File⇨Workspace⇨Load.**

   A Load Workspace query box may appear and warn you that loading a workspace replaces your existing workspace settings. It asks whether you want to save the existing workspace. Click Yes to open the Save Workspace dialog box we just described. Click No if you don't care to save the current workspace.

   The Load Workspace dialog box appears and lists workspaces by name.

2. **Click the named workspace you want.**

3. **Click Load.**

Paint Shop Pro loads any images that are part of that workspace and restores all settings.

Using Native and Foreign File Types

Most graphics files are "not from around here"; that is, they're not Paint Shop Pro files. Because you may have to open or create these types of files, knowing something about file types can be helpful. This section describes a few of the most popular file types. Each file type is identified by the *extension* (ending) it uses. For example, Paint Shop Pro files end with the extension .pspimage or .psp.

"How the FPX can I see the TIF, JPG, DXF, and other extensions?!"

An image file is often referred to by the 3-or-more letter ending (extension) at the end of its filename. The file polecat.tif, for example, is a TIF (or TIFF) file. On many computers, Windows is set up to hide these extensions, which makes your life harder when you're using Paint Shop Pro. If, when you go to open a file in Paint Shop Pro, the files don't appear to end with a period and extension (such as .psp, .bmp, or .pcx), Windows is hiding valuable information from you. To reveal the extensions, do this: On the Windows desktop, double-click the My Computer icon. In the window that appears in Windows XP, choose Tools⇨Folder Options (or in Windows 98, choose View⇨Folder Options). This command displays the Folder Options dialog box. Click the View tab there, and under Files and Folders, Hidden Files, deselect the check box labeled Hide File Extensions for Known File Types.

Most of the time, you don't have to do anything special to open a particular file type or to save your work as that type of file — and then again, sometimes you do. Paint Shop Pro, in most cases, simply asks you a few questions to resolve any problems when you're opening or saving a foreign file type.

Paint Shop Pro files (pspimage or PSP)

The native Paint Shop Pro 9 file type, pspimage, is probably the best choice for storing your own images. When you save your work as a Paint Shop Pro file, you can save everything just as it is, including any areas you have selected with the Paint Shop Pro selection tools, plus your various kinds of layers, palettes, tool settings (like current brush width), transparency, and other advanced features. You can pick up almost exactly where you left off. Paint Shop Pro files can have any color depth (maximum number of colors) you choose. Pspimage is the latest and greatest of the Paint Shop Pro native formats; earlier versions used the PSP extension.

Programs other than Paint Shop Pro and Animation Shop don't often read Paint Shop Pro files, however. You may need to save a copy of your image in a different file type for someone who uses other software, like Photoshop. Also, earlier versions of Paint Shop Pro can't read later Paint Shop Pro files (Paint Shop Pro 7 can't read Paint Shop Pro 9 files, for example.) To create files for earlier versions of Paint Shop Pro, see the instructions for saving a copy of your image in the section "Saving a Copy of Your File As Another File Type," earlier in this chapter.

Color depth

Color depth refers to the capacity of a given file type (like GIF) to store a variety of colors. Color depth is described as either the maximum number of colors an image can contain (like 256 colors) or a number of bits. The term *1 bit* means that the image contains only black and white; *4 bits* means that the image can contain 16 colors; *8 bits* corresponds to 256 colors, and *24 bits* means as many as 16 million colors.

BMP

BMP files are *Windows bitmap* files; that is, they were designed by Microsoft for storing images, and many programs under Windows can read and write them. BMP files can have color depths of 1, 4, 8, or 24 bits. (Set your color depth by choosing Colors⇨Decrease Color Depth or Colors⇨Increase Color Depth.)

BMP files that are 24-bit can be quite large. When you save a file as BMP, you can click the Options button in the Save As (or Save Copy As) dialog box to choose higher *compression* (make smaller files). Under Encoding in the Options dialog box that appears, select RLE and then click OK. (RLE stands for *Run-Length Encoding,* a way of making image files smaller.) Now, when you save the file, Paint Shop Pro asks your permission to switch to a 256-color (8-bit) version of the BMP file. The resulting file is much trimmer than the original, although the color quality may diminish slightly.

TIFF

TIFF (or TIF) stands for Tag Image File Format (which, of course, tells you nothing useful). Many graphics programs on the PC and Macintosh can read and write TIFF files, so it's a good choice of file type when you don't know what kinds of files the other person can read.

TIFF files can be quite large unless you compress them. To compress a TIFF file, click the Options button when you're using the Save As or Save Copy As dialog box. Then choose the LZW Compression option in the Compression area of the Options dialog box that appears. LZW gives you the best compression and compatibility with most other programs. (No image quality is lost by using LZW compression in TIFF files.)

For advanced users, TIFF is a good choice because it can store information in not only RGB (red, green, blue) primary colors, but also in CMYK (cyan, magenta, yellow, and black), which is used for some high-quality printed images. It can also store advanced data for color accuracy, such as gamma.

GIF

The Web uses CompuServe GIF images all over the place. GIF is the most popular of three common file types used on the Internet. (JPG and PNG are the other two.)

Many programs read GIF files. (Older programs may read only the older GIF standard, GIF87, rather than the newer GIF89a. Paint Shop Pro lets you choose which standard to use when you're saving a GIF file — just click the Options button in the Save As or Save Copy As dialog box.)

Saving your Paint Shop Pro work as GIF usually means that it loses something, but perhaps not enough to matter. GIF images have a maximum color depth of 256 colors, which allows fairly realistic images. That number of colors, however, isn't enough to enable Paint Shop Pro to do all operations, so it may at some point suggest that you let it increase the number of colors. (See the section "File Types and Auto-Action Messages about Colors," later in this chapter.)

GIF enables you to use some special features, such as a *transparent color* (which lets the backgrounds of Web pages show through), and *interlaced display* (in which the entire image gradually forms as it's downloaded from the Web).

A special Paint Shop Pro tool called the *GIF Optimizer* can help you set transparency and otherwise optimize the image for Web use. See Chapter 15 for the details of creating GIF files for the Web using this tool.

Some GIF files contain a whole series of images to be displayed as an animation. You can view these images by using Animation Shop; Paint Shop Pro shows you only the first image of the series.

JPEG

JPEG (or JPG) stands for Joint Photographic Experts Group, which sounds impressive. JPEG images are common on the Web for color photographs and other realistic color images because their files are small (relative to other file types) and download quickly.

The disadvantage of JPEG is that it uses a kind of compression, called lossy compression, to make its files small. *Lossy compression* means that the image quality is reduced a bit, especially around sharp edges, like text. Storing an image as a JPEG is kind of like stuffing a pie into a little plastic bag in your backpack for a hike. If it gets squeezed, the basic taste and nutrition are still there, and it doesn't take up lots of space, but you may not like the result.

You can choose just how much squeezing you want in the JPEG format, but first storing your work in some other format (preferably, PSP) is a good idea.

1. **Choose File⇨Save Copy As.**

   The Save Copy As dialog box appears.

2. **Select JPEG in the Save As Type box.**

3. **Click the Options button.**

   In the Save Options dialog box that appears, drag the Compression Factor slider to the left for higher quality and larger files, or to the right for lower-quality and smaller files.

4. **Click the Save button.**

The geeks at the Joint Photographics Experts Group have also come up with a lossless (unsqueezed) variety of JPEG. To save your files in this maximum-quality-but-largest-file-size format, first select JPEG 2000 in the Save As Type selection box. Then click the Options button, and in the Save Options dialog box that appears, choose Lossless. Be aware that not all software can read or display JPEG 2000 files, though.

If you're reading JPEG files, Paint Shop Pro offers an effect that removes some image distortions, called *artifacts,* that result from compression. (See Chapter 6 for instructions for removing JPEG artifacts.)

As with GIF, Paint Shop Pro offers a special tool, the JPEG Optimizer, for adjusting JPEG images for the Web. See the section in Chapter 15 about creating JPEG files for the details of fine-tuning JPEG images with this tool.

PNG

PNG (Progressive Network Graphics) was designed to take over for GIF on the Web, although it's catching on slowly. It does have some advantages over GIF and accomplishes the same functions as GIF, so it may yet take over. Because its main use is Web graphics, we discuss it a bit more in Chapter 15.

Using Vector File Types (Drawing Files)

Graphics images come in two main flavors: *raster* (also called *bitmap*) and *vector*. Here are the differences between them:

- ✔ **Raster (bitmap) images are made up of dots (pixels).** Most computer images are of this kind, and Paint Shop Pro is principally designed for this kind of image. It both reads and writes a wide variety of raster images.

- ✔ **Vector images are made up of lines, shapes, filled areas, and text.** You can change text, lines, and shapes more easily if they're stored as vectors than if they're stored as bitmaps. Although Paint Shop Pro is principally designed for raster images, it allows you to create vector layers that contain lines, text, and preset shapes. If you use these layers, store your image as a Paint Shop Pro file to retain any vector graphics you create. If you store your images as other file types, PSP may convert your vector graphics to bitmap form, which may make editing more difficult.

Vector files are typically created by popular *drawing* software (as opposed to *painting* software). AutoCAD, for example, a popular drafting application, writes DXF (Drawing eXchange Format) files. Corel Draw writes CDR files, and Corel WordPerfect uses WPG files. Many other vector file types are in use too.

Like Paint Shop Pro files, some other file types can also contain a mix of vector and bitmap graphics. These include Windows Enhanced Metafiles (EMF, a Microsoft Windows standard), Computer Graphics Metafiles (CGM, a standard by the American National Standards Institute), PICT (a Macintosh standard), and embedded PostScript (EPS, by Adobe). Some files (like embedded PostScript) may contain in some cases both a bitmap and a vector version of the same image.

Opening vector files

Paint Shop Pro can open many kinds of vector (or mixed vector and bitmap) files. You can also copy drawings, using the Windows Clipboard, from most vector programs that run under Windows and paste the images into Paint Shop Pro.

Paint Shop Pro 9 opens many types of vector files and keeps them as vector files. If you open an AutoCAD DXF file, for example, the lines and other objects are translated into Paint Shop Pro vector objects.

Because Paint Shop Pro also lets you work with bitmap graphics, however, whenever you open a vector file, you have to add information about what size, in pixels, you want the image to be. Paint Shop Pro pops up a dialog box that requires you to enter dimensions in pixels (or dimensions in inches and pixels per inch) for the resulting bitmap image. If a Maintain Original Aspect Ratio check box appears, select it if you want to keep the same proportions as the original image.

For a PostScript file, for example, Paint Shop Pro displays the PostScript Renderer dialog box. To enter the page size, we generally find the Bounding Box option (which refers to the outside of the drawing area) to be the best solution; for resolution, the 72 dpi that is already entered in the Resolution box usually does well. The image size you get (in pixels) is the image dimension (say, 8.5 x 11 inches) times the Resolution (say, 72 dpi, gives you an image that is 8.5 x 72 pixels wide and 11 x 72 pixels high). For more detail or a bigger picture, choose a higher resolution.

Because Paint Shop Pro is translating between two different kinds of image data, it may make a few mistakes that you have to clean up afterward.

Saving vector files — not

You can't save pure vector-type image files, such as DXF, in Paint Shop Pro. You can, however, save your work as one of the file types that is allowed to contain a mix of vectors and bitmaps, such as EPS or CGM.

In those instances, however, Paint Shop Pro simply stores all your edits as a bitmap image and stores nothing in the vector part of the EPS, CGM, or other combined bitmap or vector file. Your vector objects become part of a single bitmap image. Because no vector objects are stored, a program that handles only vector graphics may not be able to read the file.

Converting or Renaming Batches of Files

If you have lots of image files and need copies of them in a different file type, try the Paint Shop Pro batch processing feature. Batch processing also lets you create an ordered series of related names, like `hawaii0001` through `hawaii9579`, for your 9,579 vacation photos.

To copy a bunch of files to a new file format, follow these steps:

1. **Choose File⇨Batch⇨Process.**

   The Batch Process dialog box appears.

2. **Click the Browse button at the top of the Batch Process dialog box.**

   A Select Files dialog box appears.

3. **In the Select Files dialog box, open the folder containing your files, hold down the Ctrl key, and click all the files you want to convert.**

4. **Click Select to close the Select Files dialog box.**

   Your selected files are now listed in the Files to Process box of the Batch Process dialog box. To add files from another folder, repeat Steps 2 and 3.

5. **In the Save Options area at the bottom of the Batch Process dialog box, in the Type selection box, choose the file type you want as the result of your conversion.**

6. **To put the newly generated files in a different folder, click the Browse button at the bottom of the dialog box and choose a new folder.**

7. **Click the Start button.**

In a few seconds or minutes, you have copies in the new file type you need.

To give a bunch of files similar names, differing by only a number (as in hawaii01, hawaii02, and so on), take these steps:

1. **Choose File⇨Batch⇨Rename.**

2. **In the Batch Rename dialog box that appears, click the Browse button.**

3. **In the Select Files dialog box, open the folder containing your files, hold down the Ctrl key, and click all the files you want to convert.**

4. **Click Select to close the Select Files dialog box.**

   Your selected files are now listed in the Files to Process box of the Batch Rename dialog box. To add files from another folder, repeat Steps 2 and 3.

5. **Click the Modify button.**

   The Modify Filename Format dialog box appears. The idea is to combine various naming and numbering elements into a sort of formula for Paint Shop Pro to follow. For example, hawaii50 is a *custom text* element of our choosing, followed by a 2-digit *sequence*.

6. **Click an element in the Rename Options panel to choose the first part of the new name, such as Custom Text.**

7. **Click the Add button to add that element to your formula, which gets assembled in the right panel.**

   Depending on what kind of element you choose, a 1-line text box appears on the right for you to make a choice or enter some text. We stick with our simple example. If you have chosen Custom Text, type your text (**hawaii**, for example) in the Custom Text box that appears. If you have chosen Sequence, type a starting number in the Starting Sequence box that appears; use as many digits as you need for the batch (type **1** for as many as 9 images and **01** for as many as 99 images). For today's date, choose a date format.

8. **Repeat Steps 4 and 5 to add more elements. Make sure that one of your elements is Sequence, or else you're asking the impossible: for each file to have the same name.**

   The order in which you add elements on the right is the order in which they appear in the filenames.

9. **Click OK. When the Batch Rename dialog box returns, select the files to be converted.**

   The files are all renamed, and each name includes a different number.

File Types and Auto-Action Messages about Colors

When you try to use certain Paint Shop Pro features or save your work in a non–PSP format, you may see an Auto Actions message box from Paint Shop Pro. For example, you may open a GIF file and want to use one of the Paint Shop Pro commands on the Adjust or Effects menu. Or, perhaps you want to add a raster layer to that GIF file. Paint Shop Pro displays an error message like the one shown in Figure 1-3.

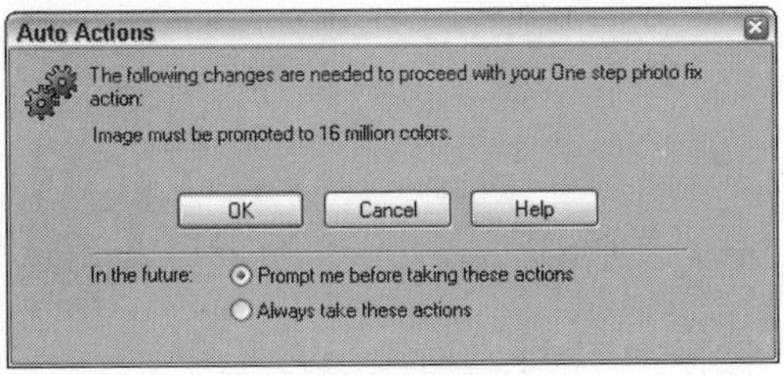

Figure 1-3: First, Paint Shop Pro may need to improve the image quality.

Don't worry — be happy; just click OK. The issue is that certain file types, like GIF, can handle only a limited number of colors (they have limited *color depth*) and many Paint Shop Pro features work only on images able to handle as many as 16 million colors. Paint Shop Pro is offering to create a 16-million-color image for you so that it can apply the tool you want to use.

If you get one of these messages, and if you later save your work in the original, color-limited file type (GIF, for example), you also get a message requesting permission to reduce the number of colors back to whatever that type of file can handle. Simply click OK in whatever dialog box or boxes result, and you're likely to be happy with the result.

If you're a professional and are picky, you understand what's going on and can take the necessary steps to control the result. You can always change the number of colors manually by choosing Image⇨Increase Color Depth or Image⇨Decrease Color Depth.

To turn off these messages and always have Paint Shop Pro proceed (or not proceed), choose File⇨Preferences⇨General Program Preferences. Click the Auto Actions tab in the dialog box that appears. For each type of conversion, you can choose to never do it or to always do it or to have the program prompt you. Or, click Never All or Always All to never or always do any of the conversions.

Obtaining Image Files from the Web

The Web is a grab bag of goodies for graphics gurus. Here's how to get your hands on these fabulous fruits.

One of the best ways to get graphics is to find a Web site offering them free and clear. Most of these sites provide instructions for downloading those image files. Other Web pages may copy-protect their images so that you can't use the procedures we list in this section.

To save an image that you're viewing in your Web browser, use either of these methods:

✔ Right-click the image and, on the pop-up menu that appears, look for Save Picture As or a similar choice. You're prompted for the location on your hard drive where you want the image saved.

✔ Right-click the image and, on the pop-up menu that appears, choose Copy. This choice copies the image to the Windows Clipboard; open Paint Shop Pro and press Ctrl+V to paste the image as a new image. (Choose the Edit⇨Paste command to see ways to paste the image into another open image.) Save the image by choosing File⇨Save.

A fair number of graphics images on the Web have transparent portions, especially their backgrounds. The transparent parts of these types of image have a hidden color (typically white), and that color may become visible in Paint Shop Pro. See Chapter 15 for more information about transparency in Web images.

Most Web images are one of only a few different file types: GIF, JPEG, or PNG. GIF and some PNG images are *palette images,* with a limited number of colors (typically, 256 colors).

Many animations on the Web are GIF files. You should open animated GIF files in Animation Shop, not in Paint Shop Pro (which displays only the first frame of the animation). Some animations are, however, in a private vector format (Flash) that neither Animation Shop nor Paint Shop Pro can read.

Chapter 2

Getting Bigger, Smaller, and Turned Around

*I*t happened several times to Alice, of Wonderland fame: She needed to be bigger or smaller or to change her orientation. Fortunately, you don't have to adopt her dubious pharmacological methods — eating and drinking mysteriously labeled substances — to change the size or orientation of your images.

No, to make your pictures bigger, smaller, rotated, or otherwise reoriented, you need to indulge in only a few clicks on well-labeled commands or icons. In this chapter, we illuminate your choices as you navigate the Paint Shop Pro rabbit hole.

If your image appears smaller than you think it should be when you first open it, Paint Shop Pro has probably zoomed the image out to fit your window. To zoom in, click the Zoom (magnifier) tool from the pan and zoom tool group and then left-click the image.

Getting Sized

Size may not be everything, but it's important. You don't need a 1024-x-768-pixel image, for example (full-screen size on many PCs), for a snapshot of your new company CEO on your Web site. If you didn't get an appropriately sized CEO (okay, an image of a CEO) in the first place, you can trim that person in Paint Shop Pro. Likewise, if you're rushing to prepare the opening screen for a company presentation and the only way you can get a logo is to scan in the tiny one on your letterhead, Paint Shop Pro can help you size it up to a more presentable image.

If you're preparing an image that someone else plans to place in a profession-ally prepared and printed document, don't scale it down yourself. Let your graphics designer or printer do the scaling to suit the printing process.

Start resizing by choosing Image⇨Resize or press Shift+S. The Resize dialog box appears in order to help you size the situation up — or down (see Figure 2-1).

Proportioning

The Resize dialog box normally keeps an image's *proportions* (relationship of width to height) constant while you resize. If you set the width, therefore, Paint Shop Pro sets the height for you (and vice versa). Keeping image pro-portions constant avoids distortion.

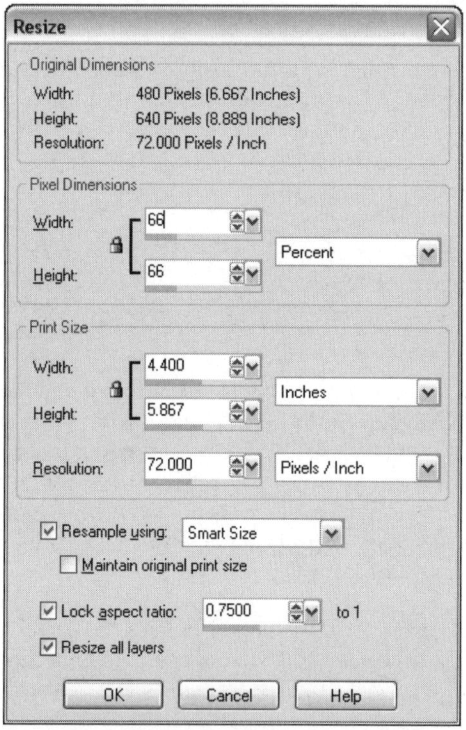

Resize ☒

Original Dimensions
Width: 480 Pixels (6.667 Inches)
Height: 640 Pixels (8.889 Inches)
Resolution: 72.000 Pixels / Inch

Pixel Dimensions
Width: [66]⇕   ⌐ [Percent]⌄
Height: [66]⇕

Print Size
Width: [4.400]⇕   ⌐ [Inches]⌄
Height: [5.867]⇕
Resolution: [72.000]⇕ [Pixels / Inch]⌄

☑ Resample using: [Smart Size]⌄
    ☐ Maintain original print size

☑ Lock aspect ratio: [0.7500]⇕ to 1
☑ Resize all layers

[OK]   [Cancel]   [Help]

Figure 2-1:
Sizing your image up — or down.

If you prefer to change the proportions (which distorts your image), you can click to clear (deselect) the check box labeled Lock Aspect Ratio to 1. (The box appears checked in Figure 2-1) Paint Shop Pro then lets you set the width and height independently.

Dimensioning

Using the Resize dialog box (refer to Figure 2-1), you can adjust the size in one of three ways, all of which do the same thing: change the image's size in pixels. Use whichever way suits your mindset:

- **Specify size in pixels:** If you're using the image on the Web or in e-mail, you most likely have a pixel size (probably a desired width) in mind. Select Pixels from the drop-down menu next to the Width and Height controls and then enter a value for Width (or Height).

- **Make it X% of its current size:** Select Percent from the drop-down menu next to the Width and Height controls and then enter a Width (or Height) value. In Figure 2-1, for example, the 66 setting makes the image ⅔ (66 percent) of its current size. To double the image size, use 200.

- **Make it *print* bigger or smaller:** Select which measurement you want to use (inches or centimeters) from the menu on the right side and then use the Width or Height controls in the Print Size section to make the image print as large as you want. Paint Shop Pro multiplies this physical size (in inches, for example) by the resolution setting (pixels per inch) in this dialog box and calculates a new image size in pixels. You can also change the value in the Resolution text box to adjust the image resolution (pixels per inch or centimeter). Don't confuse this setting with the printer's resolution (typically, 300 to 600 dpi); see Chapter 14 if you *are* confused about printing and resolution!

If your image has several layers and you want them all resized the same, make sure to check the Resize All Layers check box. If you clear that check mark, you resize only the active layer. Click OK to make the resizing happen.

Avoiding degradation

Resizing sounds easy: Just make the image bigger or smaller. What's to think about? Well, usually, you don't have to think about anything. Occasionally, however, your image's appearance degrades after resizing. It has jagged or fuzzy edges. These situations call for a little thought.

Behind the resizing issue is another difference between how computers and humans think. If you want your image to be 25 percent bigger, Paint Shop Pro has to figure out how to spread 100 pixels over 125 pixels. To get an idea of the scope of the problem, imagine dividing 100 cookies among 125 kids who don't accept broken cookies. Fortunately, Paint Shop Pro is pretty smart, so you don't have to smoosh up and bake these cookies again yourself. Unless you instruct Paint Shop Pro otherwise, it uses the *Smart Size* feature to make these decisions — it chooses the right way to do it based on what your image looks like.

If your image doesn't look so hot after resizing, try second-guessing the smart resizing that Paint Shop Pro uses by default. Press Ctrl+Z to undo the ugly resizing you just did. Then choose Image⇨Resize again. In the Image Resize dialog box that appears, click the Resize Type selection box to see the specific choices of ways to resize. Here's what to do with those choices:

- ✔ **Bicubic Resample:** Choose to enlarge a realistic-looking or complex image (like a photo) or to avoid jagged edges.

- ✔ **Bilinear Resample:** Choose to reduce a drawn image, one with well-defined edges, or one with text.

- ✔ **Pixel Resize:** Choose to enlarge a drawn image or one with well-defined edges. (Paint Shop Pro then simply removes or duplicates pixels in order to resize.)

- ✔ **Weighted Average:** Choose to reduce a drawn image, one with well-defined edges, or one with text if the Bilinear Resample option doesn't work out.

Click OK to proceed with the resizing. If your image doesn't look better, press Ctrl+Z to undo the last resize. Choose a different resizing method and try resizing again.

Bilinear and bicubic resampling work for only 24-bit color images (or grayscale images). You can use them on fewer-color images by first increasing the color depth to 24-bit: Press Ctrl+Shift+0.

Cropping (Trimming) Your Edges

Is your image a bit shabby around the edges and in need of a trim? You can improve the composition of many pictures by *cropping* (trimming) a bit off the top, bottom, or sides. Often, for example, snapshots are taken from too far away, so the subject is too small. You can enlarge the image in Paint Shop Pro, but you also need to trim it so that the overall picture isn't yards wide.

In a layered image, cropping affects all layers.

Paint Shop Pro provides a special tool for your crops. Take these steps to trim your image:

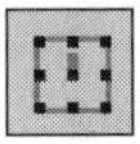

1. **Click the Crop tool (shown in the margin) on the Tools toolbar.**

   The cursor icon displays a set of crosshairs.

2. **Visualize a rectangular area that defines the new boundaries of your image.**

   For example, if you're cropping a family photo taken in the backyard, next to the trash barrels, visualize a rectangle around the family, excluding the barrels.

3. **Move the crosshairs of your cursor to one corner of that visualized rectangle and then drag diagonally toward the opposite corner.**

   As you drag, a real rectangle forms and items outside the rectangle are dimmed. The status bar at the bottom of the Paint Shop Pro window gives you the exact pixel column and row where the cursor is positioned, in case you need that information. As you drag, the status bar also gives you the cursor position and the crop's size, as shown in Figure 2-2.

   If the cropping rectangle isn't quite right, you can modify it in one of these three ways:

   - To remove the rectangle and try again, right-click anywhere on the image. The rectangle disappears.

   - To change any side or corner of the rectangle, drag that side or corner or adjust the edge values on the Tool Options palette, as indicated in Figure 2-2.

   - To position the rectangle, move your cursor within that rectangle; the cursor becomes a four-headed arrow and you can drag the rectangle to any new location.

4. **When the rectangle is correct, double-click anywhere on the image.**

   Paint Shop Pro crops the image. If you don't like the result, press Ctrl+Z to undo the crop and then try these steps again.

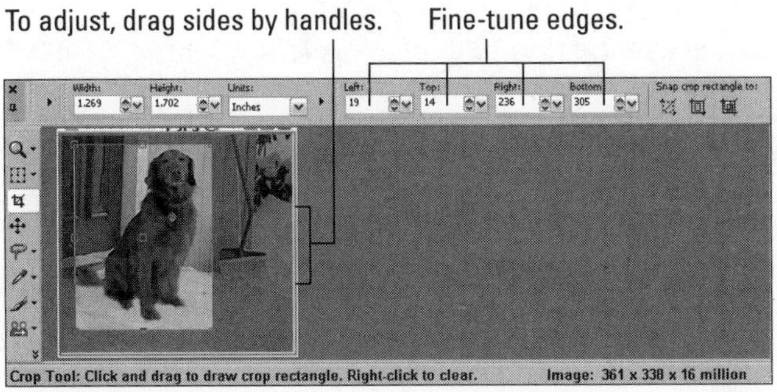

To adjust, drag sides by handles.   Fine-tune edges.

Figure 2-2:
Cropping a
furry dog.

Getting Turned Around, Mirrored, or Flipped

We can't tell you how many people we have seen bending their necks to view a sideways image! Apart from providing work for chiropractors, this habit does nobody any good.

Paint Shop Pro makes rotating, mirroring, or flipping an image simple. Mirrored or flipped images are particularly useful for imaginative work, such as creating a reflection that isn't present in the original or making a symmetrical design, such as a floral border. Mirroring can also correct a transparency that was scanned wrong side up.

Does your image have layers, or have you selected an area? As with many Paint Shop Pro functions, the mirroring, flipping, and rotating commands apply to only the active layer. If you have a selected area, mirroring and flipping also restrict themselves to that area.

Rotating

To rotate an image, choose Image⇨Rotate⇨Free Rotate or press Ctrl+R. The Rotate dialog box appears, with a variety of option buttons:

- To rotate the image clockwise, click Right.

- To rotate counterclockwise, click Left.

- Choose 90 degrees (a quarter-turn, good for righting sideways images), 180 degrees (a half-turn), or 270 degrees (a three-quarter turn) of rotation, or choose Free (see the next bullet).

- To rotate any desired amount, choose Free and enter any rotation (in degrees) in the highlighted text box.

If you're rotating an image taken with the camera turned sidewise, just choose Image⇨Rotate⇨Rotate Clockwise 90 or Rotate Counterclockwise 90.

Although you *can* use the Rotate dialog box to straighten an off-kilter photo, you have a better way: the Straighten tool, which we cover in Chapter 5.

If your image has multiple layers (or if you aren't sure whether it does) and you want to rotate the entire image, click to place a check mark in the All Layers check box in the Rotate dialog box. Otherwise, Paint Shop Pro rotates only the active layer. Click OK to perform the rotation.

To rotate a portion of an image, select that portion with a selection tool and then use the Deform tool. See Chapter 3 for help with selection and Chapter 4 to rotate a selection with the Deform tool.

Mirroring and flipping

To *mirror* an image is to change it as though it were reflected in a mirror held alongside the image. To *flip* an image is to exchange top for bottom as though the mirror were held underneath the image. Note that both transformations are unique: You can't achieve the same result by rotating the image!

If your image has layers, the mirroring and flipping commands apply to only the active layer. If your image has an area selected, these commands float that selection and then work on only that floating selection. See Chapter 4 for more information about floating selections.

To mirror an image in Paint Shop Pro, choose Image⇨Mirror. Your image is transformed into its mirror image.

To flip an image, choose Image⇨Flip. Your image is turned head over heels.

Taking on Borders

Paint Shop Pro can add a border of any color and width to any image. (If your image uses layers, however, Paint Shop Pro has to merge them. For that reason, borders are often best left as the last thing you do to your image.) To create a border around an image, follow these steps:

1. **Choose Image⇨Add Borders.**

   The Add Borders dialog box appears. (If Paint Shop Pro first displays a dialog box warning you that the layers must be merged to proceed, click OK to proceed.)

2. **Choose your color.**

   Click the color box to bring up the Material Properties dialog box and then click the shade you want to see surrounding your picture. Click OK. If this strange array of circles and boxes proves too daunting for you, check out the section in Chapter 10 about choosing a color for the very picky, where we explain the Material Properties dialog box.

3. **Set your border widths.**

   For a border that is the same width on all sides, leave the check mark in the Symmetric check box and enter your border width in the Top, Bottom, Left, or Right box. (It doesn't matter which one you use; they all change together.) For different border widths on all sides, clear the Symmetric check mark and enter the border widths in all the boxes individually. To set a border in inches or units other than pixels, choose your preferred unit from the selection box in the Original Dimensions area.

Click OK. Your image is now larger by the borders you have set.

Borders are no different from any other area of your image; they're just new and in all one color.

Achieving a Particular Canvas Size

Paint Shop Pro enables you to expand the *canvas size* of any image: that is, to add a border area around the image to achieve a particular image width and height. The Canvas Size command has the same effect as Add Borders.

"But," you say, wisely, "if Add Borders does the same thing, why would I bother with Canvas Size?" You would bother if you were looking to have an image of a particular size — and didn't want to do the arithmetic to calculate how much border to add to the existing dimensions.

You may use the Canvas Size command, for example, if you're making a catalog using images of various heights and widths and want all the images to be of uniform height and width. You can't resize the *images* because that would distort them. If you use the Add Borders command, you have to calculate border widths to fill out each image to the right dimensions. With canvas sizing, however, you can simply place each image on a uniformly sized background.

Here's how:

1. **Choose Image⇨Canvas Size.**

   The Canvas Size dialog box makes the scene.

2. **Choose your color.**

   Click the Background swatch in this dialog box to display the Material Properties dialog box. Choose the shade you want to see surrounding your picture, and then click OK. (We explain the Material Properties dialog box in Chapter 10). Alternatively, click with your cursor, which is now an eyedropper, on any color in your image.

3. **Enter in the Width and Height boxes a new width and new height for your canvas.**

   These numbers define how big your overall image will be, including its expanded canvas (borders). A selection box in this area lets you use units of pixels, inches, centimeters, or millimeters.

To keep the canvas proportions the same as your original image, check the Lock Aspect Ratio check box.

4. **Choose where you want your image positioned on the canvas.**

   As you can see in Figure 2-3, you can press one of nine placement buttons to select which corner your image will be flush with on the canvas. (The button in the center centers your image.)

   If these ten positions aren't good enough for you, you can place your image on the canvas with exacting precision by using the Placement settings. The values in these boxes tell Paint Shop Pro how far away the image should be from each of the four borders, in whatever units you chose in Step 3. For example, if you want to set your image so that it's 20 pixels away from the left side of the new canvas, enter a value of **20** in the Left Placement box.

   For artistic purposes, you may want to crop the image at the canvas edge (an effect called a *full bleed*). Using negative numbers in any of the placement boxes places at least part of the image *outside* the canvas border and effectively crops it. For example, a value of –20 pixels in the Left placement box sets your image 20 pixels *outside* the left border of the canvas. This action effectively trims 20 pixels off your image's left side.

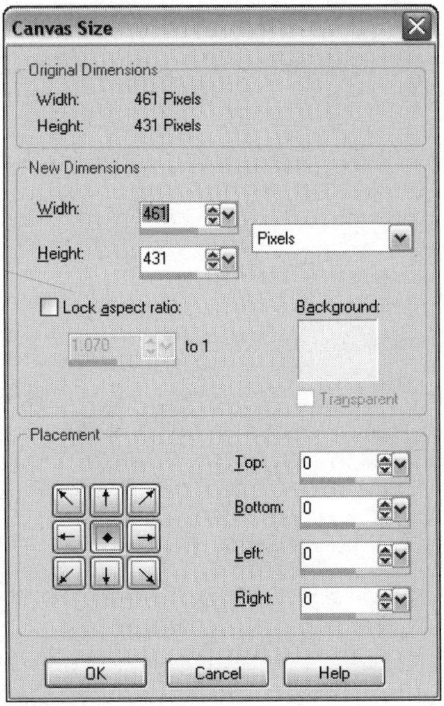

Figure 2-3: In the Canvas Size dialog box, buttons with arrows point to a corner or edge of the new canvas. Click to place your image against that edge.

Click OK and your image is mounted on a fresh canvas of your chosen size and background color. If you're trying to put lots of variously sized images on same-size canvases (as in a catalog), you may find it convenient that your preceding canvas size settings remain as you open each image. Just choose Image⇨Canvas Size for each subsequent image and click OK.

Chapter 3

Selecting Parts of an Image

*I*f Uncle Dave is the only one looking a bit dark and gloomy in your wedding picture, how can you lighten him — and only him — up? If the model in your catalog is wearing last spring's Irish Spring Green sweater, how can you make it Summer Sunset Magenta without making your model magenta too?

Sometimes, you want Paint Shop Pro to do something to just one portion of an image, like lighten Uncle Dave or color the model's sweater, and leave the rest of the image alone.

The solution is to *select* an area of the image. Just as you can select some text that you want to modify in a word processor, you can select an image area to modify in Paint Shop Pro. With that area selected, you can do, well, nearly anything Paint Shop Pro can do, such as paint the area, change its color, improve its contrast, erase it, copy it, or paste it.

You can hand-select an area by outlining it or automatically select an area by its color. You can even get Paint Shop Pro to help you outline by finding edges. Paint Shop Pro offers lots of features for getting a selection just right.

 Paint Shop Pro has two other features that let you focus your actions on certain parts: the Background Eraser and layers. If you want to erase around Uncle Dave, try the Background Eraser (see Chapter 9). Another feature, the Paint Shop Pro layers, lets you transfer selections to independent layers so that they can stay independent of the rest of the image (see Chapter 11).

In this chapter, we deal with selecting parts of your image that are *raster* (bitmap) images. We don't, however, deal with the special case of selecting *vector* objects. The text and shapes that the Text, Draw, and Preset Shapes tools make are almost always vector objects. To read about selecting vector objects, see the section in Chapter 12 about controlling your objects.

Selecting an Area

Selecting is creating a restricted area in which you want Paint Shop Pro to do its thing — a sort of construction zone. Paint Shop Pro's "thing" is whatever operation you choose, whether it's moving, changing color, painting, filling, smudging, filtering, erasing, copying, pasting, or mirroring — essentially, any image change Paint Shop Pro can perform. For example, you can select an elliptical area around Aunt Elizabeth in a group photo, copy that area to the Windows Clipboard, and then paste it as a new image to create a classical cameo-style oval image.

If you have layers in your image, selection can be slightly more complicated. See the section "Avoiding Selection Problems in Layered Images," later in this chapter.

The selected area has a moving dashed line, or *marquee,* around it. Figure 3-1 shows you Alex the Wonder Dog in his very own marquee.

Tool used here for outlining an area

Figure 3-1:
The dashed-line marquee shows you your selection. We created this selection with the Freehand (lasso) tool and chose the Smart Edge option from the Tool Options palette.

Selection tool group

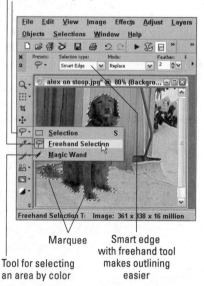

Marquee

Tool for selecting an area by color

Smart edge with freehand tool makes outlining easier

The keys to selecting an area lie in two places in Paint Shop Pro:

- ✔ **Selection tools on the Tools toolbar** (along the left edge of the Paint Shop Pro window)
- ✔ **Commands on the Selection menu** (on the Paint Shop Pro menu bar)

The three Paint Shop Pro selection tools are in the fifth tool group from the top of the Tools toolbar, as shown in Figure 3-1. They give you three different ways to select an area:

- ✔ **Selection:** Use the Selection tool to drag a rectangular, circular, or other regular shape.
- ✔ **Freehand:** Use the Freehand tool, as we did in Figure 3-1, to draw an outline.
- ✔ **Magic Wand:** Use the Magic Wand tool to click an area that has a more-or-less uniform color or brightness.

To make these tools work exactly the way you want, you need to use the Tool Options palette (press F4 if you don't see it). The Tool Options palette is where, in Figure 3-1, you see Smart Edge chosen as the selection type.

You can add to or subtract from a selection with any selection tool, so you may also find yourself switching between tools to build or carve out a selection of a particularly tricky shape.

The Selection menu on the menu bar also holds various commands for refining your selection and coping with technicalities. See the section "Modifying Your Selection," later in this chapter.

You may wonder why selecting gets all the attention it does in Paint Shop Pro. The reason is that making a precise selection is the key to editing a bitmap image cleanly. Check out Figure 3-2, which shows William's daughter's snow creation, the Snowduck. (What, you didn't recognize it? See the beak, the eyes?) It has been selected from a photograph and then copied and pasted on a white background.

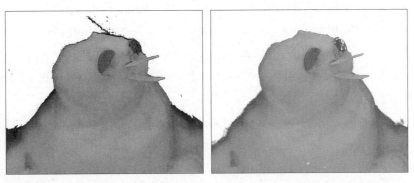

Figure 3-2: Careful selection gives you the paste job you want.

The selection pasted on the right had all the black removed from it, although a dark gray fringe remains. The figure on the left had the black color range subtracted from it, and looks much cleaner.

Selecting by outlining: The Freehand tool

We find the Freehand tool to be one of the most useful of the selection tools, especially in Smart Edge mode. It lets you define the area you want by outlining. It even helps you with that outlining so that you don't have to scrutinize every pixel you include or exclude.

On the Tools toolbar, click the lasso icon (the Freehand tool), as shown in Figure 3-1. The Tool Options palette then looks something like the one shown in Figure 3-3. (Press the F4 key to flash the Tool Options palette on or off if you have misplaced it.)

Figure 3-3:
Four ways to outline your selection with the lasso (the Freehand tool).

The Freehand tool gives you four ways to snare a selection. From the Selection type drop-down list, choose whichever of these methods best suits the area you're trying to select:

- ✔ **Freehand:** Drag an outline around the area you want to select. At whatever point you release the mouse button, Paint Shop Pro finishes the outline with a straight line to your starting point. This method is best for an area with a complex shape, especially if it doesn't have a clear edge. (If it does have a clear edge, try the Smart Edge method instead.)

- ✔ **Point to Point:** Click at points around the area you want to select. As you click, the outline appears as straight line segments connecting those points. To close the loop, double-click or right-click, and Paint Shop Pro draws the final line segment from that point back to the starting point. This method works well for areas with straight edges.

- ✔ **Smart Edge:** If the area you want to select has a noticeable edge — a transition between light and dark, such as the edge of someone's head against a contrasting background — choose this type of selection. To begin, click at any point along the edge. A skinny rectangle appears, with one end attached to the cursor. Move the cursor to another point along the edge so that a portion of the edge is contained entirely within the rectangle and then click. Paint Shop Pro selects along the edge. Continue clicking along the edge in this way; Figure 3-4 shows you the result. Double-click or right-click, and Paint Shop Pro finishes the outline with a straight line back to your starting point.

✔ **Edge Seeker:** This option works much like Smart Edge, except that you can set how wide an area it searches to find an edge (called the Range, it's measured in pixels). As with most Paint Shop Pro elements, you can change the Range on the Tool Options palette.

Figure 3-4:
Alex's coat forms an edge that Smart Edge can detect.

Here are a few tips for selecting with the Freehand tool:

✔ **Aborting:** You can't abort the selection process after you begin. Instead, right-click (or release the mouse button if you're dragging) to finish the loop, and then press Ctrl+D or right-click again to remove the selection.

✔ **Undoing segments:** If you're in the middle of using Point to Point or Smart Edge and make a mistake, you can undo segments by pressing the Delete key on your keyboard.

✔ **Being precise:** When you're using Smart Edge, click directly on or near the edge as you go around the shape. (Put another way, don't overshoot any bends in the edge or let the edge exit the rectangle from the side of the rectangle.)

✔ **Smoothing edges:** The Freehand tool provides anti-aliasing and feathering, which, if you're going to use them, you should set up before making the selection. See the later sections "Feathering for More Gradual Edges" and "Anti-Aliasing for Smoother Edges."

✔ **Using layers:** If your image uses layers, Smart Edge normally looks for the edge within only the active layer. If you want Smart Edge to look at all layers combined, click to enable the Sample Merged check box.

Selecting a rectangle or other regular shape

Selecting a rectangular area is particularly useful for copying portions of an image to paste elsewhere as a separate image. This technique is also useful for working on portions of your image that happen to *be* rectangular. The Selection tool lets you select rectangles, circles, and other predetermined shapes.

To create a selection area, click the Selection tool (see Figure 3-5) or press the S key, and then drag diagonally on your image. You determine the shape you drag on the Tool Options palette, as shown in Figure 3-5.

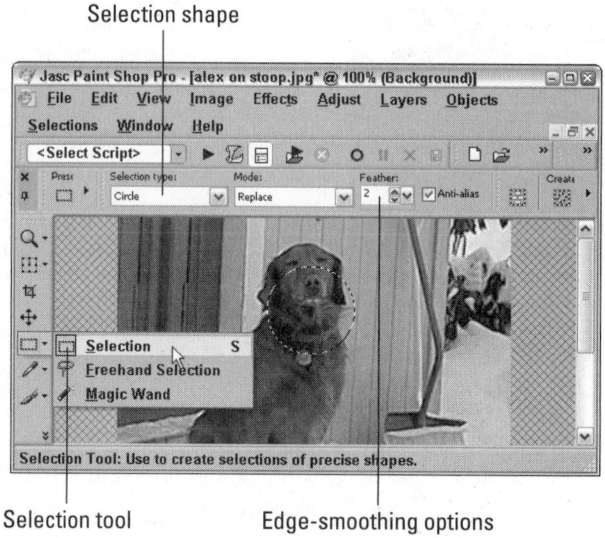

Selection shape

Figure 3-5:
Choose the
Selection
tool and
then a
shape (here,
a circle) and
any edge-
smoothing
options.
Drag to
select
an area.

Selection tool   Edge-smoothing options

Choose one of the many shape selections from the drop-down list. Drag diagonally to give your area both width and height. Here are a few tips for making and changing your selection:

✔ **Try again:** After you define a selection, you can't resize it by dragging sides or corners, as you may expect. (Try it, and you drag the entire selection instead.) Right-click anywhere to clear the shape to try again. Or, you can simply drag a fresh shape if you begin your new drag operation anywhere outside the existing selection.

✔ **Drag:** After you have selected an area, you can drag to move that portion of the image and expose whatever background color or underlying
layer lies beneath your picture. Accidental dragging is very easy, but, as
with any accident, just press Ctrl+Z to undo an accidental drag.

✔ **Modify:** To move, add to, or subtract from the selection, see the section
"Modifying Your Selection," later in this chapter.

Selecting by color or brightness: The Magic Wand tool

Sometimes, you want to select an area so uniform in appearance that you want
to simply tell Paint Shop Pro, "Go select that red balloon" or whatever it is.
To you, with your human perception, the area is an obvious thing of some
sort. In software, anything that even slightly mimics human perception is
often called *magic.* The Magic Wand selection tool is no exception. It can
identify and select areas of uniform color or brightness, somewhat as your
eye does.

One benefit of this tool is that you can select areas with complex edges that
would be a pain in the wrist to trace with the Freehand tool. For example, a
selection of blue sky that includes a complex skyline of buildings and trees
would be relatively easy to make with the Magic Wand tool.

The Magic Wand tool doesn't, however, work as well as your eye. In particular, if the color or brightness of the area you're trying to select isn't uniform
or doesn't contrast strongly with the surroundings, the selection is likely to
be spotty or incomplete or have rough edges.

Paint Shop Pro gives you lots of ways to improve an imperfect selection. See
the section "Modifying Your Selection," later in this chapter, and particularly
the subsection "Removing specks and holes in your selection."

Making the selection

To make a selection, select the Magic Wand from the selection tool group,
as shown in Figure 3-6. Your cursor takes on the Magic Wand icon. Click
the Magic Wand cursor on your image and it selects all pixels that match
(or nearly match) the pixel you clicked.

To get the selection you want when you use the Magic Wand tool, consult the
Tool Options palette. The Tool Options palette for the Magic Wand tool looks
like the one shown in Figure 3-6. The palette lets you define (by using the

Match Mode list box) exactly what you mean by *match* and lets you adjust (by adjusting the Tolerance setting) how closely the selected pixels should match the one you clicked.

Match mode Tolerance

Figure 3-6:
Choosing
tolerance
and other
options for
the Magic
Wand
before using
it ensures
better
magic.

To select a contiguous area of similar pixels around the point where you click (all of Alex, for example), make sure that Contiguous is selected on the Tool Options palette. To select all similar pixels regardless of where they are in the image — any Alex-colored pixel anywhere, for example — deselect the Contiguous check box.

If your image uses layers, be sure that the active layer is the one containing the pixels you're trying to click with the Magic Wand. If you want the Magic Wand tool to examine all layers combined, enable the Sample Merged check box on the Tool Options palette. Otherwise, the Magic Wand tool selects a totally wrong area and you wonder what's happening!

Choosing Match mode for better results

Click the Match Mode list box and you can choose exactly how you want Paint Shop Pro to select the pixels around the place you clicked. Some of the choices are shown in this list:

✔ **RGB Value:** When you choose this option, you tell Paint Shop Pro to "select pixels that match in both color *and* brightness." Clicking a red apple by using this choice may select only the highlighted side where you clicked, for example. Technically, it selects all adjacent pixels with red (R), green (G), and blue (B) primary color values that match the one you clicked.

✔ **Hue:** You're telling Paint Shop Pro to "select pixels that match in color" when you choose Hue. Hue, however, is somewhat more independent of brightness than the RGB value. Clicking a red apple with this choice is more likely to select the entire apple than if you choose RGB Value. Technically, this option selects all adjacent pixels with hues (in the Hue/Saturation/Lightness color system, or color wheel) that match the hue of the pixel you clicked.

✔ **Brightness:** Brightness disregards color and selects all adjacent pixels whose brightness matches the one you clicked. This choice is useful for selecting things that are similarly illuminated, like shadows and high-lights, or that are in a notably light or dark color compared with the background.

✔ **Opacity:** *Opacity* is a measure of how transparent your image is. Opacity mode selects anything that's suitably close to the transparency of the selected pixel. For example, if a layer contains brush strokes at various opacities, Opacity lets you select strokes of a specific range of opacity.

✔ **All Opaque:** This option is a special choice for when you're working on an image or a layer that has transparent areas — areas of no content whatever — usually displayed with a checkered background. All Opaque tells Paint Shop Pro to select the area that has content around the pixel where you clicked. For example, you may have photos of various air freshener products on an otherwise transparent layer, artistically float-ing over a cow pasture on the background layer. With this choice, you can just click one of the products to select it in its entirety.

Experiment to get the mode that works best for you! Press Ctrl+D to deselect each failed experiment, change match modes, and click again with the Magic Wand tool.

Setting tolerance to include more or fewer pixels

The Tolerance setting on the Tool Options palette helps you determine how much of an area is selected by the Magic Wand tool. You may have to undo your selection by right-clicking, adjust the tolerance, and click again with the Magic Wand tool several times to get the best selection possible. For an easier solution, see the discussion of expanding and filling in selections in the following section.

Tolerance tells Paint Shop Pro how closely the pixels it selects should match the pixel you clicked — in RGB value, hue, or brightness, depending on which match mode you chose. (Tolerance doesn't matter for All Opaque match mode. A pixel either has content or it doesn't.) Here's how it works:

- ✔ Lower the tolerance value to select fewer pixels the next time you click.
- ✔ Raise the tolerance value to select more pixels the next time you click.

In Paint Shop Pro, low tolerance means that the Magic Wand tool tolerates little variation in color or brightness from the pixel you clicked. The tolerance value itself has no particular meaning; it's just a number.

The Tolerance value box on the Magic Wand tool's Tool Options palette has a clever adjustment feature you find in similar boxes throughout Paint Shop Pro. As with these types of boxes in any Windows program, you can type a value (from 0 to 200) in its text box or click its up or down arrow to adjust the value. We find that the best way is to click the down arrow, or clever adjustment feature, and hold the mouse button down. A tiny slider appears, which you can drag left or right to set the tolerance value lower or higher.

Tolerance can be a sensitive and picky adjustment. A small change can sometimes make a big difference in what gets selected. Unless you're trying to select an area well differentiated by color, brightness, or content, you probably have to adjust your selected area afterward. We tell you how to do that in the next section.

Modifying Your Selection

If you didn't select exactly the area you want with one of the Paint Shop Pro selection tools, don't despair. You can fine-tune or completely rework your selection in any of these ways:

- ✔ Drag the selection outline to another area of your image.
- ✔ Add to or subtract from your selection by using the selection tools.
- ✔ Expand or contract the selection's boundary by a given number of pixels.
- ✔ Remove holes or specks in your selection.
- ✔ Edit the selection with the Paint Brush or Eraser tool.
- ✔ Grow the selection to include adjacent pixels of similar color or brightness.
- ✔ Select pixels of similar color or brightness anywhere in the image.

The following sections tell you how to make each one of those modifications. Read on!

Moving the selection outline

To move the selection outline (marquee) to another area of your image, first click the Move tool, as shown in the margin (or press the M key). Then hold down the *right* mouse button anywhere in the selection area and drag to move the outline elsewhere.

Adding to or subtracting from your selection

You can use the selection tools to add to or remove from your selection. You can add any area at all, and using any selection tool — not just the one you used to create the selection.

Performing the addition or subtraction is as simple as, well, arithmetic — simpler, even. Do either of the following:

- ✔ **To add areas to an existing selection:** Hold down the Shift key (or choose Add [Shift] as your mode on the Tool Options palette). Then, as with any selection tool, make a new selection outside (or overlapping) the original selection. A + sign appears next to the tool's cursor to remind you that you're adding.

- ✔ **To subtract areas from an existing selection:** Hold down the Ctrl key (or choose Subtract [Ctrl] as your mode on the Tool Options palette). Then, make a selection within (or overlapping) the original selection. A – sign attaches itself to the selection tool's cursor.

Here's an example. In Figure 3-7, we originally clicked with the Magic Wand tool on the blue clothing worn by Dave's wife, Katy, and used Brightness for the match mode. (We chose Brightness over Hue because the contrast in brightness between dark blue clothing and white snow was stronger than the uniformity of the blue.) The selection extended over to sled dog Starr's darker markings, however, which we didn't want.

To remove Starr from this selection, we held down the Ctrl key and used the Freehand tool (set to the Freehand selection type) to draw a loop around Starr. Figure 3-7 shows you this loop nearing completion. Note the – sign near the lasso cursor, indicating subtraction. When we released the mouse button, Paint Shop Pro completed the loop and subtracted Starr from the selection. We could just as easily have used the Selection tool and (with the Ctrl key pressed) dragged an elliptical selection around Starr. In real life, Starr was never this easy to lasso.

Figure 3-7:
Removing
Starr from
the selec-
tion by
outlining her
with the
Freehand
tool while
pressing
the Ctrl key.

Expanding and contracting by pixels

Expanding or *contracting* a selection in Paint Shop Pro simply means adding or removing a set of pixels around the edge of the selection area. It's like packing snow onto a snowman or melting it away. You can expand or contract a selection by as many snowflakes, er, pixels as you like. Follow these steps:

1. **Choose Selections⇨Modify⇨Expand, or Selections⇨Modify⇨Contract.**

   The Expand Selection, or Contract Selection, dialog box appears.

2. **Set the Number of Pixels control to however many pixels you want to add or remove.**

   To examine the effect closely, zoom in by clicking the magnifying glass icon marked with a + in the dialog box. Drag the image in the right panel to move it around. To see the effect in your actual image, click the Proof button (with the eye icon).

3. **Click OK when you're done.**

Removing specks and holes in your selection

If the current selection has holes in it that you want selected or has specks of selected areas you don't want, you can fix it. This feature is especially useful for selections made with the Magic Wand.

This feature works in a more understandable fashion if your selection has no feathering (see the following section).

After you have an area selected, follow these steps:

1. **Choose Selections➪Modify➪Remove Specks and Holes.**

   You're presented with a Remove Specks and Holes dialog box, as shown in Figure 3-8, which shows you the selected area on the left and the despecked or deholed area on the right. This box needs to know the maximum size of the speck or hole to be filled in (as measured in pixels, the smallest element of the picture that can be measured).

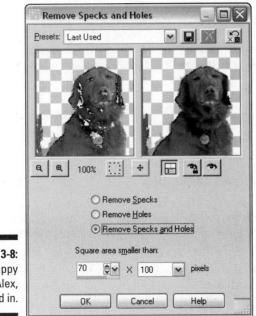

Figure 3-8:
A gappy
Alex,
filled in.

2. **To select the Remove Specks, Remove Holes, or Remove Specks and Holes option, click the appropriate option box.**

3. **In the two boxes labeled Square Area Smaller Than, enter the size (the area in total pixels) of the largest holes or specks to be removed.**

   The numbers in the boxes are a bit confusing, so think of it as a multiplication project: In Figure 3-8, the left number is set to 70 and the right number is chosen to be 100. (The number on the right goes up in multiples of 10.) Any speck of selection in Figure 3-8 that is smaller than 7,000 pixels is removed; any hole smaller than that is filled.

4. **When the picture on the right looks correct, click OK.**

   If you're not sure whether all the holes and specks are fixed, zoom in by clicking the magnifying glass icon marked with a + and move your view by dragging on the image in the right panel. To see the selection in your actual image, click the button with the eye icon. Change the left number in Step 3 to fine-tune the result.

As you can see, the holes in Alex's interior get filled in, but they're not expanded out along the border. The danger is that if you select too wide an area, Paint Shop Pro may well decide that your entire selection is one huge gap and erase it.

Editing the selection

Tired of all that adding and subtracting to get exactly the selection you want? Wish that you could just paint the selection area? Well, here's how:

1. **Choose Selections⇨Edit Selections.**

   The selected area turns a stimulating reddish orange. (This color, and in fact the procedure, should be familiar if you have used "masks" in image editing.)

2. **In the Materials palette, choose white as your foreground/stroke color and black as your background/fill color.**

   In the Foreground/Stroke Properties box or Background/Fill Properties box, you can right-click to quickly choose black or white. Choosing gray gives an intermediate degree of selection (a sort of transparency), which may confuse the heck out of you.

3. **Use the Paint Brush tool to paint the new selected area, or the Eraser tool to remove the selected area.**

4. **Choose Selections⇨Edit Selections to exit the editing process.**

Feathering for More Gradual Edges

When you copy or modify selected areas, you may notice that the edge between the selection and the background becomes artificially obvious. To keep a natural-looking edge on these types of objects, use feathering in your selection.

Feathering creates a blending zone of several pixels (however many you choose) extending both into and out of your selection. Whatever change you make to the selected area fades gradually within that zone, from 100 percent at the inner edge to 0 percent at the outer edge of the zone. For example, if you were to increase the brightness of the selected area, that increase fades gradually to 0 at the outer edge of the feathered zone. If you delete, copy, cut, or move a feathered selection, you also leave a feathered edge behind.

You can apply feathering in either of two ways:

- ✔ **Before making the selection:** On the Tool Options palette for whatever selection tool you're using, set the Feather value to something greater than zero. When you next make a selection, the feathering is applied and the marquee's enclosed area expands to include the outer feathered pixels.

- ✔ **After making the selection:** Choose Selections➪Modify➪Feather and the Feather Selection dialog box appears. Set the Number of Pixels value in that dialog box to the number of pixels you want the selection feathered, and then click OK. The area within the selection marquee expands.

The value you set in the Feather control tells Paint Shop Pro how wide to make the feather zone — how many pixels to extend it into, and out of, the selection. (A setting of 4, for example, creates a feathered zone 4 pixels into and 4 pixels out from the edge of the selection, for a total of 8 pixels wide.) A larger value makes a wider, more gradually feathered edge. When you feather, the marquee expands to include the pixels that are in the feathering zone.

If feathering in all directions is too clumsy for you, you can choose to feather the edge in one direction only, either into the interior of the selection or feathering out beyond its borders. Choose Selections ➪Modify➪ Inside/Outside Feather to display a dialog box that offers exactly the same pixel control of the regular Feather control, except that you get to choose which way you feather.

Figure 3-9 shows you the difference that feathering makes. Normally, Alex is fairly fuzzy around the edges anyway. Feathering makes his edges even fuzzier. From left to right, this is the same image copied without feathering, with feathering in all directions, with inside-only feathering, and with outside-only feathering.

Figure 3-9:
Alex, selected and pasted on a white background, with the four types of feathering.

Unfeathered   Normal (inside/out)   Inside   Outside
                   feathering,   feathering,   feathering,
                   8 pixels   8 pixels   8 pixels

When you copy or move a feathered selection, you bring along a faint border — feathered copies of the original background pixels surrounding the selection.

You can defeather your image by choosing Selections⇨Modify⇨Unfeather; unfortunately, this command isn't like the friendly Undo button, where it magically undoes any feathering you have added. Instead, this command displays a dialog box in which you can set the *threshold* of how harshly you want to strip any fuzziness from the edges of your selection; a low threshold gives your selection a light shave, whereas a high threshold reduces your selection to a sticklike skeleton of itself.

Because feathering a selection expands the marquee, it gives the appearance of filling in holes in a selection (adding them entirely to the selection). It doesn't really add those holes entirely to the selection, however; the pixels in them are simply feathered. As a result, if you feather a selection that has holes in it and then cut, delete, or move it, you leave behind faint images of those holes. If your selection has holes, try removing specks and holes or smoothing the selection *before* you feather it.

Anti-Aliasing for Smoother Edges

Because computer images are made up of tiny squares (the pixels), when a straight edge of a selection is anything other than perfectly horizontal or vertical, those squares give the edge a microscopic staircase, or sawtooth, shape known as *aliasing*. Any changes you make to the selected area, or any cutting or pasting of the selection, may make that aliasing objectionably obvious.

To avoid aliasing when you next make a selection, click to enable the Anti-alias check box on the Tool Options palette for your selection tool. Anti-aliasing is available for only the Freehand tools, not the Magic Wand or the Selection tool. (You can use feathering to reduce most aliasing problems.)

The anti-aliasing option, like other settings on the Tool Options palette, applies to only selections you make *after* choosing that option, not to a *current* selection. You can't fix an existing aliased selection by clicking that option.

Selecting All, None, or Everything But

Sometimes, you want a selection to be an all-or-nothing proposition! To select the entire image, press Ctrl+A or choose Selections⇨Select All.

The easiest way to select complex shapes

Selecting *everything but* and then inverting is a useful trick when you may have a complex object on a comparatively uniform background. Rather than spend lots of effort selecting the object, you can more easily select the uniform background with the Magic Wand tool and then, by pressing Ctrl+Shift+I, invert the selection (which selects the complex object). It doesn't work if the background is complex, but you would be surprised at how much time you can save.

However, if you do have a complex background, you can use the Background Eraser to clear a "moat" of transparent space around the shape you want selected and then switch to the regular Eraser tool to remove everything outside that moat. Then use the Magic Wand to select the transparent space around your image and invert it.

To *select none* (also known as *clearing* the selection or *deselecting*), press Ctrl+D or choose Selections⇨Select None. You can also clear selections (except when the entire image is selected) by right-clicking anywhere on the image.

Sometimes, you may want to select *everything but* the part of the image that is *not* selected. This process is known as *inverting* the selection. To perform it, choose Selections⇨Invert or press Ctrl+Shift+I.

An Example: Selecting Alex, and Only Alex

So, you have a problem: Your dog (the one in our example is named Alex) is sick of the snow. Sure, you *could* send him to a tropical paradise, but you have decided that it's much simpler to select him so that you can cut and paste him into a picture of the Caribbean. Then you show him the picture and tell him that he was in the tropics just last week.

The genius of dogs is that they require surprisingly little evidence to believe anything you tell them. So, how do you complete the transfer?

1. **Select the Magic Wand tool from the selection tool group.**

   Because you're trying to select Alex and he's the only really brown thing in the picture, set the Magic Wand tool options to a match mode of Color.

2. Set the tolerance of the Magic Wand.

Here's the trick: Even we hardened professional Paint Shop Pro experts (we're writing a book on it, aren't we?) *are never sure what number to use for tolerance* — like everyone else, we guess.

We guess 100, which, as you can see in Figure 3-10, turns out to be way too much. Right-click to clear the selection and try again. A little experimenting with the tolerance shows you that a tolerance of 25 is a solid starting point.

Figure 3-10: Alex, at 25 tolerance and 100 tolerance (selections filled in black for greater clarity).

25 tolerance   100 tolerance

3. Shift-click a few stray selections to clean up the edges.

The Magic Wand selected most of this cuddly retriever, but Alex's ear, the underside of his left foot, and his right rear foot are still not selected. Those are also the areas where the color tends to vary a little more wildly, by shifting from almost black to light green, so set the tolerance a little higher, to 50, for example — and then Shift+click in these areas to add those places to your selection. As you can see in Figure 3-11, that action adds the ears and feet, and also adds unwanted portions of the door to your selection.

Figure 3-11: Alex, with more added, and also the door.

4. **Fill in the small gaps.**

   Choose Selections⇨Modify⇨Remove Specks and Holes and set it to 70 x
   100 pixels, which automatically chooses any gap smaller than 700 pixels.
   Look back at Figure 3-8 to see the clear difference; click OK.

5. **Ctrl+click the door away.**

   Although you can create some fancy shenanigans with the Select Color
   Range option to remove that pesky door, you have a simpler solution:
   Because it's all in one place, you can just Ctrl+select it away. Remember
   that Shift+select adds to your existing selection, whereas Ctrl+select
   subtracts it. In this case, you switch to the Freehand tool, hold down
   Ctrl, and draw a ring around the door to remove it.

6. **Feather the edges.**

   Now, the edges are crisp — *too* crisp, as you can see in Figure 3-12. A little
   feathering makes the selection edge softer and blends it with any background in which you paste it. Choose Selections⇨Modify⇨ Inside/Outside
   Feather and opt to feather the inside of the selection by two pixels.

Alex before feathering:
Notice the jagged, blocky edge?

Figure 3-12:
The two
sides of
Alex: pre-
and post-
feathering.

Alex after feathering,
with his edges muted

Avoiding Selection Problems in Layered Images

Layered images can cause both the selection and the editing of those selections to go apparently screwy. The Magic Wand tool and Smart Edge features
may appear neither magic nor smart, by selecting areas not at all like what
you had in mind. Also, whatever changes you try to perform to the selected
area (such as cutting, copying, or changing color) may apparently not take
place. (If you're not sure whether your image has layers, see Chapter 11.)

The basic trick is to work on the right layer. Here are some more detailed rules you can follow to keep the selection and editing process relatively sane:

✔ **Activate the right layer:** Before you make any changes to a selected area (such as fill-painting it), be sure to activate the layer you want to change. Otherwise, you paint (or otherwise modify) whatever layer happens to be active at the time.

✔ **Use Sample Merged for combined layers:** Before you make a selection with the Magic Wand tool or Smart Edge feature, if the object you're trying to select is the result of various layers combined, enable the Sample Merged check box on the Tool Options palette. That way, the Magic Wand tool or Smart Edge feature examines the combined effect, not just the active layer. For example, if you added a party hat to Uncle Charley's head on a separate layer and now you want to select Charley-with-hat by using the Smart Edge feature, you use Sample Merged.

✔ **Consider the effect of higher layers:** If the changes you try to make to a selected area aren't visible or seem only partially effective, a higher opaque or transparent layer may contain pixels that are obscuring your work. You may have to merge layers, make your changes to the higher, obscuring layer, or rethink your use of layers altogether.

Paint Shop Pro helps keep you sane. The preview window that certain adjustments provide (such as Brightness/Contrast) shows you only the area you're affecting: the selected part of the active layer. If the wrong layer is active, you don't see the area you're expecting!

When you make a selection, it extends to all layers — no matter which one is active at the time. *Changes* to selected image areas, however (like painting), affect only the active layer. So, you can activate one layer, for example, to make a selection with the Magic Wand tool and then switch to another layer to make changes within that selected area.

Chapter 4

Moving, Copying, and Reshaping Parts of Your Image

In This Chapter

▶ Moving, floating, copying, or deleting a selection

▶ Using the Windows Clipboard

▶ Reshaping selections

*I*n Chapter 3, we tell you how to select a chunk of your image in Paint Shop Pro. In this chapter, you see how to move, copy, twist, and deform a selection — in short, how to do almost anything that changes the physical location or outline of a selection. (Paint Shop Pro also lets you rotate, flip, or mirror a selection. Just select something and follow the same directions Chapter 2 gives for rotating, flipping, or mirroring an entire image.)

✔ If your image has multiple layers, make sure that you're working on the right layer. See Chapter 12 for help with layers.

✔ You can press Ctrl+Z to undo any changes you make. The changes you can undo include selecting, floating, moving, copying, pasting, or defloating.

✔ The instructions in this chapter deal only with selections to bitmap or raster images (images made from dots, not objects like rectangles or text). To deal with vector selections (typically, text, lines, and geometric shapes), see Chapter 12.

Floating, Moving, and Deleting Selections

After you have made a selection, you can easily move it anywhere within your image, move a copy of it, or delete it altogether. Here's how to do it:

✔ **To move a selection:** Choose any selection tool (Selection, Freehand, or Magic Wand) and then drag the selection. Selection tool cursors become 4-headed move arrows when you position them over a selection, as shown in Figure 4-1. On the Background (main) image layer, dragging a selection in this way leaves behind background color. The image on the left in Figure 4-1 shows you the effect.

✔ **To float a selection (make it moveable):** A *floating* selection simply means a moveable one. You can float a selection in one of two ways. When you click an existing selection with a selection tool (as the preceding bullet describes), that selection is floated automatically. Alternatively, you can choose Selections⇨Float or press Ctrl+F. Floating a selection in that way (manually) leaves a copy of it behind. (Note that any floating selection also appears on the Layer palette.)

✔ **To move a selection and leave a copy behind (as the right side of Figure 4-1 shows you):** *Float the selection manually first* (choose Selections⇨Float or press Ctrl+F) and then move it with the Mover tool (the 4-headed arrow) or any selection tool.

✔ **To defloat the floating selection (or glue it back down):** To *defloat* a selection, press Ctrl+Shift+F or choose Selections⇨Defloat. You can also *deselect* (press Ctrl+D) to defloat. The defloating command leaves the area selected in case you want to do additional work on it. Whichever way you defloat the image, defloating glues the image down. It's now part of the underlying image (or image layer), and its pixels replace whatever was there. If you move the selection again, you find that the original underlying pixels are no longer there.

Simply dragging leaves background color

Figure 4-1:
Dragging a selection. Float the image first with Ctrl+F to drag a copy.

Float, then drag to move a copy

✔ **To delete the selection:** Press the Delete key on your keyboard. If the selection is on the background layer, the Paint Shop Pro background color appears in the deleted area. If the selection is on a layer, the pixels within the selection simply go away. (Okay, technically, they're made transparent — same thing.)

✔ **To move a floating selection to another layer:** Drag the *Floating Selection* layer up or down on the Layer palette. (Press F8 to display the Layer palette if it's not showing.) Leave the selection immediately above the layer you ultimately want the selection to join. When you defloat the selection, it joins the closest underlying (raster) layer.

You can also flip or mirror a selection. See the section in Chapter 2 about getting turned around, mirrored, or flipped for information about using the Flip and Mirror commands. Both commands leave a copy of the original image underlying the selection.

Cutting, Copying, and Pasting from the Windows Clipboard

To make lots of copies of a selection, use the conventional cut, copy, and paste features that employ the Windows Clipboard. You can use these features for copying selections to or from other Windows applications too because nearly all Windows applications make use of the Clipboard.

If your image has multiple layers, first make sure that you have selected the right layer to cut, copy, or paste the image you want. Click the layer's name on the Layer palette. (Press F8 if the palette isn't visible). See Chapter 12 for more help with layers.

Cutting and copying

In Paint Shop Pro, *cut* and *copy* work much the same as they do in any Windows program. First, select an area in your image. Then, do any of these tasks:

✔ **Cut a selection:** Press Ctrl+X, choose Edit⇨Cut, or click the familiar Windows Cut button (scissors icon) on the Paint Shop Pro toolbar. Paint Shop Pro places a copy of the selected area on the Windows Clipboard. If you're cutting on the main (Background) layer of the image, Paint Shop Pro fills the cut area with the current background color on the color palette. On other layers, it leaves behind transparency.

- ✔ **Copy a selection:** Press Ctrl+C, choose Edit⇨Copy, or click the Copy button (2-documents icon) on the Paint Shop Pro toolbar. Paint Shop Pro puts a copy of the selected area (of the active layer) on the Windows Clipboard. Nothing happens to your image.

- ✔ **Copy a merged selection from a multilayer image:** The normal Edit⇨ Copy command copies only from the active layer. If your image is made up of multiple layers, you may want to copy the combined effect of all layers. If so, choose Edit⇨Copy Merged (or press Ctrl+Shift+C).

- ✔ **Cut or copy from other applications:** Most Windows applications offer the same Edit⇨Copy and Edit⇨Cut commands, so you can place text or graphics on the Windows Clipboard. Paint Shop Pro enables you to paste a wide variety of Clipboard content from other programs, such as text, vector graphics, or raster graphics.

Pasting

After your selection is on the Windows Clipboard, choose Edit⇨Paste to paste it into Paint Shop Pro (or nearly any other application). When you choose Edit⇨Paste in Paint Shop Pro, however, you get several different paste options.

If you're in the habit of using Ctrl+V for pasting in other programs, you need to retrain yourself. In Paint Shop Pro, Ctrl+V creates a new image rather than pastes your selection to the existing image, which is what you probably expect to happen.

One pasting option we cover elsewhere in this book is Paste As New Vector Selection. This command is used only for pasting text and shapes you create by using the Paint Shop Pro Text tool and various shape tools. For more about vectors, see Chapter 12.

For better paste jobs, see the section in Chapter 8 that gives you tips for natural-looking pastes.

Pasting to create a new picture: As New Image

The Paste As New Image option creates a new image containing the Clipboard contents. The image is just big enough to contain whatever is on the Clipboard. The background of the image is transparent, which means that if your copied selection isn't rectangular, you see transparent areas; erasing also leaves transparency behind.

Choose Edit⇨Paste⇨Paste As New Image or press Ctrl+V (the nearly universal keyboard command for Paste). Your new image appears in a new window.

If you prefer your new image to have a background color or to be slightly larger than the contents of the Clipboard, create the new image first, separately (refer to Chapter 1). Then paste a selection or new layer rather than use the Paste As New Image command.

Pasting on an existing image: As New Selection

The Paste As New Selection option pastes the Clipboard contents as a floating selection on your image. This pasting option is the one most people want for editing an image because it is the simplest and most intuitive.

If your image uses multiple layers, make sure to first activate the layer where you want to paste (refer to Chapter 12).

Because the selection is floating, you drag the selection to move it anywhere in the image. To defloat the selection (paste it down on the underlying layer), press Ctrl+Shift+F or choose Selection⇨Defloat. See the earlier section "Floating, Moving, and Deleting Selections," for details about moving and defloating a floating selection.

Pasting for maximum flexibility: As New Layer

Pasting directly on another image is fine, as far as it goes. For maximum flexibility in making future changes, however, paste on a new layer instead. When an image is on a layer, you can modify it to your heart's content without worrying about surrounding or underlying image areas. (In Chapter 12, we discuss the whys and hows of layers in detail.) Here's how:

1. **If your image already has more than one layer, activate (choose) the layer above which you want the new layer to appear.**

   For example, click the layer on the Layer palette to activate it. See Chapter 12 for more details on activating layers.

2. **Choose Edit⇨Paste⇨Paste As New Layer (or press Ctrl+L).**

   Your pasted image appears on a layer of its own.

If the background of the image you pasted was transparent, the underlying image layer shows through those background areas. Otherwise, the pasted image and its background color fill an opaque rectangle. If you want to delete the background (make it transparent), use the Magic Wand tool, or another selection tool, to select it (refer to Chapter 12) and press the Delete key on your keyboard. Alternatively, see the following section.

Moving or pasting without the background color: As Transparent Selection

The most straightforward way to move or paste something (a picture of your kid, for example) without the background is to make sure that you don't select the background in the first place! Refer to Chapter 3 for instructions on making precise selections.

If, however, the background color is uniform (and this is almost never true of a photograph — only a painting or drawing), Paste As Transparent Selection may be faster.

This approach is the same as pasting a new selection, but any color in your selection that matches the current background color is made transparent. Suppose that you have painted a black dot on a white canvas. You can select the dot with a simple rectangular selection, copy and paste it, and not worry about pasting the surrounding white too. Follow these steps:

1. **Make the background color in the Materials dialog box match the image's background by right-clicking the background with the dropper tool.**

2. **Select around the thing you want to copy and don't fret about including the background. Use a rectangular selection, if you like.**

3. **Choose Paste As Transparent Selection (or press Ctrl+Shift+E).**

For most work, where the background is somewhat, but not entirely, uniform, we prefer to remove the background from the selection with the Magic Wand tool. Refer to Chapter 3 for instructions on using the Magic Wand. Select a rough area, as described in Step 2. Then, while holding down the Ctrl key, click the background within that rough area with the Magic Wand. Holding down the Ctrl key removes whatever you click from the selection. Then, copy and paste (or move), background-free, to your heart's content.

Pasting while scaling to fit: Into Selection

If you select an area in your image, you can fit the Clipboard contents exactly into the height and width of the selection and scale the contents up or down as needed. This process is useful for copying the head of Person A onto the body of Person B because rarely are their heads the same size!

Copy the image you want to paste (for example, the head of Person A from Photo A) to the Clipboard by choosing Edit➪Copy. Then, select the area you want to paste into (the head of Person B in Photo B) and choose Edit➪Paste➪Paste Into Selection. The image doesn't fit exactly because of irregular shapes, but you can finesse the edges with other Paint Shop Pro tools.

Resizing, Rotating, Deforming, and Perspective-izing

Okay, so perspective-izing isn't a real word. Perspecting? In any event, you can resize, rotate, deform, or move your selection by using the deformation tool group, as shown in Figure 4-2.

Figure 4-2:
The deformation tool group, where everyone has a skewed perspective.

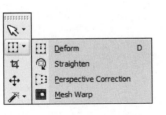

Making a shape look as though it's seen in perspective is one of the cool kinds of deformation you can do. You can make a rectangular area, for example, look like a wall or road receding into the distance. You can paint a railroad track running vertically, flat, as though it's on a map, and then make it lie down realistically by applying perspective.

Preparing for deformation

The deformation tools are picky: They need a separate layer (other than the background layer) to work with. If you're trying to deform a selection, Paint Shop Pro asks you whether it's okay to promote that selection to a layer.

Are you using layers? These tools work on the active layer and encompass all nontransparent areas in that layer. In other words, if you have a blob of pixels on a layer, the tool encompasses (rather neatly, in our opinion) just that blob. If you have multiple blobs separated by transparency, it encompasses all blobs. If you want to deform just one blob, select it.

Doing the deformation

The easy and fairly intuitive way to make a deformation is by dragging various parts of the deformation grid with the Deform tool. See "Deforming by dragging," coming up next.

The geeky, but precise, way to do the deformation is in the Deformation Settings dialog box. See "Deforming by dialog box," a bit later in this chapter.

Deforming by dragging

Select the Deform tool from the deformation tool group(if it's grayed out, refer to the earlier section "Preparing for deformation" for instructions), and your cursor turns into that icon. Click your selection to get this cool-looking *deformation grid* with tiny squares (called *handles*) on it, as shown in Figure 4-3.

Drag anywhere inside grid to move selection

Resizing handles

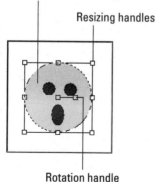

Figure 4-3: The Deform tool's grid for stretching, rotating, and dragging the victim.

Rotation handle

This figure shows you what to drag for resizing, rotating, or moving the image. Note that you can move the selection with this tool by dragging anywhere *except* on one of the handles. (In areas where dragging is possible, the cursor changes to a 4-way arrow.) Here's how to do various operations, by using the handles of the deformation grid:

✓ **Resizing or repositioning sides:** Adjust the width and height by dragging the handle in the center of any side. Drag corner handles to change both the height and width at the same time. (The Deform tool provides no way to automatically keep the proportions constant while you drag, so see the following section for help.)

✔ **Rotating:** Drag the handle, marked Rotation handle in Figure 4-4, in a circular motion around the center of the grid. (When your cursor is over the rotation handle, the cursor depicts the pair of curved arrows shown in the figure. The center of rotation is marked by a square that is at the face's nose.) Only the grid rotates until you release the mouse button; then, the selection rotates.

✔ **Adding perspective:** In the real world, the farther away an object is, the smaller it appears to your eye. Here's how to create that illusion with your selection so that one end looks farther away:

- To shrink any side of the selection as though it were farther away, first hold down the Ctrl key. With that key down, drag one of the two corner handles that terminate the side; drag toward the center of that side. To expand the side, drag away from the center. The side shrinks or expands symmetrically about the center (both corners move). The perspective this distortion creates is symmetrical, as though your eyes were level with the middle of the selection, as the left side of Figure 4-5 shows you.

- To shrink or expand any side asymmetrically (move one corner only), first hold down the Shift key. With that key down, drag a corner handle toward or away from the center handle of that side. When you apply this effect to the left or right side, as shown on the right in Figure 4-5, the result is as though your eyes were at a level above or below center. For example, to get the illusion of a tall wall, drag the upper corner down.

Cursor

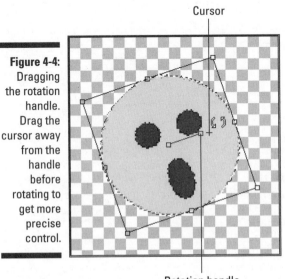

Figure 4-4: Dragging the rotation handle. Drag the cursor away from the handle before rotating to get more precise control.

Rotation handle

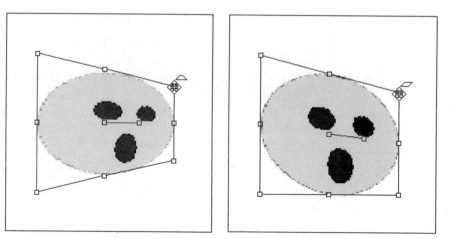

Figure 4-5:
Getting
perspective
by dragging
a corner
while
pressing Ctrl
(left image)
or Shift
(right
image).

✔ **Shear (or *skew*) distortion:** We created the shear effect shown in Figure 4-6 by dragging the right side of the selection down. To drag a side of your selection, hold down either the Ctrl or Shift key and drag the center handle on the side you want to move.

Shear is useful for perspective when you want the virtual horizon (the vanishing point, in drafting terms) to be higher or lower than dead center. Apply perspective distortion to shrink a left or right side first, and then use the shear effect to drag one of those sides up or down. Dragging down, for example, makes the image appear as it would if a viewer were looking up slightly (it lowers the horizon).

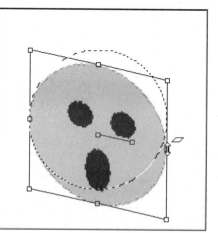

Figure 4-6:
Shear
brilliance!
Dragging a
center
handle with
Ctrl or Shift
pressed
applies
shear
distortion.

Deformation consternations

The Deform tool can occasionally wrinkle your brow with certain weirdnesses. Here are a few typical problems and their solutions:

The tool encompasses the wrong area: You probably have the wrong layer active. Here's what happens: If you're on a layer that's transparent in the selected area, the Deform tool chooses the nontransparent area instead. Press the F8 key to open the Layer palette and click the layer that contains the image you want.

You can't find the deformation grid; you see only two squares and a connecting line: The grid is there, all right, but you have applied the Deform tool to a layer or selection that covers the entire image. Change layers or make a new selection.

An annoying background appears in the area the selection outline has vacated: Well, Paint Shop Pro has to put *something* there, and it can't invent a background image. (Refer to "Preparing for deformation," earlier in this chapter, for more information about backgrounds.) If Paint Shop Pro could stretch the surrounding area to stay continuous with your newly deformed selection, that would be nice, but it isn't so.

Deforming by dialog box

Dragging handles is convenient and intuitive, but not particularly precise. What if you know that you need to rotate something 31.5 degrees, for example? Or scale it down to 85 percent of its original dimensions?

Press F4 to bring up the Tool Options palette, and you can type the settings you want. It provides a column for X, or horizontal values, and Y, or vertical values, and rows for each of the various changes that the Deform tool can make. Here's how to choose the values you need:

- **Position:** To move the selection, enter the X and Y coordinates where you want the upper-left corner of the deformation grid to go. (Remember that X and Y both equal 0 in the upper-left corner of the image.)

- **Scale:** Enter X and Y scale factors. Enter **80** in the X% scale box, for example, to reduce the horizontal size of the selection to 80 percent of the original. To keep the original proportions, put the same value in both the X and Y columns.

- **Shear:** To slide the top edge to the right, enter a positive value; enter a negative value to move the edge the other way.

- **Perspective:** To make the right edge appear to recede into the distance by pulling the upper-right corner down and inward, enter a positive number in the Perspective X box. To make the top edge appear to recede, do likewise in the Y box. Use negative values to make those same edges appear to approach the viewer instead.

✔ **Pivot:** Normally, when you rotate a selection or layer, it rotates around the center. If you want your image to revolve around a different point — around the upper-left corner of the selection, for example, or even around a point that's outside the selection entirely — adjust the pivot values. The numbers in the X and Y boxes vary, but unless you have changed the pivot in the past, those numbers are the exact center of the image. Lower X numbers move the pivot to the left, whereas higher Xs shift it right; lower Y numbers move the pivot up, and higher numbers drop it down.

✔ **Angle:** To rotate the selection clockwise, enter a positive number of degrees (45, for example) into the text box. Use a negative value to rotate the selection counterclockwise.

Other handy deformities

You should know about three other tools in the deformation tool group:

✔ **Mesh Warp:** Using this tool covers your image with a grid of warp points; you can click and drag each of these points to deform your image in specific ways, as you can see in Figure 4-7.

In the left picture, the grid is untouched; in the right, however, we have moved the warp points around and the image has stretched itself to fit the new warp points. (You can control the number of warp points by changing the Mesh Horizontal and Mesh Vertical controls on the Tool Options palette; larger values mean more points. As usual, press F4 if you don't see the Tool Options palette.)

Figure 4-7:
Warping Amy and Alex; the left image is what you see when you first open the Mesh Warp tool, and the right is what happens after some of the points have been shifted about.

You can accomplish some mighty strange effects with this feature, given time and lots of patience; the most common use is to warp an existing image to fit on another image's contour.

✔ **Straighten:** Did you ever spend an afternoon hanging paintings and taking painstaking care to ensure that the bottom edges of the frames were all perfectly parallel with the floor? This tool is an automatic picture adjuster. Most images are at least a little tilted when they're scanned, so we discuss this tool in Chapter 5, in the section about scanning into Paint Shop Pro.

✔ **Perspective Correction:** This tool does the reverse of the Deform tool: If you have an image that's already a little skewed or sheared, you can use this tool to attempt to *remove* the skew or shear. Dragging the Perspective tool around an image creates a box; you can then drag the points on the edge of the box, just as you would with the Deform tool — but in this case you're trying to re-create the shear or skew that's already present. Align the box sides with vertical and horizontal edges in your image. When you're done, double-click the image and Paint Shop Pro attempts to remove the shear. See color plate C-8 in the center of this book for an illustration.

Part II
Prettying Up Photographs

The 5th Wave   By Rich Tennant

"Why don't you try blurring the brimstone and then putting a nice glow effect around the hellfire."

In this part . . .

*E*ver since Kodak sold its first Brownie camera, folks have been snapping pictures like mad — and often, not liking them much. They're too dim, too bright, scratchy, speckly, or simply contain far too much Aunt Martha. But, even Aunt Martha can get an extreme makeover in Paint Shop Pro, even without (much to the disappointment of certain relatives) ever going under the knife. And, if the makeover doesn't work, this section tells you how to remove her altogether and get rid of that terrible wallpaper behind her, too.

The problem goes beyond family snapshots. There's nothing uglier than a bad screen capture of some image or an amateurish scan of a printed image (except perhaps for Uncle Dave). And, of course, you need to be able to get your digital picture into Paint Shop Pro in order to use it. No matter if your problem is unsightly blemishes or looking a bit green, you can hack your way to beauty in Part II.

Chapter 5

Capturing Pictures from Paper, Camera, or Screen

*W*here do your pictures come from? From your new digital camera? From a piece of paper? Or, from your PC screen?

Ironically, most people don't *paint* pictures in Paint Shop Pro. They get an image from somewhere and then mess around with it. This chapter tells you how to use Paint Shop Pro to get that image onto your hard drive. After the image is on your computer, *then* you can start making your pictures prettier.

Connecting to Your Scanner or Camera

Paint Shop Pro has lots of built-in ways to transfer images from a scanner or camera to your hard drive — but the most common methods involve a software program called TWAIN. Much like a career bureaucrat, TWAIN doesn't do anything by itself; instead, it acts as an interpreter, translating your scanner or camera's language into native Windows-speak. If your camera or scanner came with an installation disc, chances are good that the software it installed is TWAIN-compliant, which means that Paint Shop Pro (a Windows program) can use TWAIN to get images from your scanner or camera.

Another method of getting computers and cameras to talk to each other is the Microsoft Windows Image Acquisition (WIA) method, which serves the same function as TWAIN but isn't quite as popular. If your scanner or camera supports WIA, follow the instructions that came with the device for installing and using WIA.

In this chapter, our instructions usually assume that you're using the long-time standard, the TWAIN software interface. However, the instructions also give general scanning tips for everyone, regardless of what form of connection you use.

Getting Images from a Digital Camera

Digital cameras were *made* for family get-togethers. You can preview your photo seconds after you have taken it and share the fun with your friends. You can take 200 snapshots over the course of an afternoon without changing film. And, if an unflattering photo highlights your bald spot, you can quietly delete the evidence before anyone else sees!

The good news is that Paint Shop Pro can be a great tool for enhancing your digital photos. First, however, you have to get the pictures off the camera and onto your PC, which means that you need to get your PC and camera talking to each other. They have to connect (or *interface,* in geekspeak) both physically and with their software.

Getting RAW power from your camera

On certain high-end cameras, you can elect to save your pictures in RAW format, which is a special file type that sidesteps the automatic corrections that most digital cameras make to fix photos taken by everyday doofuses like you and us. Most digital cameras automatically perform rudimentary sharpening and color correction before saving a file. When a camera saves an image in RAW format, however, it does no processing to the image. What you saw is what you get.

Professional photographers refer to RAW files as "true digital negatives" and prefer them because

they feel that the autocorrected images are too synthetic and artificial. If you too rage against the machine, rejoice! Paint Shop Pro 9 can now read RAW files. (You have to read your camera's manual to find out how to get your digicam to produce them, however.)

For most people, however, regular ol' JPEGs or TIF files — the two formats that cameras usually save in — are just fine. If all you want is photos of your latest cookout, RAW is probably irrelevant.

Connecting hardware-wise

We wish that we could give you exact instructions on how to hook your camera into your PC, but digital cameras — particularly, older ones — connect in all sorts of mysterious ways. Your physical connection may be a serial port (a connector on the back of most PCs, if a modem or something else isn't already using it), a parallel (printer) port, a USB port, a FireWire port, a memory card that plugs into your computer, a floppy disk, an infrared beam, X-rays, semaphore flags, or magical auras — who knows what the camera people will come up with next? You have to consult your camera manual for precise details.

However, the way *most* cameras connect to your computer these days is via a *USB port* — a small, rectangular socket about the size of a Chiclet held sideways. You simply plug one end of a USB cable into your camera's input port and plug the other end into the USB port, and you're ready to go.

Some cameras save their pictures on a small chip called a *flash card* (or, sometimes, *memory stick*). If that's the case, you need to remove the stick from your camera and insert it into a small device called a *flash card reader*. You then plug the reader into your computer.

Many cameras also require you to flip a switch or open the camera lens to put the camera in "upload pictures" mode. Again, check your friendly manual if simply plugging it in isn't enough.

Connecting software-wise

You can use one of four methods to move pictures from your camera to your PC. All but one of them (the easiest way) involves installing the camera's interface software, which comes on a disc with the camera. Most cameras use either a TWAIN-compliant interface or a Windows Image Acquisition (WIA) interface; Paint Shop Pro knows how to use both to transfer your pretty images from your camera's memory to your hard drive.

If the installation program lets you, avoid installing any freebie image software (basically, a cheaper Paint Shop Pro) that comes with the camera. If you do, the installation process may assign certain image file types to that program rather than to Paint Shop Pro. If that happens, refer to the Chapter 1 sidebar that talks about the secrets of opening a file by double-clicking, for making Paint Shop Pro open the right file types when you double-click.

Copying pictures from mounted drives

If your camera is *plug-and-play* enabled (a fancy way of saying that it's smart enough to work with Windows automatically), Windows thinks of your camera as nothing more than a separate hard drive. When you plug in your camera and turn it on, a new drive — helpfully named something like E: or F: — appears in My Computer, as shown in Figure 5-1.

You can copy, delete, or move files on and off your digital camera just like it were any other drive. Simply copy the files to a folder on your computer and open them in Paint Shop Pro — or, if you like, you can even open and edit files while they're still on your camera!

It's not a good idea to edit files while they're still on your camera — not that it does any harm. But, if you're anything like us, you may forget that the image you're altering is still on your camera, and you won't save a copy of your carefully tweaked photograph to your hard drive. Later, when you absent-mindedly clear your camera's memory in order to take more pictures, you lose *everything*.

Using TWAIN to transfer photos

TWAIN, which is the industry standard software that acts as a go-between to Windows and your digicam, is used widely to translate native camera dialects into fluent Windows-speak. If your camera isn't plug-and-play, chances are excellent that TWAIN can get the photos off your memory stick and onto your hard drive.

If you want to import photos directly from Paint Shop Pro, you can sometimes use TWAIN even if your camera supports plug-and-play.

Figure 5-1:
When you have a plug-and-play–enabled camera, your digicam is just another hard drive as far as Windows is concerned. That thing labeled Removable Disk E is one of our cameras!

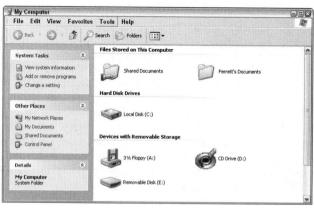

If you have on your computer more than one TWAIN device (a scanner and your camera, for example), first choose File⇨Import⇨TWAIN⇨Select Source. In the Select Source dialog box that appears, click the camera and then click Select.

To begin the downloading process, choose File⇨Import⇨TWAIN⇨Acquire. Some form of dialog box, similar to the one shown in Figure 5-2, arrives on the scene.

Figure 5-2:
Transferring
one or more
photos to
your PC with
a TWAIN-
compliant
camera —
in this case,
an Olympus
D-560.

If you have more than one TWAIN source set up (like a scanner and a camera on the same computer), choosing From Camera or Scanner starts up the scanner rather than the camera. Yes, that *is* irritating if you use your camera more than your scanner.

If that's the case, choose File⇨Import⇨TWAIN⇨Select Source to access your camera; a small dialog box appears that shows you all your TWAIN-compliant devices. Click the one that has a name something like your camera model (ours was Olympus Digital Vision 3.0 33-32) and click OK. Then, choose File⇨ Import⇨TWAIN⇨Acquire to start your camera's download.

Alas, we can't tell you exactly how this happens because the interface that downloads the pictures is unique to each camera. Fortunately, most of them are similar; they present a selection of thumbnails or preview images that you can flip through in some manner.

If you don't see a set of thumbnail images, you may need to hunt for a Get Previews button or menu option.

You see buttons or menu options that allow you to accomplish these common camera tasks:

✔ **Download photos — the whole enchilada:** Look for a Download All, Save All, or perhaps (as in our Olympus example) Select All command before you can click the Download button. *Downloading* means that your photos go directly to your PC's disk drive, as files. You don't see them in Paint Shop Pro. You then can open them in Paint Shop Pro by choosing File➪Open, as you can any other image file (refer to Chapter 1).

✔ **Download selected images — the ones where your child isn't sticking out his tongue:** Browse through the thumbnails (which are sometimes also called *previews*), which you can generally do by clicking the left and right arrows under the thumbnail image or scrolling up and down. The exposure number, date, and time appear next to the image in some cameras, and others may have an Information or Details button to display details.

When you come to a desirable photo that you want to download to your PC, click the image you like and then look for a Save to Disk or Download button or something similar. (You can select multiple images by holding down Ctrl while you click.) You then can open them in Paint Shop Pro by choosing File➪Open.

✔ **Erase the images where your child *is* sticking out his tongue:** Browse through the thumbnails and find the offending images. Click that image and first try pressing Delete, and then look for a Delete, Erase, or Trash button. Clicking this button removes the image from your camera.

✔ **Open a particular image in Paint Shop Pro:** Browse through the thumbnails (as the preceding bullets describe) to that image. Click the image and then look for an Open button. You can also open *all* images in Paint Shop Pro if you select them all and then press Open. That choice may use so much memory, however, that Paint Shop Pro becomes sluggish. To save an open image to disk, refer to the instructions for saving a file in Chapter 1.

For most makes of digital cameras, downloading images doesn't delete them from the camera. Erasing images, however, generally does wipe them from the camera, which you want to do to clear out space for future photos.

Retrieving pictures with WIA

WIA serves the same function as TWAIN, but was never as popular. However, some digital cameras only use WIA, so Paint Shop Pro supports it.

In Paint Shop Pro, choose File➪Import➪From Scanner or Camera to open camera files by using the WIA method. Depending on your camera's make, the program either shows you the photos as though they resided on a hard drive (in which case you would follow the instructions in the earlier section "Copying pictures from mounted drives") or presents you with some sort of preview interface (in which case events are similar to what happens in the earlier section "Using TWAIN to transfer photos").

EXIF, stage left

Once upon a time, taking a photo was an intensely complicated process: You had to be able to set a camera's F-stops, whatever *those* were, read lighting exposures, and, um, snorkel the defibrillating valve. If any of those cryptic settings was set wrong, your pictures of Aunt Flo may have developed as blurry brown smears.

Fortunately, today's digital cameras handle those fine details automatically. Normally, this is a good thing — but sometimes you want to know why one picture looks fantastic and another photo, taken seconds later, looks as though it were taken from behind the glass of an uncleaned aquarium tank. The difference is usually because, for some reason, the camera quietly changed one of its many settings.

If you want to study differences in camera settings to find out what sorts of F-stops and focal lengths create the clearest pictures, you can find out by examining the image's EXIF (Exchangeable Image File) data. EXIF data is saved as part of a JPEG file on most cameras, and it contains all the camera's settings at the time the photo was taken.

One other part of EXIF files is handy, even if you don't give a darn about metering patterns: It stores the date and time the photo was taken and can contain optional extras, such as the artist's name, the artist's comments, and the make of the camera that took it. Some photo albums use EXIF data to help sort through thousands of stored pictures; for example, you can search through keywords stored in the EXIF comments to find a specific photo, even if you don't know the name of the file.

You can edit some parts of a JPEG's EXIF information by choosing Image⇨Image Information and selecting the EXIF Information tab. The editable bits are marked with asterisks.

Your last resort: The camera's native software

If all else fails, it may be that your camera is either very old or very cranky, and it allows you to snarf photos off it *only* via its custom-written interface software. In that case, Paint Shop Pro can't get the images for you; read your camera's manual's for the directions. Sorry 'bout that. You can still save the image from that software to your hard drive by using its File⇨Save command; then open the file in Paint Shop Pro.

Making E-Mail-Ready Photos

William's family *means* well. About twice a month, they send him pictures of his niece, Amanda. Unfortunately, the pictures are the size of billboards and take about an hour-and-a-half to download, which prevents him from doing anything else while he waits for the new picture to arrive.

He loves Amanda, but it's not worth waiting 90 minutes just to see a picture of her.

Chances are, your friends feel the same about your pictures: They want to see your little bubbeleh, but they want to see her quickly. Unfortunately, scanners and digital photos, left to their own devices, give you the biggest, the most detailed, and, above all the *largest* files they can possibly produce. On the Internet, large files mean large download times — and long waits.

Shrinking Photo Download Times

Your friends never tell you that they hate waiting four hours for a picture of your newborn; they just force a smile and say "Those humongous photos were *lovely.*" Be proactive and take these steps to condense your photos — and save your friendship!

1. **Crop the photo so that it shows you only the important parts.**

   If Amanda is on the right side of the picture, there's no sense in showing everyone the wallpaper in the left half of the room. Cropping is ridiculously easy, and we show you how to do it in Chapter 2.

2. **Reduce the physical size of the photo.**

   Most digital cameras produce photos roughly the size of this page; the smaller the photo, the quicker it downloads. Again, this information is in Chapter 2.

3. **Reduce the quality of the image.**

   It sounds horrible: Our darling Amanda, in a *low-grade image?* — but the fact is that most images can have their quality reduced by 10 or 20 percent without anyone noticing a thing — and it saves *lots* of download time. We show you how to compress photos in Chapter 15.

Scanning into Paint Shop Pro

With digital cameras so cheap these days, you may wonder why anyone would use a scanner. After all, putting a photo on a flatbed and going through the hassle of aligning it properly is *much* more trouble than simply clicking Download in your camera's software program. Why would you bother?

For one thing, digital cameras are still a recent development. Chances are good that you have a drawer full of old, paper photos that you want to send to your friends. Or, maybe you have a magazine cover that you want to share with the world. Other scanning candidates are line drawings, original artwork, and documents that you have only in paper form. If that's the case, your only option is a scanner.

Many people are surprised to discover that scanning is a fairly involved process. Getting an image *from* paper isn't quite as simple as putting an image *on* paper — unless quality isn't all that important.

If your PC is equipped with more than one TWAIN-based image-acquiring device (scanners or cameras, for example), you need to tell Paint Shop Pro which one you're using before going through the following steps. Choose File➪Import➪Twain➪Select Source. The Select Source dialog box appears. Select your scanner (source) and then click Select.

In most instances, these steps scan an image from a properly installed scanner that has a TWAIN interface (although your scanning software may differ):

1. **Launch the scanning software that came with your scanner.**

   To do that, choose File➪Import➪TWAIN➪Acquire. (If your scanner uses WIA, choose File➪Import➪Scanner or Camera.)

   Or, press the Scan button on your scanner, if it has one.

   Some special software designed to run your scanner should appear, and Paint Shop Pro enters into a special TWAIN mode. (If the software doesn't appear, read the literature that came with your scanner and check to make sure that your scanner is properly installed.) Because that software depends on the scanner manufacturer, we can't tell you many details about it. We give you some tips, however, in the following section.

   Figure 5-3 shows you the software that appears if, for example, you're using a Canon Multipass.

Figure 5-3:
An example of scanning software. Your software may be different.

2. Find and click the Preview button.

In Figure 5-3, for example, the Preview button is in the Preview window. If you don't find a button labeled Preview, look for a similar word. The scanner starts to scan and then shows you a small preview image, as shown in the Preview window in the figure. This preview image shows you the entire scanning area of the scanner (the glass area in a flatbed scanner).

3. Define the area you want to scan.

In most scanner software, you create a rectangle in the Preview area to define the area you want to scan. (Drag from one corner of the part you want to the opposite corner.) Usually, you can then drag this rectangle to adjust its position or drag its sides or corners to adjust its size. If you don't define the scan area in this way, you may end up with an enormous image (your scanner's entire field of view) that you have to crop (trim) to the area you want. (Chapter 2 shows you how to crop a photo after it's in Paint Shop Pro — a vital skill that everyone should know.)

Most scanner software allows you to enlarge (zoom in on) the preview image. Look for a magnifying glass icon, click it, and then click the image.

4. Adjust settings that control the resolution or number of colors or that improve the appearance of the preview picture.

Scanner software often offers important features and controls, including whether you want color or black-and-white scanning. In the ScanWizard software shown in Figure 5-3, the controls are in the right window. We describe these and other useful controls in the following section.

5. Find and click the Scan button.

If you can't find a Scan button, look for a Start or Begin button. Figure 5-3 shows you a Scan button under the Preview button. The scanner begins to scan again. (It may take longer or shorter than it did in Step 2.)

After the scanner is done, an image appears in Paint Shop Pro. You can now close the scanner software window or continue to scan more images (starting with Step 2). Each image gets its own window in Paint Shop Pro.

6. When you're done scanning, close the TWAIN session.

If you're using TWAIN software to run your scanner, as we suspect, Paint Shop Pro will have put you into a special TWAIN-handling session where you can save files but not edit them. To return to "normal" mode, choose File➪End TWAIN Session. You return to Paint Shop Pro, where your scanned images are waiting for you.

Getting the most from your scanning software

Whatever software your PC uses to control your scanner, it undoubtedly offers certain settings to play with. For casual scanning of images that don't have problems (such as underexposure), you can often ignore lots of those settings and do all your fiddling in Paint Shop Pro. Sometimes, however, the controls in your scanner software can improve your image in ways that Paint Shop Pro alone can't — especially with moiré problems that occur when you scan newspaper photos. (Although Paint Shop Pro has an adjustment that removes moiré patterns, it's not nearly as effective as fixing it at the source. See "Forever plaid: Scanning printed images," later in this chapter, for more about moiré.)

You can usually adjust these settings *after* you do the preview. Except for resolution and color settings, the preview image reflects the changes without running your scanner again.

Choosing the number of colors

To achieve the best quality possible with color photographs (and other images that have either many colors or gradual, subtle shadings), you want the maximum number of colors the scanner can produce. Usually, this maximum is expressed as 24-bit or 32-bit color. If your PC has disk space for the large files this produces, scanning at this number of colors is best even if your final application requires fewer colors.

Here are some scanner settings you may find, labeled Type or Color Depth in the scanner software, that usually work well for the following uses:

- **Business or highest-quality personal use:** Choose 16 million colors (24- or 32-bit). (You can then color-reduce these images in Paint Shop Pro for faster downloading in Web or e-mail applications; see Chapter 15.)

- **Casual family or business Web page illustrations or snapshots to be sent by e-mail:** Choose 256-color if it's available, although it's not always offered as a scanner option. Use 16 million colors if the 256-color option isn't available.

- **Black-and-white photos, pencil drawings and sketches, or line drawings with lines of varying weight:** Choose 256 shades of gray, or sometimes Newsprint. Scanners typically scan these types of image by looking for one particular color. If your drawing is all in one color of pencil, such as green, it may not appear! Check your scanner manual for notes on scanning grayscale (black-and-white) images or line drawings, or avoid red, blue, or green pencils.

> ✔ **Clear, original printed text with good contrast or line drawings in dark ink or with thick lines:** Choose two colors (1-bit), or *line art,* if it's available; otherwise, choose 256 shades of gray. If you have a line drawing with uneven line darkness, you can sometimes turn it into good line art by adjusting either the Line Art Threshold or Highlight/Midtone/Shadow settings. See the section "Setting contrast and other adjustments," later in this chapter, for more information about the latter setting.

Choosing resolution

Resolution is the number of dots (or *samples*) per inch that your scanner reads from the paper image. Your scanning software has a control for resolution.

Higher resolution means that you get more detail — more pixels — which is generally A Good Thing. For example, if you scan a 4-inch x 6-inch snapshot at 300 dots per inch (dpi), you get an image of 4×300 (1200) pixels high and 6×300 pixels (1800) wide. (That's even more pixels than most PC screens can show at the same time.) You can always make a picture lower in resolution (reduce its size in pixels) in Paint Shop Pro, if necessary, but you can't add detail that isn't there in the first place.

Higher resolution also poses some problems. First, high resolution means bigger files! If you're just scanning a photo to e-mail to someone or to put on the Web, the people viewing your photo won't appreciate the long wait for a large photo to download — especially if it's bigger than their screen! You can reduce a photo in Paint Shop Pro, of course, but why bother if you don't need to? Besides, sometimes the shrinking process (also called *resampling*) doesn't give quite as good a result as if you had chosen the lower resolution in the first place.

To judge which resolution to use, answer these questions:

> ✔ **"How big an image do I need?"** For most Web and e-mail work, an image 300 to 400 pixels on a side is plenty. Multiply the width or height of the region you're scanning (6 inches wide, for example) by the scanner resolution you're thinking of using (300 dpi, for example) to figure out the resulting width or height in pixels (1800 pixels wide, in this example). Select a lower resolution to get a smaller image in pixels.

> ✔ **"How big a file do I want?"** Scanning a 4-inch x 6-inch color snapshot at 300 dpi (and 24-bit color) can give you a file as large as 6 megabytes. Cutting the resolution in half can reduce the file size by as much as a factor of four.

> ✔ **"How finely detailed does the image need to be?"** With the setting at 300 dpi, you can begin to see an individual human hair placed in your scanner.

You probably won't see any changes you make to the resolution in your pre-view image . To see the effect of resolution settings, you have to scan an image into Paint Shop Pro (click the Scan button in your scanner software).

Setting contrast and other adjustments

Some other adjustments that are available in your scanner software can make an enormous difference in the quality of your image. Fiddle with these after you have clicked the Preview button in your scanner software so that you have a preview image to look at as you make your adjustments. You may have to poke around to find a button or command (usually Advanced or More Options) that reveals these adjustments, or even discover that your software doesn't offer them.

Many adjustments that scanning software offers are technical. We don't have room to fully do them justice here, but you probably don't need them anyway. We describe here a few of the important ones you may find:

- **Brightness:** Brightness makes all areas darker or lighter to the same degree.
- **Contrast:** The Contrast adjustment makes dark areas darker and light areas lighter.
- **Exposure:** Increasing the Exposure setting makes dark pixels dispropor-tionately darker and brings out detail in the light areas.
- **Shadow/Midtone/Highlight:** The Shadow and Highlight values are also called the black and white points, respectively. Sometimes they're unnamed and appear as sliding arrows under a histogram chart. These three settings are something like Contrast and Exposure, but more pre-cise, which make an image's dark areas darker and its light areas lighter. The settings also bring out detail in the middle ranges of darkness and adjust a too-dark or too-light image to a more pleasing appearance. Each setting ranges from 0 to 255 (the numeric values correspond to bright-ness: 0 is black and 255 is white). The choices are shown in this list:
  - **Shadow:** To make the darker areas as dark as possible, adjust the Shadow value upward. All pixels *below* that value become as dark as you can make them without radically changing any colors.
  - **Highlight:** To make light areas as light as possible, adjust the Highlight value downward. All pixels *above* that value become as light as possible without radically changing their colors.
  - **Midtone:** If the rest of the image is, overall, kind of dark, adjust the Midtone value downward; if the image is light, set the value higher.

✔ **Descreen:** Some software has special *descreen* capabilities, which means that they can minimize the moiré patterns that arise when you scan printed images. Generally, the software offers several settings that depend on whether you're scanning from a newspaper, magazine, or higher-quality printed source, like a book. (You probably have to scan to see the result of descreening — it's unlikely that you can see it in the preview.)

✔ **Unsharp Mask:** Try this feature (it often lurks in an area named Filter or something similar) if your photo doesn't look quite as sharp as it should. Without making the image sharper, this feature gives the illusion of sharpness. It raises the contrast around edges (where the pixel values change). Unsharp masking usually has four settings:

   • **Strength:** Adjusts the degree of contrast enhancement (sharpness).

   • **Radius:** Determines how far from an edge the effect extends.

   • **Clipping:** Sets a limit, below which an edge isn't enhanced. A setting that's too low may make the image speckly.

   • **Luminance Only:** Sometimes, unsharp masking may mix up the colors and produce strange new hues that have no place in your image. If that's the case, set the Unsharp Mask to Luminance Only, which means that it changes only the black-and-white bits and leaves the colors alone. Although this option sounds horrible, often it produces a much clearer picture.

(The numbers used in these settings have no intuitive meaning, so don't look for one. Just adjust them up or down.)

If you forget to use Unsharp Mask *while* scanning, you can use the Paint Shop Pro Unsharp Mask effect *after* scanning. Choose A̲djust⇨Sharpness⇨Unsharp Mask and the Unsharp Mask dialog box appears. Make the same adjustments listed in the last bullet in the preceding list. Figure 5-4 shows you the Unsharp Mask effect, as shown on a picture of one of the authors as a young Gene Simmons.

Many scanner programs offer check boxes to turn on automatic features (typically auto contrast and auto color correction). These features attempt to adjust various settings for you, based on the preview scan. Sometimes they work well and sometimes they don't. Try enabling and disabling their check boxes to see the result in the Preview area.

You can find an excellent, detailed guide to using the features of scanning software — in fact, to using your scanner in general — on the Web at www. scantips.com.

Figure 5-4: KISS and makeup — unsharp masking refers to the effect illustrated by this before-and-after pair of images.

Before   After

Forever plaid: Scanning printed images

When you scan a printed image from a newspaper, magazine, or book, your image often acquires a blurry checkered plaid or barred pattern. This pattern, called a *moiré* ("mwah-RAY") pattern, is caused by conflict between the dots used to print your image and the dots that happen during scanning.

The next time you put your window screens up or down, you can see this same effect if you look through two screens at the same time. Or, if you have a screen porch, stand outside and look through the two screens where they meet at a corner.

TECHNICAL STUFF

Dots not nice!

Why do scans of printed images get moiré patterns? Unlike photographic prints and painted or drawn artwork, printed images are made up of ink dots of varying sizes at a certain spacing. This effect wouldn't be a problem, except that your scanner also uses dots — and they're of a different size and spacing.

Your scanner reads the image by *sampling* it (looking at tiny spots on the image) at some spacing (your chosen resolution in dots per inch). The samples don't align exactly on the printed dots, except every 10 or 20 pixels, for example; the rest of the time, they align partly on the dots and partly on the white background. The usual result is a checkered or barred patterning on the image. Something similar can happen when Paint Shop Pro displays the image on your PC screen, which also uses dots.

The moiré pattern may exist only on your PC screen in Paint Shop Pro and not in your image file, as Figure 5-5 illustrates. In this figure, the zoom of 1:3 (noted on the title bar) is responsible. Try viewing the image at full scale (press Ctrl+Alt+N) or larger. If the pattern disappears, the pattern is just the effect of using a zoom of less than 1:1. Don't worry about it. When the image is printed at a high printer resolution or used on the Web at full size, that pattern probably doesn't appear. If the pattern is still visible at a 1:1 zoom, it's permanent and you need to do something about it.

Figure 5-5:
A moiré pattern appears on this roof, but isn't an image flaw.

Permanent moiré pattern problems? Try these solutions:

- **Higher resolution:** The pattern may fade if you set the resolution of your scanner's software (the dots-per-inch value) higher.

- **Descreening:** If your scanner software provides descreening, use this option. See the section "Setting contrast and other adjustments," earlier in this chapter, for more information.

- **Special filter:** Choose Adjust➪Add/Remove Noise➪Moiré Pattern Removal (see Chapter 6).

Printed images pose more problems than just moiré patterns. Although the images appear to have a wide variety of tones, printed images are composed of alternating dots of primary colors (black-and-white photos have only two colors, for example). When these images are scanned (particularly at high resolution), they retain that spotty, dotty character. Zoom in to see them.

As a result, Paint Shop Pro features that use color selection and replacement don't work as your eye would lead you to expect. An area that looks uniformly green, for example, may be made up of blue and yellow dots. You can't select that green area of your scanned-in logo, for example, because it's not really green! This problem gets worse at higher resolutions.

To partially solve this problem, you can apply the Paint Shop Pro blur adjustment (see Chapter 8) to make the dots blur together. If you have problems selecting a colored area with the Magic Wand tool (refer to Chapter 3), try increasing the Tolerance setting in the Tool Options dialog box.

Straightening crooked scans

Lining up your photos neatly across the bottom of most scanners is a pain — and even *then* you normally don't get it quite right, which leads to a tilted picture of your sweet snookielumps. Fortunately, Paint Shop Pro has a useful tool that straightens your pictures for you.

Here's how to get your pictures to straighten up and fly right:

1. **Select the Straighten tool from the deformation tool group, as shown in Figure 5-6.**

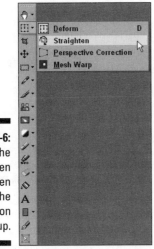

Figure 5-6:
The Straighten tool, hidden among the deformation tool group.

2. **Find a horizontal line in your crooked picture that should be level, but isn't.**

In Figure 5-7, which we show you momentarily, that line is the top edge of the photo. In other images that don't have easily accessible photo edges to work with, try looking for flat horizons (oceans disappearing against the sky are usually a good bet), pictures, benches, kitchen counters, or windows.

Image rotation angle 0.00 degrees   (x:237 y:63) 0.0

Figure 5-7:
The
Straighten
line, and a
truly twisted
image.

This tilted straight line is your way of telling the Straighten tool, "If you rotate the image until *this line* is perfectly level, the image will be fixed." So choose it carefully!

If your image has no horizontal lines that you can use but it does have vertical ones, you can use the Straighten tool on a vertical line as well. Paint Shop Pro notices that your baseline is vertical, not horizontal, and instead rotates your image so that the baseline is perfectly north-to-south.

3. **Position the Straighten line so that it's next to your baseline.**

   A straightening line, complete with a handle on each end, appears in your picture. Move your mouse over it until the cursor becomes a four-headed arrow with a line over it, as shown in Figure 5-7.

   Click and drag the Straighten line to the tilted line you have chosen to use as a baseline.

4. **Click and drag the handles on each end of the Straighten Line until both of them are on the tilted line you have chosen.**

   When you're finished, the Straighten tool should be lying along the edge of your baseline.

   If you want to have your image automatically cropped to snip out the blank spaces around the edge of the picture after it has been straightened, check the Crop Image box on the Tool Options palette (press F4 if you don't see the palette).

Double-click your image to straighten it (and crop it, if you have chosen to).

5. **Make sure that it's straight!**

For the picture shown in Figure 5-7, we chose to use the top edge of the photo as a baseline for straightening . . . and we were wrong. As you can see in Figure 5-8, we have adjusted the image so that the photo is level, but the photo itself was taken at an angle (as though it weren't embarrassing *enough*)! On the right side of the figure, William is on the level — a feat he would not manage to duplicate until years later.

Press Ctrl+Z to undo any changes. Note that when we went back and straightened the image again using the top line of the television set as a baseline, it came out much better.

Figure 5-8: The image on the left has been adjusted so that the photo is straight, but the photo itself is crooked.

Capturing Images from Your PC Screen

There it is, onscreen: the exact image you need. But it's in some other program, not Paint Shop Pro. You figure that there must be some way to get it into Paint Shop Pro — after all, it's already in your computer.

You're right. Paint Shop Pro has several different ways to capture that image.

When an image appears in a window on your PC, it comes with all kinds of other stuff that is part of the program displaying the image: toolbars, status bars, a title bar, and a sushi bar, for example. Maybe you want that stuff, and maybe you don't. Paint Shop Pro helps you capture only the part of the window you really want: It's most likely an image, but if (like us) you're illustrating software, you may want to see just a toolbar from the program window or where a mouse cursor is pointing. For all these captures, use the Paint Shop Pro capture features, on the Capture menu.

Preparing to capture

To set your snare, follow these steps:

1. **Choose File⇨Import⇨Screen Capture⇨Setup from the menu bar.**

   The Capture Setup dialog box, as shown in Figure 5-9, comes to your aid.

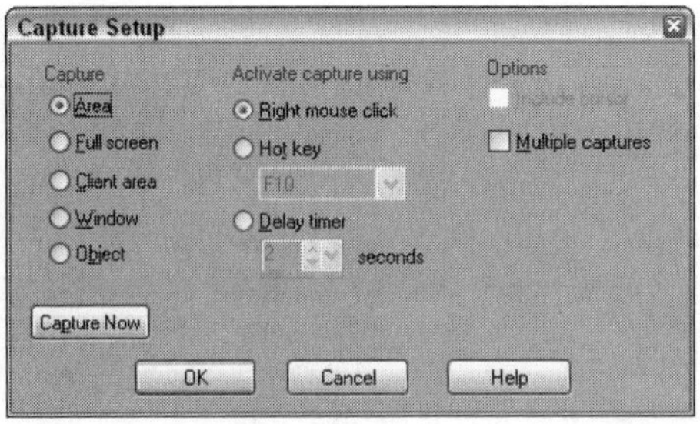

Figure 5-9:
Setting your
snare for
elusive
Windows
wildlife.

   From left to right in the figure, you can see that you have three kinds of choices: what you want to capture, how you want to *trigger* (activate) the snare, and a couple of options (Include Cursor or Multiple Captures).

2. **Choose what to capture.**

   Paint Shop Pro can capture five different species of Windows wildebeest. In the Capture Setup dialog box, choose one of the possibilities listed in Column 1 of Table 5-1.

Table 5-1	Using Different Types of Capture
Type of Capture	*What It Does*
Area	Captures a rectangular area that you define anywhere onscreen.
Full screen	Captures the whole nine yards, the entire enchilada, the full Monty — everything onscreen.

Type of Capture	What It Does
Client area	Captures everything in a window except the title bar.
Window	Captures the application window you specify (don't use for a document window; use Object for that).
Object	Captures an application window, a document window, or any individual feature in a window, like a toolbar — a useful catchall category that works for toolbars, menu bars, scroll bars, palettes, and sometimes portions of those objects.

3. **Choose your trigger.**

   You must choose a *trigger,* which is an action (such as pressing a particular key) that you take, after setup finishes, to tell Paint Shop Pro to start capturing images. Without a trigger, the capture would start immediately. All you would ever capture is Paint Shop Pro itself! In the Capture Setup dialog box (refer to Figure 5-9), you can see that you have three choices for triggering the capture. Select one of these options:

   • **Right mouse click:** A right mouse click begins the capture.

   • **Hot key:** From the Hot Key selection box, choose a key to serve as a trigger. You can choose any of the function keys, F1 through F12, alone or in combination with Shift, Alt, or Ctrl. F10 is initially chosen for you.

   • **Delay timer:** Select this option and then enter a delay time (in seconds) in the Delay Timer box.

4. **Choose options.**

   Paint Shop Pro gives you two options:

   • **Capture multiple images:** If you plan to capture a series of onscreen images, select the Multiple Captures check box in the Capture Setup dialog box (refer to Figure 5-9). You then can simply snap a series of images without returning to Paint Shop Pro each time. If you're creating a tutorial for using some software, for example, you can set up Paint Shop Pro and then easily capture a screen for each step.

   • **Include mouse cursor in capture:** You may want to show the mouse cursor in your screen captures to point out some feature. If so, select the Include Cursor check box in the Capture Setup dialog box (refer to Figure 5-9).

Using the Include Cursor option may not work if you're only capturing an object. You need to use your cursor to select the object and place the cursor somewhere other than where you want it in the picture. If you're capturing a client area or window, you have to be sure that your cursor is within the captured area.

Making the capture

After you're set up to capture from the PC screen in Paint Shop Pro, you're ready to make the capture. To capture an image, follow these steps:

1. **Click the Capture Now button in the Capture Setup dialog box.**

   The Capture Now command starts the capture process. (Or, you can press Shift+C.) Paint Shop Pro discreetly shrinks to a button on the taskbar to get out of your way.

2. **Make any last-minute changes to the thing you want to capture.**

   You have a final opportunity to adjust the appearance of the screen area that contains the image — before you trigger the capture. If you have chosen the option of capturing the mouse cursor, position the cursor now.

3. **Trigger the capture (or wait for the timer to trigger it).**

   Depending on the kind of trigger you chose (refer to Step 3 in the preceding section), either right-click with your mouse, press the hot key (F10, for example), or wait for the time interval to elapse.

   If you're capturing a full screen, Paint Shop Pro restores itself to full window size now. You're done and can skip the following steps. Otherwise, Paint Shop Pro waits for you to choose your capture area.

4. **Choose the capture area (unless you're capturing the full screen).**

   How you choose the capture area depends on what kind of capture you have chosen, as shown in Table 5-2.

   After you choose the capture area, the capture occurs instantly. Paint Shop Pro immediately restores itself to its original window size (unless you have chosen the multiple capture option) and displays the capture as a new image.

5. **Repeat Steps 3 and 4 if you have chosen the multiple capture option.**

   Paint Shop Pro acquires each capture as a separate image. You don't see them because Paint Shop Pro remains minimized as a button on the taskbar. To restore Paint Shop Pro, click its button on the Windows taskbar.

Table 5-2	Pointing Out Your Quarry to Paint Shop Pro
Type of Capture	*What to Do after Triggering the Capture*
Area	Left-click once where you want one corner of the area. Then, with your mouse button released (don't drag), move your cursor diagonally to where you want the opposite corner and click again.
Full screen	Do nothing, except for switching back to Paint Shop Pro if you want to edit your images.
Client area	Left-click the window you want.
Window	Left-click the window you want.
Object	A black rectangle encloses whatever object is directly under the mouse cursor. You don't have to keep that object. Move your cursor around and, when the black rectangle encloses the object you want, left-click.

For better and easier captures, read and heed these tips:

✔ Set up your screen the way you want it to look before you enable the trigger (before you press the Capture Now button or press Shift+P). If you try to make adjustments after you set the trigger, you may accidentally trigger the capture.

✔ To enhance colors — for those captured colors that come out fairly accurate, but faded, murky, or otherwise less than satisfactory — see Chapter 7.

✔ If you're capturing an image from your Web browser, use the browser's Save As or Copy command rather than the Paint Shop Pro screen capture. To save an image as a file in Internet Explorer, for example, right-click the image and choose Save Picture As.

Chapter 6

Fixing Broken Pictures: Removing Scratches, Blurry Parts, and Red Eye

● ●

● ●

Common wisdom states that beauty is in the eye of the beholder, but common wisdom is wrong. Beauty is in the lens of your camera — because when you have broken photos, *nobody* looks good. Your cousin Freddy may be a heartthrob, but if your photos of him are scratched and his eyes are glowing a dim red, who can tell the difference between Freddy-your-cousin and Freddy-the-stalker from *Nightmare on Elm Street?*

Fortunately, Paint Shop Pro has many tools to fix common photo mistakes. The problems that Paint Shop Pro is good at fixing are shown in this list:

✔ Scratch removal

✔ Red-eye removal

✔ Tinted photos

✔ Blurry areas

✔ Grainy photos

✔ Moiré patterns

✔ JPEG artifacts

Note that this chapter is dedicated to fixing *broken* photographs — pictures where something is obviously very wrong. If you have an otherwise-unremarkable image and you want to make it look better, that's easily done. But, you have to find out how in Chapters 7 and 8.

If your image has a color depth of fewer than 16.7 million colors, Paint Shop Pro needs to increase the number of colors in your image before you can use any of these tools and adjustments; if you're tired of it always asking you whether it's okay to increase the colors, see Chapter 16.

Removing Scratches

Photographic scratches usually fall into one of two categories:

- *Individual scratches* that arise from creased photos or scratches on the negative
- *Masses of tiny scratches* that arise from a photo being stored in a drawer for a long time, where it has been rattling around with dusty pencil shavings and spare screws.

Fortunately, Paint Shop Pro is adept at handling either type of scratch. (Then again, if it weren't, we probably wouldn't be writing this section.)

Patching up single scratches

Having photos come back from the developer with a scratch is heartbreaking. Usually, it means that a scratch is on the negative, so making a new print can't help. Equally traumatic is having a valued print creased, torn, or scratched when you don't have a negative and can't replace the print. Thankfully, Paint Shop Pro has an answer for all your folds, creases, and scratches. After you scan the picture into Paint Shop Pro (refer to Chapter 5), here's what to do:

1. **Zoom in on your scratched area so that it fills the screen.**

   Select the magnifying-glass icon from the pan and zoom tool group and zoom in; refer to Chapter 1 for details.

2. **Click the Scratch Remover tool from the clone tool group, as shown in Figure 6-1.**

   This tool is the trowel-looking icon shown in the margin.

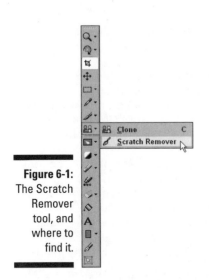

Figure 6-1:
The Scratch
Remover
tool, and
where to
find it.

3. **Position your mouse cursor at one end of the scratch and drag along the scratch.**

   As you drag, a frame area stretches to follow your mouse cursor and extends across the width of the scratch, as shown in Figure 6-2.

Figure 6-2:
Having a
dog requires
familiarity
with
scratching.
Here, Alex
looks
pleased as
we remove
a scratch.

4. **Release your mouse button at the end of the scratch.**

   If you're following a curved or irregular scratch, release your mouse button at the point where the curve can no longer fit within the frame. (Later, you can go back and remove remaining segments of the scratch.)

   When you release the mouse button, the Scratch Remover tool picks up paint from either side of the scratch and pushes it into the scratch. If you had to stop short of the end of the scratch, drag a second time to cover the remaining portion.

That's it! You now have a slightly fuzzy band where the scratch was, but it's probably much better than a scratch.

If the scratch wasn't completely filled in, you may need to repeat your action for another segment of scratch or adjust some tool options and try again. For irregular scratches, remove the scratch in sections. To adjust options, first undo any failed attempt (press Ctrl+Z). Next, open the Tool Options palette (press F4 to toggle the window on or off). Follow one of these methods:

- **If the scratch didn't fill in because the scratch was wider than the tool's frame:** A value box on the Tool Options palette allows you to adjust the Scratch Remover's width in pixels. Increase the value in that box and again try to remove the scratch. With tool settings larger than 20, the frame exhibits an inner and outer zone as you drag. As you drag, make sure that the scratch fits in the inner zone and that the outer zone is completely filled with the bordering colors you want to use for filling in.

- **If you end up with an unacceptably wide, fuzzy band where the scratch was:** The tool's width was set too high. Lower the width value on the Tool Options palette.

- **If the end points of the scratch didn't properly fill in:** An outline option gives you an alternative shape to drag; one that has pointed ends rather than square ones. That shape is good for clicking in tight spaces or corners. Click that alternative shape button and then try scratch removal again.

If the scratch runs along an edge in the image, use the smallest width possible to avoid blurring that edge. For example, in Figure 6-2, the scratch grazes Dave's shoulder, where his shirt ends and the trees begin. The scratch remover blurs that edge. Rather than remove the entire irregular scratch in one broad attempt, he may do better to remove that shoulder-grazing portion of the scratch separately, with the width value set very low. If all else fails, use the Clone Brush tool, as shown in Chapter 8.

Smoothing masses of scratches

Some photos or their negatives can get pretty seriously abused, picking up tiny scratches, pits, or other imperfections while being handled, while living in suitcases or sandy beach bags, or while being badly processed. Hey, who wouldn't get a little abraded under those circumstances?

Choose Adjust⇨Add/Remove Noise⇨Automatic Small Scratch Removal to display the Automatic Small Scratch Removal dialog box. You can see its effects on your screen, as shown in Figure 6-3.

Figure 6-3:
Automatic
Scratch
Removal
helps this
neglected
photo look
less rough.

Scratchy image   Post-Automatic Scratch Removal

If only a part of your picture is scratched, you can use the selection tool group to restrict the Scratch Removal tool to a limited area. For further selection details, see Chapter 3.

First, determine whether your scratches are light or dark or both. Next, select Remove Light Scratches, Remove Dark Scratches, or both. If the preview image on the right side isn't already adequately cleaned up, change the Strength setting from Normal to Aggressive. If the effect is removing things that aren't scratches or making your photo too fuzzy, try changing Strength to Mild. (A necessary side effect of cleaning up scratches with this effect is a bit of added fuzziness, so you can't be too picky.) If the effect is removing too many tiny features, try adjusting the Local Contrast Limits option. To restore low-contrast features, drag the pointer at the left end of the line to the right. To restore high-contrast features, drag the pointer at the right end of the line to the left.

If the result is still too fuzzy, check out the section "Removing Noise from Grainy Shots," later in this chapter, for alternative methods, like the Salt-and-Pepper filter.

The Red-Eye Remover

In our youth, we longed for something to remove the telltale morning red eye that bespoke a long, hard night out. Regrettably, Paint Shop Pro doesn't remove *that* kind of red eye, where the blood vessels in the whites of your eyes throb reproachingly.

The Paint Shop Pro red-eye remover *does,* however, fix the evil red glow that sometimes appears in photographs and emanates from the pupils of the eye as the result of a camera's flash. In animals, that glow may not be red, but, rather, yellow or other colors.

The red-eye remover in Paint Shop Pro is a red-eye *replacer.* Rather than attempt to restore the original pupil of the eye, Paint Shop Pro says "The heck with it!" and paints a whole new pupil, complete with the glint of the flash bulb. In fact, the red eye remover can even construct a new iris (the colored portion of your eye) if the camera's flash has obliterated it!

Reconstructing the pupil

Usually, red eye affects only the pupil. If it has affected the iris in your photo, see the section "Replacing pupil and iris," later in this chapter. Here's how to get rid of red eye if the flash hasn't affected the iris area:

1. **Choose <u>A</u>djust⇨Photo Fix⇨Red E<u>y</u>e Removal.**

   The amazingly complex-looking Red Eye Removal dialog box appears. Figure 6-4 gives you the picture.

2. **Zoom in close on one of the red eyes, in the preview windows.**

   To zoom in, click the button displaying a magnifying glass with a + sign, underneath the left window. Repeat until the eye practically fills the windows.

   To move the photo around behind the window, drag in the *right* (not left) window. Your cursor displays a hand icon when it's over the right window.

Figure 6-4:
If this figure were in color, the left eye's pupil would be a scary red. Color Plate C-1b in the color insert of this book shows the actual color.

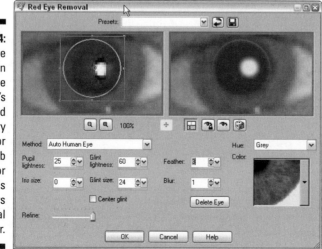

If you mistakenly drag or click in the left window, click the Delete Eye button to remove the replacement iris you have accidentally created.

3. **Choose Auto Human Eye (if you're working on a human) from the Method selection box.**

   If you're working on an animal, choose Auto Animal Eye.

4. **Set Iris Size to zero.**

   Or, if you have changed your mind and decided that the red really does afflict the iris, see the section "Replacing pupil and iris," later in this chapter.

5. **Click once on the dead center of the (red) pupil of the eye in the left window.**

   A circle appears, with a dot in the center and a square frame surrounding the circle. The circle has *handles* on it (tiny squares you can drag). Figure 6-4 shows this tool.

   You want the circle to just cover the red pupil and be centered over it.

6. **Adjust the circle's position or size if the circle doesn't cover the red pupil.**

   You can drag the circle by the dot in its center. To resize the circle, drag one of the handles on the box surrounding the circle.

7. **Looking at the right window, adjust the Refine control left and right until the red is just covered by a dark spot (the new pupil).**

   The Refine control determines to what extent the new pupil covers the red. When you're done, little or no red should be showing. For precise control of Refine, click the slider and press the left- and right-arrow keys on your keyboard to decrement or increment the slider. The new pupil should be no larger than the original and shouldn't cover the eyelid. If you can't achieve a result you like, return to Step 5 and resize the circle.

8. **Adjust the Pupil Lightness value box to set the lightness of your new pupil to your liking.**

   Decrease the value for a darker pupil. For a normal appearance, the pupil should be darker than the iris.

9. **Check the new, white glint in the right window against the original in the left window.**

   If the new glint isn't roughly the same size as the original, adjust the Glint Size control up or down until they match. Feel free, however, to make the new glint any size you like, including removing it altogether by setting the glint size to zero. If you prefer the glint in the center of the eye, click to enable the Center Glint check box. Otherwise, the glint tracks the original one. Adjust the Glint Lightness control up or down to match the brightness of the original glint. If the new glint has a noticeably sharper edge than the old, adjust the Blur control upward.

10. **Increase the Feather control to get a softer edge or to mute any remaining red spots around the edge.**

    Alternatively, if the original photo is a bit blurry, try adjusting the Blur control upward instead. Fool around with these two controls until the edges look properly blended into the rest of the eye.

11. **Click the Proof button (with the unlocked eye icon) to check your results in the main image window.**

    (Drag the Red Eye Removal dialog box out of the way, if necessary; don't close it yet.)

    Return to any earlier steps that seem necessary to adjust size, darkness, coverage, glint, and so on.

    If you decide that you need to give up and start again, click the Delete Eye button. If you want to return all the settings to their original positions, click the Reset button in the upper-right corner.

    If you can't get acceptable coverage of the pupil, click the Cancel button and see the following section.

12. **Click OK.**

When you're done with one eye, repeat those steps for the other eye. When you proof your work in Step 10, make sure that the eyes match!

Outlining problem pupils

As you undoubtedly remember from school, some pupils are troublemakers. They don't cooperate if you try to doctor their red eye. In that case, change from using automatic red-eye removal to *manual outlining*.

Open the Red Eye Removal dialog box and zoom in as directed in Steps 1 and 2 in the preceding section. Rather than choose Auto Human (or Auto Animal) Eye in Step 3, which tells Paint Shop Pro to automatically outline the red area, choose one of these two manual outlining options:

✔ **Freehand Pupil Outline:** Choose this option if you prefer to drag a continuous line around the red area to outline it. (This technique requires a steady hand, but can give a more rounded outline.) When you release the mouse button, Paint Shop Pro connects the line's end with its beginning.

✔ **Point-to-Point Pupil Outline:** Choose this option if you prefer to click a series of points around the red area. Paint Shop Pro draws a straight line between the points. When you're ready to complete the circle, don't click the starting point again. Instead, double-click somewhere short of that point. Paint Shop Pro completes the circle for you.

Drag or click an outline, according to your choice of options. After you outline the pupil, resume with Step 7 in the steps in the preceding section to refine the red-eye correction.

Replacing pupil and iris

If the flash has affected the colored iris of the eye, first follow Steps 1 through 4 in the steps in the section "Reconstructing the pupil," earlier in this chapter. (In those steps, you open the Red Eye Removal dialog box, zoom in on an eye, and click in its center.)

Then, after Step 3, follow these steps:

1. **Enlarge the circle in the left window to cover an area equal to the *iris* (not just the pupil) you need.**

   Drag any corner handle of the square frame surrounding the circle to enlarge the circle. Often, the circle needs to overlap the top eyelid and possibly a bit of the bottom.

2. **Adjust the value in the Iris Size value box up or down, a little at a time, until the iris and pupil size either matches the other eye or simply looks correct.**

   Click the tiny up arrow or down arrow adjoining the Iris Size value box to change the value by one.

3. **Click the Hue selection box and choose an iris color from the list.**

   Choose from Aqua, Blue, Brown, Grey, Green, or Violet.

4. **Click the down arrow to the right of the Color sample box and choose a precise shade of color from the gallery that appears.**

5. **Adjust the Refine control left or right to set the shape and extent of the iris.**

   The optimal setting of the Refine control occurs when the iris doesn't significantly overlap an eyelid and is reasonably round elsewhere. A black spot with a white glint should cover the pupil of the eye.

Resume with Step 8 in the earlier section "Reconstructing the pupil." From here, you adjust the darkness of the pupil, set any feathering or blurring you need, and adjust the glint size, if necessary.

Color-Correcting Photos

Sometimes, you take a photo and the entire thing is tinted with a color that wasn't there when you took the picture. The white drapes look a milky green, the yellow sunflowers are a bright emerald, and your family now possesses an alien skin tone that makes them look like they're auditioning for *The X-Files*.

Would you recognize the correct color of that skin if you saw it? If so, you have an easy way to correct the color of your photo: the Paint Shop Pro Manual Color Correction effect.

Note that the Manual Color Correction effect adjusts the color of the *entire* image so that your selected object (skin or fur, for example) is then the correct color. It presumes that every object in your photograph was shot in the same terrible light. If it gets your selected portion of the image correct, the entire image is then correct.

As with any other Adjustment tool, you can select a part of the image and then color-correct only that area. So, if you *want* to keep your family a sickly green while making the sunflowers yellow again, you can. Refer to Chapter 3 for details.

Ready? Choose Adjust⇨Color Balance⇨Manual Color Correction to give this targeted tool its instructions. The Manual Color Correction dialog box appears, as shown in Figure 6-5. (Refer to the color section of this book to see the difference in colors.)

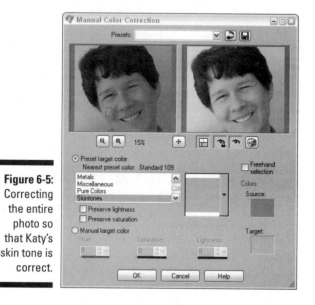

Figure 6-5: Correcting the entire photo so that Katy's skin tone is correct.

1. **Click the Preset Colors radio button and choose a likely-sounding category from the menu that matches some portion of your object, like Skintones or Hair.**

2. **Click and drag in the left preview window to select a small swatch in your image that matches the menu selection.**

   In this case, we have selected Skintones and have selected a tiny box of skin on Katy's cheek. We could also have selected Hair and selected her bangs, if we had wanted.

   Drag diagonally to define a rectangular area. For example, drag across the forehead of your subject, to create a rectangle that surrounds a fairly uniform skin color, if you intend to match the person's skin tone to a color. Choose an area that isn't strongly affected by highlights or shadows. Drag again if you want to change your selection.

   If the area you want to define is irregular in shape, enable the Freehand Selection check box. Then, drag (draw) the irregular shape you want to use on the left window.

   Use the zoom, drag, and locating features in the dialog box (see the section in Chapter 7 about understanding the Paint Shop Pro dialog boxes) to get to the right place in the left preview window, if necessary.

3. **Click the down arrow to the right of the colored box next to the Preset Target Color radio button.**

   A gallery of color appears.

4. **Choose a color from the gallery that is what that swatch *should* look like.**

   If you can't find the color you want, click the Manual Target Color button and then click in the Target box to choose a color from the Paint Shop Pro Color dialog box. See Chapter 9 for the details of using this dialog box.

Paint Shop Pro then alters the image in the right preview window, to match the hue of your selected area to the hue of the color you chose in Step 4.

"But," you may say, "the color doesn't match exactly." Don't panic. Unless you have previously fiddled with the check boxes in the Options section of the Manual Color Correction dialog box, the color *shouldn't* match exactly — yet. The Preserve Lightness and Preserve Saturation check boxes, which are initially selected, cause your photo's color to be corrected only to the *hue* (a kind of fundamental color) of the color you have selected, and not to its saturation or lightness. If you want to make the color match your chosen sample exactly, you must clear both check boxes. However, you may find that you get good results more easily by leaving both check boxes selected and choosing different colors.

Bringing Your Photo into Focus

Paint Shop Pro offers three ways to clarify a blurry photo — though none of them is a complete fix for a bad shot. Remember that Paint Shop Pro can work with only the information you have given it, and although it can make some educated guesses about what a picture should look like, there are limits to its power. If your picture looks like a patch of white fog, all the sharpening in the world won't turn it back into the Leaning Tower of Pisa.

That said, Paint Shop Pro does a bang-up job of fixing photos that are slightly out of focus. You can deblurrify a picture with two methods: sharpening and edge enhancing.

How do sharpening and edge enhancing compare? The Enhance effect is more dramatic, by focusing directly on even the tiniest edge, as shown in Figure 6-6. The Sharpen adjustment makes a subtler (and usually more effective) change that influences a range of pixels around the edges of items in your photo.

Figure 6-6:
The picture on the right is sharpened; the picture on the left is edge enhanced. The picture in the middle is William's godchild Andy, and you should bow to his cuteness.

Sharpening your snapshots

Sharpening is the first method you should try for fixing blurry photos, mainly because it's the most effective. To give it the old college try, choose Adjust⇨ Sharpness and then choose one of these options from the menu that appears:

- ✔ **Sharpen:** Does a little bit of metaphorical grinding and filing on the various edges of your photo, by boosting the contrast at those edges. No dialog box appears — your image simply gets sharper.
- ✔ **Sharpen More:** The same as Sharpen, but more so.

✔ **Unsharp Mask:** Sharpens like its two siblings (Sharpen and Sharpen More), but operates incognito, like the Lone Ranger. No, just kidding. It wears not a mask, but rather an adjustment dialog box. To use this box's controls, refer to Chapter 5, where we discuss unsharp masking for setting contrast and other adjustments in scanning software.

As with all these other photo fixers, you can apply them to a selected area. Refer to Chapter 3 for details.

Edge enhancing

The Paint Shop Pro Enhance Edge effect is a close cousin to its sharpening effect. Both find adjoining pixels that contrast in lightness (an edge) and then make the contrast stronger by darkening or lightening those pixels. The pixels gradually move toward fully saturated primary colors, plus white and black.

Choose Effects⇨Edge Effects⇨Enhance or its more powerful sibling, Enhance More. Neither uses an adjustment box, but just immediately does its thing.

Removing Noise from Grainy Shots

Removing noise from an image sounds a bit illogical, like subtracting apples from oranges or removing odor from a TV program. Okay, you can perhaps imagine ways to do the latter, but apply that same imagination to how your TV looks when you run a vacuum cleaner: The screen is covered with speckles. That's *graphical noise:* pixels altered at random locations and in random colors.

The trick with removing speckles is to avoid removing freckles or other speckly stuff that's supposed to be in the picture. (Unless, of course, you *want* to get rid of the freckles!) For that reason, Paint Shop Pro offers several choices, depending on what you need. Choose Adjust⇨Add/Remove Noise and then one of these menu selections:

✔ **Despeckle:** Removes smaller, isolated speckles altogether and is good for removing a light coating of dust. Speckles that are closer to each other tend to form clumps, however.

✔ **Edge-Preserving Smooth:** Gives an effect like rubbing carefully within the shaded areas of a pastel drawing, using your finger. Speckles disappear into a uniform shade, and you keep the sharp edges of those larger areas. This effect is also good for removing the random discoloration of pixels that often results from shooting digital photos in low light. In the adjustment dialog box that appears, drag the Number of Steps slider to the right to make a smoother image.

The Edge-Preserving Smooth effect, turned up high, creates a nice oil-painting-like effect on photos! See Color Plate C-11 in the color insert in this book.

✔ **Median Filter:** Removes speckles by removing fine detail, a kind of blurring process in which each pixel is recalculated to be the average of its neighbors. Contrast is lost at the detail level. An adjustment dialog box appears in which you drag the Filter Aperture slider to the right to remove increasingly large details.

✔ **Salt-and-Pepper Filter:** Removes speckles of a particular size (or up to a particular size) you choose. A Salt-and-Pepper Filter adjustment dialog box appears, with these adjustments:

> **Speck Size:** Adjust this value to match or slightly exceed the size of the speckles you're trying to get rid of. (You may have to zoom in close to figure out how big your speckles are.)

> **Sensitivity to Specks:** If the right preview window shows clusters of specks remaining, increase this value. Too high a value blurs your photo.

> **Include All Lower Speck Sizes:** Enable this check box to remove specks of Speck Size and smaller. Otherwise, you just remove specks close to Speck Size.

> **Aggressive Action:** Enable this check box to remove specks more completely. Otherwise, you may simply reduce the specks' intensity.

✔ **Texture-Preserving Smooth:** Sounds like a sophisticated grade of peanut butter, but in reality blurs and reduces the contrast of tiny specks while preserving the larger variations that give texture to grass, wood, water, and the like. The result is sort of like a crunchy peanut butter without small, gritty chunks. An adjustment dialog box appears in which you adjust the Amount of Correction value upward to minimize specks.

You can always select an area by using the Paint Shop Pro selection tools, to add or remove noise from only that specific area (refer to Chapter 3).

Don't Want No Moiré

Scanned-in photos from print media (books, magazines, newsletters, and PC-printed images, for example) often have moiré patterns. (Refer to Chapter 5 for more information about moiré and ways to avoid it in the first place.)

You can fix moiré patterns by choosing Adjust➪Add/Remove Noise➪Moiré Pattern Removal. The rather simple Moire Pattern Removal dialog box arrives, to do your bidding.

The Moire Pattern Removal dialog box offers two controls: Fine Details and Remove Bands. Adjusting Fine Details upward (sliding it to the right) blurs your image and removes fine, grainy moiré patterning. Adjusting Remove Bands upward counters the distracting bands that often are part of moiré patterning.

Unearthing JPEG Artifacts

When photos are stored in JPEG format, as they often are, the result is nice, small files. But JPEGs that have been heavily compressed to save space often exhibit strange patterns and checkerboard patterns around text and other objects with sharp edges. Figure 6-7 shows those patterns, also called *artifacts*.

Figure 6-7: This dog grew a few artifacts when it was stored as a JPEG image. The JPEG Artifact Removal effect uproots them.

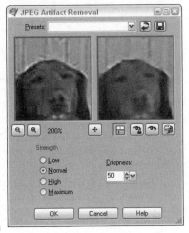

Compressing JPEG files is normally something you *should* do — done correctly, it squeezes the file size down to as much as 10 percent of its original size without noticeable image degradation. To find out how to compress a JPEG file effectively, see Chapter 15.

To clean up JPEG images, choose Adjust➪Add/Remove Noise➪JPEG Artifact Removal. The JPEG Artifact Removal expert appears on your doorstep, in the form of the dialog box shown in the figure.

After checking your image by either looking in the right preview window or proofing your choice, choose the strength (Low, Normal, High, or Maximum) needed to clean up your artifacts. Another casualty in JPEG files is a certain amount of detail, which you can restore by increasing the value in the Crispness value box.

Chapter 7

Adjusting Your Picture's Brightness, Contrast, and Color

When William does his own laundry — which, thankfully, isn't often — the colors in his clothing all run together. Pure white socks become a dull gray, bright red shirts lighten to a washed-out pink, and we don't discuss what happens to his underwear.

But, if you hadn't seen the way William's shirts looked originally, you may not realize that anything was wrong. You may think that his shirt was *supposed* to be an ugly pink and that he had chosen to wear gray socks. Eventually, William's wife, Gini, would sigh and do his laundry for him, at which point you would be amazed at how much better William looks when someone competent cleans him up.

Photos are much like William in that their colors are usually a little off by default. Although some photos are obviously miscolored, like being too bright or too murky, almost *all* pictures benefit visibly from a good color adjustment. With very little effort, you can make the colors in your picture "pop" and turn an ordinary photo into a portrait-quality image.

The secrets to brightening your family's dirty laundry lie within Paint Shop Pro. Be warned that not all remedies are intuitive. The remedy for what you may call a brightness problem, for example, may turn out to be something called lightness, or both lightness and contrast.

Some photographs are tinted a specific hue, where everything is a shade of sea blue. If that's the case, we consider the photo to be almost unusable, which is why we show you how to fix that image in Chapter 6, in the section about color-correcting photos, which deals with fixing broken photos. After you have chased the blues away, come on back to see how to improve it even further.

The One Step Photo Fix

If you're in a hurry and don't want to read the rest of this chapter, here's some good news: You don't have to! Paint Shop Pro has a one-click solution that solves many common color problems, and it's called the One Step Photo Fix.

On the Photo toolbar, at the top, you should see a drop-down menu that says Enhance Photo; select it and choose One Step Photo Fix. (If for some reason you don't see it, choose View⇨Toolbars⇨Photo.) Paint Shop Pro then adjusts your picture's color, sharpens the image, fixes the contrast and clarifies it, does an Edge-Preserving Smooth for good measure, and then tops off your gas tank. (Okay, we're just kidding about that last one.)

Be warned, however, that the One Step Photo Fix isn't a universal solution. For one thing, it doesn't fix photographs that have obvious flaws, like red eye and scratches. (To fix those problems, refer to Chapter 6.) Also, sometimes pictures have specific problem areas, like underexposed shadowy places underneath a tree or a single wall that's too bright. To spot-fix problems like that, you need to use the Backlighting and Fill Flash tools, as shown later in this chapter.

Lastly, much like baking store-bought chocolate chip cookie dough, the One Step Photo Fix isn't *quite* as good as doing it by hand — it tends to err on the light side, which creates slightly washed-out photos. But, if you're pressed for time, it can be a lifesaver.

If you don't like the results of the Photo Fix, read on! Sometimes, you just have to roll up your sleeves and get a little dirty to create the vibrant picture that your friends deserve to see.

Understanding the Paint Shop Pro Dialog Boxes

All the dialog boxes for color adjustments have similar controls, and sometimes they can be confusing. So, it can't hurt to walk you through it first. The

Brightness/Contrast dialog box, as shown in Figure 7-1, provides an example. Note that the slider shown in the figure appears only when you click and hold down the mouse button on the larger down arrow at the far right end of a value box.

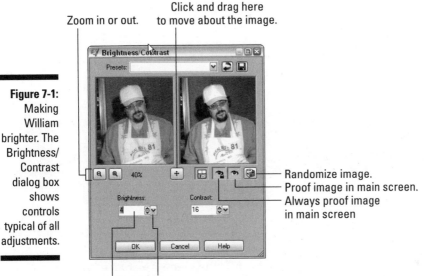

Figure 7-1:
Making
William
brighter. The
Brightness/
Contrast
dialog box
shows
controls
typical of all
adjustments.

Making color adjustments

You have several ways to adjust settings in the dialog boxes:

✔ In adjusting value boxes, you may type a value, click the associated up and down arrows, click in the value box, and press the up- and down-arrow keys on the keyboard or click and hold the larger down arrow to the right of the box and drag the slider that appears.

✔ Some adjustments appear as sliders: Drag sliders to the left or right or up or down. Dragging varies an associated value (number) that appears in a text box to the right of each slider. Dragging left or down reduces that value, and dragging right or up increases it. Alternatively, click a slider and then press the up- and down-arrow keys on the keyboard to increase or decrease its value by one.

✔ To give precise values, double-click in the box where the value appears and type a new value.

 ✔ To take a chance and see what happens, click the Randomize Parameters button. Your new settings are chosen at random.

 ✔ To reset adjustments to their original (default) levels, click the Reset to Default button (refer to Figure 7-1).

After you make an adjustment, click OK to apply it to your image. Before you apply it, however, use the proofing or previewing tools that we describe in the following section.

Changes are rarely final in Paint Shop Pro because you can undo them by pressing Ctrl+Z or clicking the History palette (see Chapter 18).

Proofing or previewing your adjustments

All the color adjustment dialog boxes let you see the effect of your adjustments in the main image window, a feature called *proofing*. The change isn't permanent until you click the OK button. If you cancel out of the dialog box, the change doesn't occur. You have two ways to proof:

 ✔ Click the Proof button, the one with the eye icon, after every adjustment.

 ✔ If you find yourself clicking the Proof button too often, try using Auto Proof. Click the Auto Proof button, the creepy eyeball with a padlock, as shown in Figure 7-1. Paint Shop Pro now shows the effect of your changes in the main image window every time you make a change. For large images, however, you may find this proofing method slow.

The dialog boxes for commands on the Adjust menu also have preview windows that let you see the effect of your adjustments without the long wait that proofing sometimes entails. Here's how to preview your changes:

 ✔ To zoom in or out within the preview windows, click the Zoom In button (marked with a +) or Zoom Out button (with a –), as shown in Figure 7-1.

 ✔ To move the image in the preview window so that you can see a new area, drag the image in either window.

 ✔ To quickly move to a new area of the image, click the Navigate button, as shown in Figure 7-1, and keep the mouse button depressed. A small version of the entire image is displayed, with a rectangle representing the preview area. Drag the rectangle to the area you want to preview and then release the mouse button.

Like most Paint Shop Pro effects, every color adjustment we cover in this chapter can be applied to a specific area within an image, which allows you to lighten a darkened entryway or make Uncle Vania's shirt color more vibrant. Here are a few points to keep in mind about that phenomenon:

- ✔ If you have made a selection, only the selected area is affected by your adjustments. For a complete rundown on the selection process, check out Chapter 3.

- ✔ If you're using multiple layers in your image, commands on the Adjust menu affect only the selected layer.

- ✔ If you're using multiple layers in your image, consider using an adjustment layer so that you can affect color across multiple layers.

- ✔ If a feature doesn't appear to be working, check to see whether you have selected an area or have made a particular layer active. If you have, the tool is working only within that selection, or layer, and not necessarily in the area you're trying to change. Read all about selections and layers in Part III.

Correcting Trouble Spots

Quite often, the problem with a picture is that only *part* of it is wrong, particularly in outside snapshots, when bright sunlight comes into play. A picture taken entirely in sunshine isn't a problem — although when you have some people sitting in the shade and others standing in the sunshine, digital cameras have to choose between one of the two lighting styles.

Your camera may decide to optimize for the people standing in the sun — in which case the sun people look normal and the folks in the shade are lost in shadow. Or, your camera may highlight the people in the shade, in which case the folks standing in the sun look overly white and washed out.

If this happens, Paint Shop Pro has two tools to correct these common errors: the Backlighting Filter and the Fill Flash Filter.

Despite the fact that the Fill Flash Filter and the Backlighting Filter do largely opposite things, nothing is stopping you from using both of them on the same image. That trick works better than you may think.

Shedding light on shadows

Technically speaking, when a picture has an area that's too murky to see because it didn't get enough light, that phenomenon is called *underexposure*. To correct the underexposed segments of *your* photo, choose Adjust⇨Photo Fix⇨Fill Flash. The Fill Flash Filter dialog box appears, as shown in Figure 7-2.

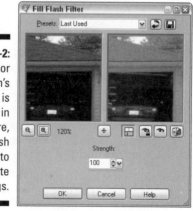

Figure 7-2:
The interior
of William's
garage is
too dark in
this picture,
but Fill Flash
helps to
illuminate
things.

The Fill Flash filter attempts to re-create your image as though it had been taken with a stronger flash bulb. Appropriately, it has one setting: Strength. A larger strength setting means that the shadowy portions of your picture are more visible, although it has a hidden cost: The rest of your image is brightened, sometimes resulting in artificially bright colors outside the underexposed area.

You can select a specific area of your image — in Figure 7-2, the garage interior would be a good bet — and have the Fill Flash filter apply its artificial flashbulb to only that portion of your picture. For details on how to select the *right* parts, refer to Chapter 3.

Preview your image with the Proof button. If everything looks all right, click OK.

Reducing glare and overexposure

Sometimes, a flash reflects off a white wall and pours too much light into the room. When that happens, not only is everyone *way* paler than they need to be, but you also have pools of glare (also known as ugly white smears) everywhere.

To help you compensate for this lighting overload, Paint Shop Pro offers the Backlighting Filter, as shown in Figure 7-3. The Backlighting Filter attempts to even out the amount of light in the photo and usually darkens it.

Like the Fill Flash Filter, the Backlighting Filter has one setting: Strength. Higher strength values reduce the glare and also make your image darker and more shadowed. Experiment to find the value that works for you, and then click OK.

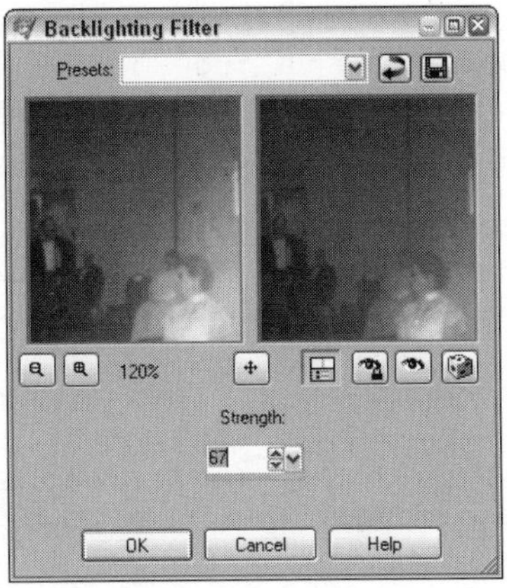

Figure 7-3:
The room is amazingly white, thanks to the flash bouncing off William's thumb, although the Backlighting Filter should help the image.

If someone's skin has glare spots so white that they don't even show up as skin colored, the best the Backlighting Filter can do is make that skin an unhealthy charcoal gray. In that case, you may want to use the Smudge Tool or the Clone Brush to copy a healthy skin color into the glare spot. Chapter 8 shows you how.

Correcting Lighting Color

Despite automatic flashes, lighting is still one of the prime photographic problems. Your flash fails to go off, the room is lit by incandescent or fluorescent light, the sunset casts an orange light, the forest reflects green, or the swimming pool reflects blue. Many of these problems go away almost magically with the Paint Shop Pro Automatic Color Balance effect.

Choose Adjust⇨Color Balance⇨Automatic Color Balance. The Automatic Color Balance dialog box makes the scene (refer to Figure 7-1).

Adjust the slider left or right in the grandiosely named Illuminant Temperature area, or edit the value in the Temperature text box. Dragging the slider left (to a lower Temperature value) makes the color of your photo visually warmer, or more orange. (Yes, lower temperature makes color warmer.) Dragging right makes the color visually cooler, or bluer. Notice that the Temperature scale is labeled with various light sources, such as Sunlight; position the slider at a given label to simulate that light source.

Adjust the Strength value higher for greater effect — generally, a brighter picture. Adjust it down for the opposite effect.

You want to check the Remove Color Cast option whenever a picture is predominantly one color — for example, when both your wife and the back porch are tinged ever-so-slightly with green. Paint Shop Pro then analyzes the image to try to find what the dominant color is and then attempts to mute that color to bring out the other hues.

This feature works well for subtle color changes — but, if your spouse is as blue as a Smurf, you're better off using the Manual Color Correction tool, as described in Chapter 6, in the section about color-correcting photos.

The temperature thing is about the illumination term *color temperature,* which refers to the temperature of an incandescent light source. A lower-temperature light source generally gives a warmer (more orange) light. You can see the effect in a fireplace or barbecue; as the fire dies down, it gives off a more orange glow.

Bringing Your Picture's Colors to Life

One problem in showing you how to improve your colors is that unless you're a professional photographer, most of the photos you enhance *don't look that bad to start with.* Most people don't look at the images on their digital camera and mutter, "Wow, this picture could use more saturation and increased coloration in the midtones." But, after you have laundered your image's colors, you may be surprised at how much better your pictures look.

To help you understand the problem, the color section of this book has before-and-after pictures taken of William's wife, Gini. Go ahead and look. Notice how the preenhanced picture of Gini isn't notably awful — you would probably just shrug if someone showed it to you — but the enhanced image is *much* more vibrant and alive.

That's how you want your photos to look.

Sadly, that's not as simple as saying "Fix the colors." *Color* is a catchall term that describes the three elements of luminance and shade that combine to create a color's "look:"

- ✔ **Hue:** *Hue* is the base shade of color, the element that differentiates one color from another. Hue is the core setting that makes something blue or red or turquoise.

   Paradoxically, hue isn't that important in the scheme of things. Hue controls only the *base* color of an object in your image; it doesn't account for the two other color-related elements that stack on top of it. Put another way, although the essential hue can be "red," adding more brightness can turn that hue into light pink and subtracting saturation can turn it into a murky red.

You almost never fiddle with hues because you usually don't want to *change* the core colors. You want to make your hues brighter or more vivid or have them stand out more. Change the hue and you risk turning your sister's lovely brown skin into an ugly fuschia with the exact shades and tones as the old color.

✔ **Brightness:** *Brightness* is a measure of how *light* your colors are, independent of their actual hue. A basic blue hue with lots of brightness may be a sky blue, whereas that same blue with low levels of brightness may become a dark navy. Taken to its logical limits, a 100 percent bright image is pure white, whereas an image with no light is jet black.

Adding more brightness makes a picture lighter; subtracting brightness makes it darker. You want to change the brightness in your images a lot.

✔ **Saturation:** Technically, *saturation* measures the amount of gray in a color. (Yes, most colors have some gray in them.) Realistically speaking, saturation measures how *pure* a color is; high levels of saturation mean that very little gray is mixed in. (An image with *no* saturation, incidentally, is a black-and-white photo — all grays, no colors.)

Hues with too much saturation look artificial and garish, like an Andy Warhol painting. On the other hand, hues with too little saturation are muddied and indistinct.

Most digital photographs suffer from too little saturation, incidentally. Reducing the saturation levels can make your image pop!

In addition, color has a secret fourth element. This element doesn't define a specific color; instead, it looks at all the colors in your image as a whole. *Contrast* measures the range of lights and darks that exist in the colors in your photo. A high-contrast image has lots of high- and low-brightness colors, with little in between, which makes it look kind of like the image shown in Figure 7-4.

A *low*-contrast image, on the other hand, has colors that are almost entirely composed of the same brightness. This sounds good, but you need contrast to be able to distinguish things — witness what happens in Figure 7-5.

Quite often, changing the contrast of your image makes things more visible and sharper.

Where do you start? Well, here's a guilty confession: Even though we're big-shot authors of *Dummies* books, quite often *we* can't pinpoint the exact problem with our family snapshots. Usually, the problem gets solved via a quick adjustment of contrast and saturation — but, sometimes we have to go delving through pretty much all the items listed in this chapter before our photos are changed to our satisfaction. Don't be afraid to roll up your sleeves and muck around until everything's picture perfect!

Figure 7-4:
In this image with ridiculously high contrast values, notice how it's almost all black or all white.

Figure 7-5:
A low-contrast image; if this looks like a big gray box on the page, that's because it pretty much is.

Tweaking contrast and brightness

We have been trying for years to be brighter, and now Paint Shop Pro has shown us the light. Just what is brightness, though? If you increase the brightness of an image, it looks whiter. This whitening affects all shades uniformly, sort of like using bleach in mixed laundry: Lights get whiter, and so do darks.

Because brightness alone rarely does the job, Jasc puts the Paint Shop Pro adjustments for brightness and contrast together. Contrast is a bit like a laundry brightener that makes the lights lighter and the darks darker. (It isn't too picky about keeping your colors exactly right, though.)

Although Paint Shop Pro offers several ways to adjust contrast, for photos, the Automatic Contrast Enhancement effect is a great place to start. It simultaneously fiddles with brightness and contrast — two interlinked attributes — to optimize your photo's appearance. Whether your photo has too little contrast or too much, this tool can help.

Choose Adjust➪Automatic Contrast Enhancement and the Automatic Contrast Enhancement control, as shown in Figure 7-6, rushes to your aid. This effect has three control areas: *Bias* (or lightness), *Strength* (amount of effect), and *Appearance* (amount of contrast).

Figure 7-6:
The "cardinal" rule for contrast problems is to try the Automatic Contrast Enhancement dialog box first.

In the figure, a photo we took of a cardinal (through a window) suffers from poor contrast — a dark fate for such a bright bird. The Automatic Contrast Enhancement effect restores his outstanding appearance. Use the controls of this effect in the following ways:

 ✔ If your photo needs contrast adjustment, use the Appearance controls. If your photo needs more contrast, click Bold; for less contrast, click Flat; and, if it's just right, click Natural.

✔ If your photo needs lightening or darkening, use the Bias controls. If it's overall too dark, click Lighter; if it's too light, click Darker; if it's just right, click Neutral.

✔ For a greater effect on contrast and brightness, click Normal in the Strength area. Otherwise, choose Mild.

Intensifying (or dulling) colors through saturation

The more common problem with photos is dull colors that need more intensity. However, if you're shooting Ronald McDonald, for example, at a sunny tulip festival, we can imagine that you may need duller colors, too. Either way, the Automatic Saturation Enhancement effect fills the bill.

Choose Adjust➪Automatic Saturation Enhancement to enter the land of more intense (or dimmer) colors. The Automatic Saturation Enhancement dialog box glimmers onto your screen.

Figure 7-7 shows the dialog box in action. Showing you intensified colors in a black-and-white illustration is a bit too much of a challenge, however, so please turn to the color section of this book for some examples of the kinds of results you can achieve.

Controls in the Bias area determine whether you intensify or dull your colors. Choose Less Colorful to dull your colors or More Colorful to intensify colors. Normal may intensify or dull your colors, depending on how intense they are now.

Figure 7-7: Brightening up a dull day at the farm with Automatic Saturation Enhancement.

Controls in the Strength area determine to what degree you dull or intensify colors (according to your choice in the Bias area). Choose Weak to barely affect colors, Normal to moderately affect them, or Strong to have the most effect.

If you have people in your image, the Automatic Saturation Enhancement may brighten their faces by mistake, by amplifying a healthy pink into a drunkard's blush. Or, it may dampen a vibrant brown into a sallow gray. If you have people in your picture, check the Skintones present check box to warn Paint Shop Pro to leave those pinks and browns alone!

Altering an overall tint

Are your overalls the wrong tint? Paint Shop Pro can't fix that laundry problem — unless, of course, you have a picture of your overalls.

Images, whether the subject is overalls or not, sometimes have — or need — an *overall tint.* Portraits taken in a forest setting, for example, tend to make people look a bit green because of the light reflected off the leaves. Or, you may want to add a slight orange tint to a sunset picture.

Paint Shop Pro, as it does with most color controls, gives you several ways to alter tint:

- **Choose Adjust➪Color Balance➪Red/Green/Blue:** The Red/Green/Blue dialog box that appears is the simplest control for altering overall tint.

- **Choose Adjust➪Color Balance➪Color Balance:** Color Balance and Curves tint shadows, midtones, and highlights separately.

Choose Adjust➪Color Balance➪Red/Green/Blue and the Red/Green/Blue dialog box appears. Like all dialog boxes for commands on the Adjust menu, it has preview windows and proofing controls, plus one sliding control for each primary color: Red %, Green %, and Blue %.

To make your image more red, green, or blue, the solution is straightforward: Increase the value for that color. (Decrease it for less of that color.) Values range from –100 to +100.

Choose Adjust➪Color Balance➪Color Balance and the Color Balance dialog box appears. It works much like the Red/Green/Blue dialog box, but you get to choose whether the controls apply to shadows, midtones, or highlights. Choose by first clicking the corresponding radio button (such as Shadows) for the tonal range you want to change; then move the sliders toward what-ever tone you want more of (Red, for example).

Fun with Colors

Not all color adjustments have to *improve* your photos. You can also alter photos by turning them black-and-white, tinting them with shades, or turning them into silk-screen paintings!

Going gray with a tint: Colorizing

We all go gray. Some of us try to add an attractive tint when that happens. The same scheme can be even more attractive when applied to images.

Paint Shop Pro calls this process *colorizing*. But, unlike the colorizing you may have seen used to make old black-and-white movies look as though they were shot in color, colorizing in Paint Shop Pro imparts only a single hue to the image. In effect, the result is a grayscale (monochrome) image done in your chosen hue rather than in gray — kind of like all of those Che Guevera pictures, where he's standing against a red background.

The best Paint Shop Pro tool for this process is the Colorize tool, and it works like this: Choose Adjust➪Hue and Saturation➪Colorize to display the Colorize dialog box. The Colorize dialog box grabs its crayons and reports for duty.

The Colorize dialog box sports two adjustments:

- ✔ **Saturation:** Increase this value to determine how much color is applied. If you set it to 0, the image is strictly grayscale (black and white). At 255, the image has no gray, but is purely the hue you choose by adjusting the Hue control.

- ✔ **Hue:** Click and hold the tiny down arrow at the right end of the Hue value box. A rainbow-colored slider appears. Drag to the hue you want and then release the mouse button.

Going totally gray or negative in one step

You're just one step away from going as gray as William's grandfather or becoming as negative as a political ad. The Paint Shop Pro commands for Greyscale and Negative Image, on the Adjust menu, are simple enough to do their work in a single step: You get no dialog box and have no adjustments to make.

Choose Adjust➪Color Balance➪Negative Image and Paint Shop Pro gives you the negative of your image. Lights become darks, darks become lights, and colors switch to their opposing colors on the color wheel. Reds become cyans, yellows become blues, and so on. Changing an image from positive (normal) to negative isn't often useful, but sometimes you need to go the other way. That event occurs when you (or whoever is supplying your images) is using a film scanner and scans a film negative. The Negative Image command gives you the normal (positive) image you want.

To turn your color image into shades of gray (like a black-and-white photo), choose Image➪Greyscale. Going grayscale affects the entire image, even if you have selected an area. If you want to turn just a certain area grayscale, select that area and use the Hue/Saturation/Lightness dialog box, as described earlier in this chapter, to set the Saturation control to the minimum.

Posterize

The Posterize control isn't on the Adjust menu, like the other advanced controls we discuss in this section, but it does interesting things with colors. Choose Effects➪Artistic Effects➪Posterize to launch the Posterize dialog box.

In *posterizing,* an image takes on the appearance of a silk-screened poster, made up of areas of a few uniform colors. Posterizing reduces the number of colors that appear and results in blocks of color, like a paint-by-numbers painting.

The dialog box for posterizing has only one adjustment, named Levels. Reduce the value to reduce the number of colors or increase it to increase colors. The value in Levels determines the number of levels of brightness in the image.

Threshold

The threshold control (choose Adjust➪Brightness and Contrast➪Threshold) gives you images in pure black and pure white, as shown in Figure 7-8. With a threshold control, you're telling Paint Shop Pro, "Turn any pixel with a brightness below a given threshold black, and turn any pixel above that threshold white."

The dialog box for this layer has a single adjustment. Reduce the Threshold value for a lower threshold (more white) and increase it for a higher threshold (more black). You can use a threshold value between 1 and 255.

Figure 7-8:
Threshold
allows you
to turn an
everyday
William into
a poster for
*Night of the
Living Dead.*

Chapter 8

Heavy-Duty Photo Alterations: Adding People and Removing Zits

*T*he problem with photos is that they are, in the end, depressingly accurate. In William's mind, he is a slim 180 pounds, has a full head of hair, and possesses white teeth bright enough to make the Osmond Brothers jealous. But when his photos show up on-screen, they always reveal William to be a man with a generous pot belly, a growing bald spot, and yellowing teeth. (This is, incidentally, why Wiley does not allow author signings for *Paint Shop Pro For Dummies.*)

William can improve the quality of his pictures all he wants — but in the end, that just makes his bald spot clearer and more vibrant. What William wants to do is to change the *nature* of his photo.

Fortunately, Paint Shop Pro is extremely good at altering details. With Paint Shop Pro, you can remove zits, cover up ugly carpets, and even put people in photos who weren't there when you took the picture. Wouldn't it be nice to have a pimple-free photo of you standing next to Britney Spears?

If that sounds interesting, let's rock on!

Retouching Skin Blemishes and Other Small Ugly Spots

Making small changes to an image to improve it is called *retouching*. Not surprisingly, if you want to spruce up your images, your best friend is the friendly finger of the retouch tool group, as shown in Figure 8-1. The retouch tool group, which lurks on the toolbar, is kind of a virtual fingertip with which you can rub away many defects, like Mom rubbing a bit of soot off your nose.

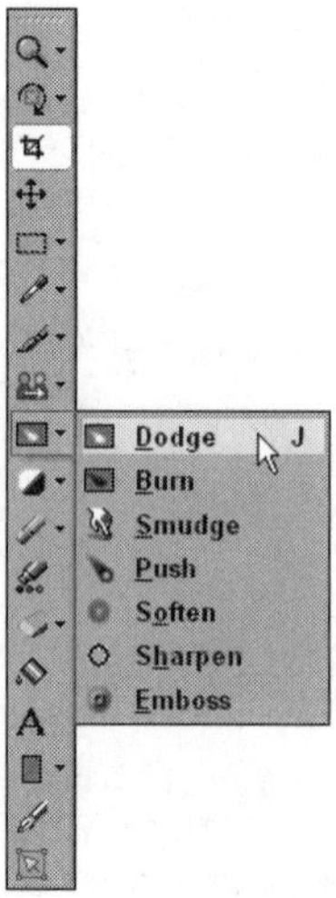

Figure 8-1: When I think about you, I retouch myself: the retouch tool group.

The retouch tool group offers many tools to choose from. Some of them require a fair amount of technical insight into computer graphics in order to use them properly. In this chapter, we cover the effects you're likely to use most.

Removing wrinkles with the Soften tool

One of the most useful Paint Shop Pro effects is great for retouching portraits: the Soften tool. The Soften tool, well, softens sharp edges — wrinkles, for example. Just brush the tool across those edges or click them.

Figure 8-2 shows a frighteningly close shot of the left eye of wrinkled, old Uncle Dave, a friendly author. On the left is an unretouched copy; on the right is the Soften tool softening his wrinkles.

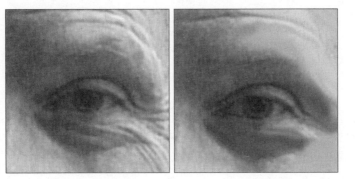

Figure 8-2:
The Soften tool removes a few years from Dave's left eye.

You could get the same result by selecting the wrinkled area and applying the Blur or Blur More effect, but that's more work. (We give you details later in this chapter, in the section "Adding Blurs and the Illusion of Motion.") If you want a nice, soft, angelic glow to your entire image, the Soft Focus Adjustment (see the later section "Bringing Someone into Soft Focus") makes everything radiant.

To work more gradually and do less softening in each stroke, set the opacity to a lower value on the Tool Options palette.

Zapping warts and pimples with the Smudge tool

The Smudge tool picks up paint from the place where you set it down and smears that paint as you drag to other areas, to make it the closest thing Paint Shop Pro has to finger painting. As the tool smears, it loses paint just as your finger would. You can use smudging to soften edges, rub out pimples, cover up glare spots, or even blend in a dot of rouge (in the form of low-opacity red paint) that you have added to the cheek of your CEO's portrait.

To minimize moles, pimples, and similar imperfections, start not *on* the discolored area, but rather off to one side. Smudge across the discolored area and release the mouse button after you've smeared skin tone through the imperfection. Repeat in the opposite direction, again starting on clear skin.

Figure 8-3 shows the smudge effect as the Retouch tool is dragged from left to right, starting with white and passing through the center of three differently colored squares in a single stroke. Notice how the paint fades as the tool moves from left to right. The tops of the three squares have also been smudged, but with repeated, circular strokes.

Figure 8-3:
Figure 8-3:
The Retouch
tool in
Smudge
mode. A
single stroke
through the
middle
creates a
"bullet
through an
apple" look,
and a
circular
motion
smudges
the tops.

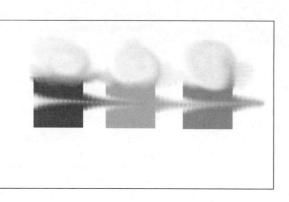

As shown in the center of Figure 8-3, a single stroke may reveal the inherent dottiness of computer stroking, which you can minimize by reducing the Step value on the Tool Options palette (press F4 if you don't see it). Repeated strokes, as indicated along the tops of the squares in Figure 8-3, tend to smear out those dots.

If your wart, pimple, or mole is too big to smudge — and some are — consider using the Clone Brush tool to cover up the offending blemish with pristine skin taken from elsewhere in your image. See the section "Removing People, Places, and Things from Your Image," later in this chapter.

Miscellaneous retouch tools

Not all retouching tools are useful; some are obscure, and others are more creative than restorative. Still, they may be worth a try. This list provides brief synopses of what they do:

- ✔ **Sharpen:** Amplifies edges, wrinkles, and other sudden transitions (the opposite of Soften).

- ✔ **Emboss:** Creates a grayscale image that appears to be embossed, like George Washington's face on a U.S. quarter.

✔ **Push:** Picks up the image area where you begin dragging and pushes it along, leaving a trail of finely overlapping copies of that area. (Overlap is controlled by the Step value on the Tool Options palette.)

✔ **Dodge:** A term taken from photographic darkroom work that means to lighten areas that are already somewhat light. It lightens the image and enhances contrast at the same time.

✔ **Burn:** The opposite of Dodge; darkens pixels that are already somewhat dark. It darkens the image while enhancing contrast.

Burning and dodging are frequently used by professional photographers to draw attention to parts of an image. For example, if you want your cousin to stand out in her graduation picture, you might burn the people surrounding her (as horrid as that sounds) and darken the rest of the assembly. The viewer's eye is then drawn to the light spot (namely, your cousin) in the middle of a dark crowd.

Adding People, Places, and Things to Your Image

Using the Paint Shop Pro selection commands makes it very easy to cut people out of one image and paste them into another. For example, in Figure 8-4, we have cut the faithful Alex from Dave's snow-covered doorstep in Maine and placed him next to Amy, William's daughter, as she kneels next to her fantastic creation: the Cleveland Snowduck.

Figure 8-4: Paint Shop Pro: Bringing people (and animals) together.

Layers: Really, incredibly useful

If you're going to be adding new people, places, or things to your image, you probably want to add them as new *layers.* When something is on a layer, you can edit it separately from the rest of the image.

For example, when we created the Alex-and-Amy fake in Figure 8-4, we put the picture of Amy and her Cleveland Snowduck on one layer and then pasted Alex the dog into another layer. That allowed us to resize Alex, making him smaller, without changing Amy's size. We also erased a little around Alex's edges *without* erasing any of the snow on Amy's layer. Whatever we did to Alex's picture didn't affect Amy's image, and whatever we did to Amy didn't affect Alex.

Layering is so amazingly powerful that we have an entire chapter devoted to it; Chapter 11 opens up a whole new world to you.

This part of the program is a great deal of fun, and Paint Shop Pro aficionados frequently get hours of enjoyment by inserting themselves into movie posters so that they're costarring with Salma Hayek. In fact, an entire underground Internet movement is devoted to taking pictures from the news and doing as many strange and bizarre things with them as possible. The Web site www.fark.com, for example, holds PG-13–rated contests to see who can "Photoshop" pictures of Alan Greenspan and Ludacris into the funniest places. Some results are quite impressive.

We cover the mechanics of selecting a portion of an image in Chapter 3, and we tell you in Chapter 4 how to cut and paste those portions into other photos. That's a good place to start — but a simple cut-and-paste doesn't create realistic fakes. Not that you need your photos to hold up to the eye of conspiracy theorists — but plopping a picture of you, jaggies and edge halos and all, into some random image just looks amateurish. Your completed pastiche should look plausible at first glance, if not the second or third.

With that in mind, we here on the *Paint Shop Pro 9 For Dummies* staff offer the following advice to make your images blend seamlessly:

1. **Use the Magic Wand to select.**

   Yes, it's easier to just draw a line around your target — but unless you have a steady hand and a *ridiculously* exacting eye, the Magic Wand does it better after some fine-tuning. Get used to it.

2. **Get rid of the holes and specks in your selection.**

   This task used to be difficult, but Paint Shop Pro makes it so easy now with its Remove Specks and Holes command that it's a crime not to do it.

3. Feather a little.

Usually, you want to leave off those crisp edges. Feather one or two pixels on the inside to help the selection blend into the background.

4. Eliminate the background color entirely.

We show you how to remove a color from a selection in Chapter 3, in the section about removing the background or other colors from your selection — and we show you an ugly image that shows what happens if you don't. Learn the lesson!

5. Resize appropriately.

When we first put Alex in the picture in Figure 8-4, he only came up to Amy's shoulder, making Amy look freakishly huge. A little downsizing made a large difference.

6. Match the blur.

Most photos aren't perfectly clear, and dropping a crisply focused image into the middle of a slightly blurry pic looks wrong in a way that most people can't quite put a name to. Sharpening or Gaussian-blurring your selection just a tad helps it to blend in.

7. Adjust the color.

Having a sunlit image brought into a fluorescent background makes the image stick out like a throbbing thumb. Adjust the contrast, hue, and brightness to match it as closely as you can. To find out how to adjust contrast, hue, and brightness, look no further than Chapter 7.

8. Don't forget the shadows!

A touch of low-opacity black paint can serve as a quick-and-dirty fake shadow — as we did in the example shown in Figure 8-4. If you want to go all out, you can even paste in another identical selection as a layer, deform it so that it's twisted sideways and elongated like a real shadow, position it so that it's spreading out from the bottom of the image, erase the layer so that it's transparent — and *then* fill it in with low-opacity paint. But that's a great deal of work for a quick fake!

Removing People, Places, and Things from Your Image

The Clone Brush tool is a *wonderful* thing that allows you to erase someone from an image without leaving a blank hole the way the Eraser tool does. The Clone Brush requires you to select an area of your image — also known as "the source" — before you start painting. When you paint with the Clone Brush, you paste copies of the pixels from the source area into the area you're painting.

This tool is frequently used in photograph retouching to "erase" areas in a picture. If you don't like your Uncle Fred, paint over him with a section of the wall that's off to his left.

This process is easier shown than described — so suppose that you have decided that the green blanket that Alex is sitting on in Figure 8-5 just *has* to go. You had better cover it up with some snow!

Figure 8-5:
The original
image,
complete
with green
blanket.

1. **Click the Clone Brush tool (shown in Figure 8-6) on the Tools toolbar.**

   If you don't see the Clone Brush tool, you may have selected the Scratch Remover tool earlier. If that's the case, click the arrow next to the Scratch Remover tool and select the Clone Brush tool from the drop-down list.

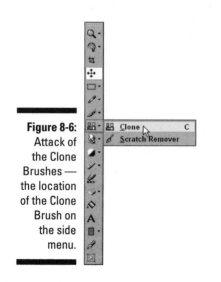

Figure 8-6:
Attack of
the Clone
Brushes —
the location
of the Clone
Brush on
the side
menu.

2. **If necessary, adjust the size and hardness of the Clone Brush tool on the Tool Options palette (see Figure 8-7).**

Figure 8-7:
The Tool
Options
palette,
Clone
Brush–style.

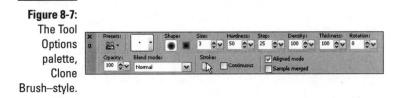

Sometimes, you want to have a very large clone selection to replace huge areas of a picture — or, you want a small selection to make sure that you can get right in between Alex's paws. You can adjust the size on the Size control on the Tool Options palette; large numbers mean that you copy a large sample of the picture, and smaller numbers mean tiny samples. You want a teeny selection, so choose 20.

The *hardness* is a percentage that determines how crisp the edge of a cloned copy is; 100 percent is a razor-sharp edge, whereas 0 percent is a fuzzy selection that looks almost blurred and blends easily into the background (see Figure 8-8). We keep ours at 50 percent.

Figure 8-8:
Values of
100 percent,
50 percent,
and 0
percent
hardness.

100 percent
hardness

50 percent
hardness

0 percent
hardness

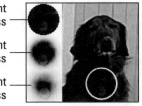

If you don't see the Tool Options palette, press F4 on the keyboard.

3. ***Right*-click the source area (the area you want to copy).**

Clicking an edge or corner of the object you want helps you with the next step. In this case, because you want to cover up the green blanket with a fluffy coating of snow, right-click the snow in the lower-right corner, as shown in Figure 8-9.

Cloning between images or layers

The Clone Brush tool copies just as well from one image window to another window as it does within one image. It also copies between layers, if you want. (If you don't know what layers are — and you should — flip to Chapter 11.)

To clone between images, open both images. They appear in separate windows in Paint Shop Pro. Just right-click the source image where you want to copy, and then left-click or drag where you want to paint on the destination image.

To clone between layers, select your source layer on the Layer palette. Then, right-click the image you want copied. Select the destination layer on the Layer palette, and then left-click or drag on the image.

Figure 8-9:
A small section of the blanket has been replaced with a copy of the snow from the lower-right corner.

4. **Brush (*left*-click or drag) on the destination area (the area you want to paint).**

   As you brush, keep an eye on the source area too. An X marks the spot on the source image where the Clone Brush tool is picking up (copying) pixels. As you move your brush, the X on the source image tracks your movement. Move so that the X sweeps across the object you want to copy, as shown in Figure 8-10.

   If you ever want to choose another area to clone, all you have to do is right-click a new section.

If, in Step 3, you right-clicked the upper-left corner of the area you're copying, begin painting where you want the upper-left corner of the clone to appear in Step 4. Stroke down and to the right so that the X traverses the original object.

Figure 8-10:
Thanks to the magic of the Clone Brush, the blanket has vanished, replaced completely with cloned snow!

Other Clone Brush options

As you have already seen, the size of the area and the hardness can be set on the Tool Options palette. In fact, by using the Tool Options palette, you can set *all* the usual variations available to Paint Shop Pro brushes: shape, opacity (transparency), step, and density (speckliness). You can find more information on these settings in Chapter 9.

Cloning versus selection

When you copy individual people or objects, you can either use the Clone Brush tool or copy and paste. Which to choose? The Clone Brush tool isn't really the best tool for copying objects because constraining the tool to just the object you're copying is difficult — although sometimes it's the fastest tool to use.

TIP

Cloning neatly within the lines

You can paint neatly within a precisely defined area by selecting that area in the destination image. (We describe selection in Chapter 3.) Paint Shop Pro paints only within the selection marquee.

To paint Alex behind a palm tree, for example, you can select the palm tree's trunk and then invert the selection to select everything *except* the palm tree. Then, your brush stroke can slop right over the tree without leaving paint on it.

Creating a selection around the *source* area doesn't help you copy *from* a precise area, however. A selection works on only the *destination* area.

Here are three tips to tell you when the Clone Brush is the way to go:

- ✔ **When you have a large enough background to clone:** If you left-click very near where you originally right-clicked, you may soon start cloning your clones. (Your X may traverse areas you just painted.) You don't lose quality, but a pattern becomes apparent more quickly. If you look carefully at Figure 8-11, where we have begun to clone over Alex, you can discern a pattern in the slats we have cloned.

- ✔ **When you want to put an object behind something:** For example, you may want Alex to appear behind a palm tree at Club Med. With the Clone Brush tool, you can paint his image on either side of the palm tree. Paint Shop Pro has ways of doing this job that give cleaner results, but the Clone Brush tool is often simpler.

- ✔ **Only when backgrounds are similar:** Copying an object without picking up a few border pixels is difficult using the Clone Brush tool, so it works best when the backgrounds match.

Figure 8-11:
Bad
patterning,
Indy.

Bringing Someone into Soft Focus

Directors learned long ago that smearing the lens with Vaseline produces a soft, gentle look that gives everything a faint glow and makes the leading lady look angelic. (Not coincidentally, it also hides wrinkles on aging marquee stars, like Doris Day.) If you want to put the romance back in your photos, you too can simulate this effect!

Choose Adjust➪Softness➪Soft Focus to bring up the Soft Focus controls, as shown in Figure 8-12, which allow you to smear all the virtual Vaseline you want.

This list describes the controls shown in the figure:

- ✔ **Softness:** This option controls how blurry you want your image, much like defocusing a camera. Slide the control to the right to give the image that total I-forgot-my-glasses look.

- ✔ **Edge Importance:** Blurring the image may cause faces to turn into peachlike, fuzzy mushes; sliding this control to the right attempts to keep the edges (and eyes) distinct. It also helps to produce halos that surround objects, as opposed to a more general haze.

✔ **Halo Amount:** You can produce halos that lend an angelic look to the items in your image. Slide this control to the right for halo effects that surround just about everything, or yank it all the way to the left to turn off halo-ing altogether.

✔ **Halo Size:** Sliding this control to the right creates large, wide bands of halos, and moving it to the left produces tighter, "borderlike" halos.

✔ **Halo Visibility:** To create halos of pure white light, move this control to 100 percent; for softer, more background-colored halos, pull it leftward.

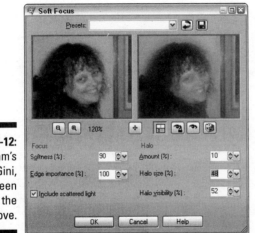

Figure 8-12: William's wife Gini, seen through the eyes of love.

Adding Blurs and the Illusion of Motion

"Why would I want to add blurs to an image?" you may ask. "Didn't I spend the big bucks to buy a digital camera that takes nonblurry photos?"

We have to admit that you have a point. But, sometimes, you're trying to paste an image into a slightly blurry photo and you need to match the larger picture's fuzzy background. At other times, you need to add a motion blur to something to make it look like it's moving very fast.

Blurring effects, although many and varied, are simple to use. Choose Adjust⇨Blur to access these menu items:

✔ **Average:** Pops up an adjustment dialog box with a single control, Amount of Correction. Drag right for more blur.

✔ **Blur:** Applies a moderate amount of blurring. No adjustment dialog box appears.

- **Blur More:** Like Blur, only more so.

- **Gaussian Blur:** Pops up a single-control adjustment dialog box. Drag the Radius control to the right for more blurring, or left for less. To the trained eye of the blur aficionado, this blur is a bit more refined than Average blur. To the rest of us, it's just a blur.

- **Motion Blur:** Produces an artistic effect that most people can understand if they have tried to take a photo of a fast-moving child, a car, or an animal and ended up with a motion blur. This effect, using an adjustment dialog box, *produces* a motion blur! Drag the clock-hand-like Direction control in that box to point in the direction you want motion. Then set the Strength slider and move it to the right if you need more blur (see the following Tip paragraph).

Blur is often most effective when applied selectively to a particular area of your image. Select an area with any of the selection tools we discuss in Chapter 3 and then apply the Blur effect. Applied selectively, Blur can help focus attention on the subject of your photo and away from a confusing background.

The Motion Blur effect is sometimes best applied to the background area *around* the object you want to appear speedy, so the object of interest isn't blurred. It's a great way, for example, to make Speedy, your lethargic retriever, appear to live up to his name. Take a photo of Speedy in his fastest pose — moseying toward his dinner bowl, for example. In Paint Shop Pro, select the area around Speedy before choosing the Motion Blur effect. Apply the motion blur in the head-to-tail direction. Your photo looks like your camera tracked Speedy as he sped heroically to save his Gravy Train from a watery demise. Figure 8-13 shows this effect applied to Alex, with a slight feathering to make him blend better into the blurred background.

Figure 8-13:
Speedy
Alex.

Spot-Changing Colors within an Image

Although Paint Shop Pro offers a dizzying variety of ways to change colors and intensities, the hue tool group, as shown in Figure 8-14, is the easiest. You can lighten or darken areas of your image, swap colors in a target area, intensify the colors, or leach them to a dull gray.

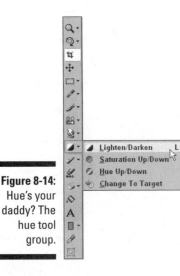

Figure 8-14:
Hue's your daddy? The hue tool group.

 The hue tool group doesn't do anything you can't do by selecting an area and then applying any one of the color adjustments we describe in Chapter 7. However, it's often much quicker to swipe a couple of strokes with a paint-brush-like object across your area than it is to carefully . . . select . . . the right . . . part and *then* adjust it.

Removing unsightly gleams and glares

You can lighten or darken in lots of different ways in Paint Shop Pro — but the most basic is the Lighten/Darken tool in the hue tool group. You're given two options here: RGB and Lightness. In most cases, RGB works just fine. Hold down the left mouse button and drag to lighten an image; hold the right button and drag to sink it into the shadows.

 Lightness adjusts the lightness portion — the *L* in HSL — and RGB adjusts the red, green, and blue portions. If you really want to know what the difference is, check out Chapter 7.

Figure 8-15 shows an image of Dave's trusty golden retriever, Alex, that was taken a bit too close to the camera's flash. On the copy on the right side, we have right-clicked with the Lighten/Darken tool in RGB mode to tone down the gleam on his nose and reduce the flash's reflection in his eyes.

Figure 8-15:
Lightening strikes as the Lighten/ Darken tool takes the shine off Alex's nose and the glare off his right eyeball.

To darken more gradually and gain more control over the results, set the opacity to a lower value on the Tool Options palette.

The rest of the hue tool group

Other tools are in the hue tool group, but they're not used much:

- **Saturation Up/Down:** Holding down the left mouse button and dragging while you have the Saturation tool selected amplifies the inherent colors in your image; holding down the right button leaches the colors out and renders the image a lifeless gray. (For more information on what saturation is, see the section in Chapter 7 about bringing your picture's colors to life.)

- **Change to Target:** You can use the Change to Target tool to transform all the colors under your brush into shades of the color in the Foreground Materials box. If you're really feeling comfortable with the whole HSL thing (as shown in Chapter 7), you can replace the hue, saturation, or lightness instead.

- **Hue Up/Down:** This option pushes colors counterclockwise (red, yellow, green, cyan, blue, violet, and magenta) or clockwise on the Paint Shop Pro color wheel. We don't know when you would use it, but, hey — it came with the program, right?

Part III
Painting Pictures

The 5th Wave   By Rich Tennant

"I'VE GOT SOME IMAGE EDITING SOFTWARE, SO I TOOK THE LIBERTY OF ERASING SOME OF THE SMUDGES THAT KEPT SHOWING UP AROUND THE CLOUDS. NO NEED TO THANK ME."

In this part . . .

Finally, someone has gotten serious about digital artwork, without charging an arm or an ear. The Paint
Shop Pro painting materials and its new Art Media tools
give you some incredibly jazzy effects without ever having
to open a can of turpentine. Oil paint? Pastels? Canvas?
You want it, you got it — or at least a darned good digital
simulation of it.

Chapter 9

Basic Painting, Spraying, and Filling

Of course, Paint Shop Pro does all the basics you have seen in garden variety "paint" programs (like the Paint program that comes with Windows). For example, it lets you brush or spray lines, blobs, and colors and fill in areas.

This is Paint Shop *Pro,* however, and *pro* means that you get a heck of a lot more control than those simple programs offer. It also means more sophisticated editing abilities, like replacing one color with another or erasing background areas. This tool is the one that Dave's house painter, Phil, would use if Dave's house were digital — and Phil's a pro.

As with most jobs you do in Paint Shop Pro, painting affects only the active layer and only the selected area. If it appears that a painting or retouching tool isn't working, make sure that you're on the right layer and working within a selected area (or clear the selection by pressing Ctrl+D). If you don't use more than one layer or don't have any current selection, don't worry about those restrictions. Also, remember that by pressing Ctrl+Z, you can undo any painting or erasing.

Starting a Fresh Canvas

You can paint on an existing image in Paint Shop Pro, but if you're starting a work of art from scratch, you need a fresh canvas, or *background layer.* Here's how to start a fresh canvas:

1. **Choose File⇨New or press Ctrl+N.**

   The New Image dialog box appears.

2. **Specify the size of your image by using the Width and Height value boxes, and choose inches, centimeters, or pixels in the adjacent Units selection box.**

   If you use inches or centimeters for your units, specify in the Resolution box how many pixels you want per one inch or centimeter. Set the adjacent Units selection box to Pixels/cm or Pixels/inch.

3. **Under Image Characteristics, choose Raster, Vector, or Art Media.**

   For purposes of this chapter, choose Raster. Vector is for text or shape objects, and Art Media is for special artsy stuff, which we talk about in Chapter 10.

4. **For color depth, choose 16 million colors unless you know that you have a special need for fewer colors.**

5. **For a solid background, deselect the check box marked Transparent.**

   If the color sample box displayed above the check box isn't the background you want, click that sample box. In the Color dialog box that appears, click a hue in the circle; adjust its lightness or darkness by clicking in the rectangle in the center of the circle. Or, click any standard color in the colored grid. When the Current box is the color you want, click OK.

Finding Your Tool

Before you can do much of anything, you need to be able to find your tools! Figure 9-1 shows the Paint Shop Pro Tools toolbar, where painterly tools, like brushes, live. This toolbar has a slightly confusing design. It doesn't give every tool its own spot on the bar. The bar would be way too long.

Instead, the toolbar groups similar tools into what we call tool groups. A tool group (or toolset) exists wherever you see a tiny downward-pointing triangle (or down arrow) to the right of an icon.

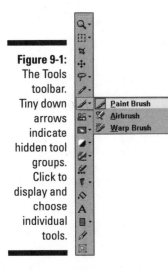

Figure 9-1:
The Tools
toolbar.
Tiny down
arrows
indicate
hidden tool
groups.
Click to
display and
choose
individual
tools.

The Tools toolbar is normally sort of magnetized *(docked)* to the left side of your Paint Shop Pro window, although you can drag it elsewhere — to the top, the right side, or the bottom or even floating free in the middle of the screen! Drag the toolbar by the faint dotted line at its top to place it to wherever you want. To place it back along the left side, drag first to the center of the side until it grabs, and then slide it up into its original position.

Click the small down arrow next to the tool group and then select its icon from the tool group menu that flies out. Your cursor then *becomes* that tool (it displays that tool's icon) whenever the cursor is over your image.

Disappearing toolbars and palettes

The Tools toolbar and other toolbars and palettes in Paint Shop Pro have the ability to get out of your way automatically. They can shrink to nothing more than a title bar when you're not using them. We find that this behavior drives us nuts, but you may like it.

Click the tiny pushpin icon at the top or left end, which turns the icon sideways. (For the Tools toolbar, first drag the toolbar to a floating position.) Now, whenever your cursor leaves the toolbar, the toolbar shrinks to a title bar (labeled, for example, Tools for the Tools toolbar). To restore the toolbar, position your cursor over the

title bar. To restore normal behavior, restore the toolbar by positioning the cursor over the title bar, and then sneak up along the toolbar to the pushpin and click it.

A completely different way that a toolbar or palette may disappear is if you close it by clicking the X next to the pushpin or by pressing a function key. You can restore (or turn off) any toolbar by choosing View⇨Toolbars, and then your desired toolbar from the menu that appears. For palettes, choose View⇨Palettes. Each line on the palette menus also lists the function key that turns the palette on or off.

Brushing, Airbrushing (Spraying), and Erasing

Using the Paint Brush, Airbrush, and Eraser tools is much like using real paint, paper, and erasers. Okay — you would never use an eraser on *paint* in real life, but you get the idea.

Like most Paint Shop Pro tools and commands, the Paint Brush, Airbrush, and Eraser tools do their things on the active layer of your image. If they don't seem to be working correctly or are grayed out, you may be on the wrong layer. See Chapter 11 for more information about layers.

Brushing or spraying

The Paint Brush tool, like a real paint brush, paints a spot of paint when you click it on your image or a line when you drag it. The Airbrush works similarly, but like a can of spray paint, it puts down a speckly spot or line that gets denser as you hold the button down.

The Airbrush tool paints speckly and the Paint Brush tool paints solid for a reason: Jasc initially gives the two tools different density settings on the Tool Options palette. You could easily change their density settings and make the Paint Brush tool paint speckly or the Airbrush tool paint solid. The real difference between the tools is that if you pause the Airbrush tool or move it slowly while keeping the mouse button pressed, paint continues to fill in the speckles. As a result, you increase the paint density just as you can with real spray paint. Not so with the Paint Brush tool: You would have to click repeatedly to get that effect.

The two tools work similarly. Here's how to paint with the Paint Brush or Airbrush (spray) tools:

1. **Click a color from the Materials palette, as shown in Figure 9-2.**

   Press F6 to turn on the Materials palette if you don't see it. Click the middle tab of the three tabs that appear there to see the easy-to-understand "rainbow" display of colors, and then click your color. To use more complex paint materials, see Chapter 10.

   Your chosen color appears in the foreground color box.

2. **Select the Paint Brush or Airbrush tool from the brush tool group.**

   Refer to the first section in this chapter and Figure 9-1 for help in locating your tool.

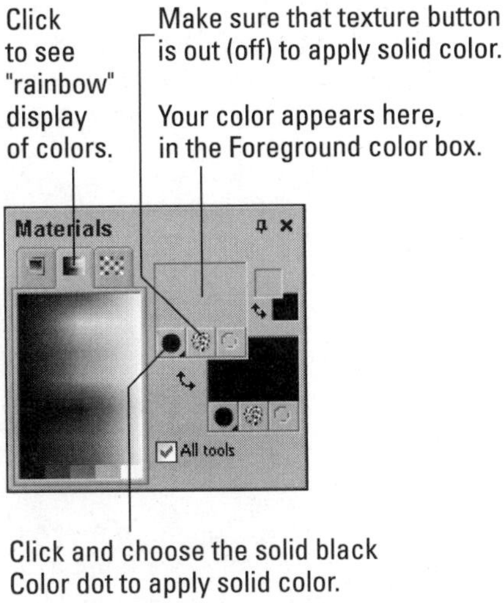

Click to see "rainbow" display of colors.

Make sure that texture button is out (off) to apply solid color.

Your color appears here, in the Foreground color box.

Figure 9-2:
Choose a color from the Materials palette. Press F6 to make the palette appear.

Materials

All tools

Click and choose the solid black Color dot to apply solid color.

3. **Set the brush size and other options on the Tool Options palette.**

   Press F4 to turn on Tool Options if it's not visible, and adjust the Size value box. If the industry standard Paint Shop Pro brush doesn't tickle your fancy, here's where you get to change the kind of brush you paint with; you can make it a tiny, crisp square or a ghostly, rocket ship-shaped brush or a watercolorish schmearer. We go over this technique in the next section, but feel free to experiment. It's fun!

4. **Drag on your image (or click to make just a single spot).**

   As you drag or click with the left mouse button, you apply whatever color (material) you have selected as the foreground in the Materials palette.

   If you're using the Airbrush tool, you can keep the cursor in one place and hold down the mouse button. The paint density gradually builds up.

Painting or erasing a straight line

Can't draw a straight line? Paint Shop Pro comes to your rescue. The starting point of the line is the last place you clicked, or wherever your last brush stroke ended.

To create a straight line from that point, hold down the Shift key and click where you want the line to end. This trick works with all the tools from the brush tool group (Paint Brush, Airbrush, Warp Brush) and with the Eraser tool.

If the spot or stroke doesn't look right, press Ctrl+Z (or click the Undo button on the toolbar) to undo it; you may need to use the Tool Options palette to change the brush features. See the later section "Controlling Strokes, Sizes, Shapes, and Spatters: Tool Options," for details on changing appearances.

Picking up colors from an image

You can pick a color to paint with from the Materials palette, as shown in Figure 9-2, but picking color from the image is sometimes much more convenient. Cohabiting with the Color Replacer in the color selection tool group is an eyedropper icon. Shown in the margin here, it's called the Dropper tool, and is the sixth button from the top of the Tools toolbar.

Click the Dropper, and then click any color in the image to make that your current working (that is, foreground) color. To pick up a background color (used by some tools and paint brushes), right-click. Here are a few tips for picking up color:

- ✔ If you're using any brush, painting, or eraser tool, you don't need the Dropper to pick up paint. Just Ctrl+click with your current tool to pick up color.

- ✔ The Dropper initially is set to pick up color from only a single pixel. Sometimes, however, apparently continuous color is mottled, and no single pixel is the right color. In that case, average the color of an area by choosing a larger sample size on the Tool Options palette. (Press F4 if it's not visible.)

- ✔ The Dropper normally gets its color from all layers combined. To pick up color from just the current layer, enable the Active Layer Only check box on the Tool Options palette.

Erasing with the Eraser tool

The eraser tool requires a little caution to get the results you want. Here's how to erase:

1. **Click the Eraser tool, as shown in the margin.**

   Alternatively, press the X key rather than click the Eraser. Make sure that you have chosen the Eraser shown at the left, not the Background Eraser.

2. **Set the Size of the eraser on the Tool Options palette.**

   Press F4 to turn the Tool Options palette on if it's not visible. Then, adjust the Size value box. A higher number is bigger.

3. **Hold down the Ctrl button and right-click your image somewhere that the background color (typically, white) appears.**

   You can skip this step if you're erasing on a layer that is transparent. This little precautionary trick ensures that when you erase on a background layer (which is typically nontransparent), the Eraser leaves the correct color behind. It sets the official background color on the Materials palette, which is what the Eraser leaves behind on nontransparent layers.

4. **Drag on your image to erase, or click to erase a single spot.**

   The Eraser leaves behind background color on an opaque background. On transparent backgrounds or other layers, it leaves transparency.

If the size, shape, and density (speckliness) of your eraser aren't what you want, press Ctrl+Z (or click the Undo button on the toolbar) to undo. Then, see the section "Controlling Strokes, Sizes, Shapes, and Spatters: Tool Options," a little later in this chapter.

Erasing backdrops with the Background Eraser tool

A common problem in any Paint Shop Pro project is erasing specific areas; for example, you want to erase an ugly wallpaper print — but not Cousin Charlie, who's standing in front of it. You *could* carefully erase that ghastly wallpaper, pixel by pixel. Not only is that method incredibly time-consuming, though, but also one slip of the wrist and you accidentally remove his left elbow.

The incredibly handy Paint Shop Pro Background Eraser tool makes this process easy by doing some complex calculations to determine what is Charlie and what is the background *behind* Charlie and then automatically erasing that background. (You can also select *around* Charlie to make normal erasing easier; refer to Chapter 3 to read about selection.)

For example, as you can see in Figure 9-3, erasing the background behind both Dave and Alex is a snap. The Background Eraser recognizes the difference between Dave and a coniferous tree — not always an easy task.

Just to confuse you, Paint Shop Pro calls this tool the Background Eraser, even though it has nothing to do with the Background Material box, discussed in Chapter 10. Whereas *background* in every other aspect of Paint Shop Pro means "the secondary color that's used to fill the middle of a shape," here it means what most people think it does: the stuff behind the interesting things in a picture. Why they didn't call it something like the Erase to Edge tool in order to keep the terminology consistent is beyond us.

Figure 9-3:
Man, dog,
and tree.
The Back-
ground
Eraser
appreci-
ates the
distinction.

Here's how to erase the background behind Uncle Charlie:

1. **Click the Background Eraser tool, as shown in the margin.**

2. **Set the size of your eraser by adjusting the Size value on the Tool Options palette. (Press F4 if you don't see the palette.)**

   To control other brush-like aspects of the Background Eraser, see the following section.

   If the background is the result of multiple layers, enable the Sample Merged check box. To improve the Background Eraser's behavior, see the nearby sidebar "Tweaking the Background Eraser."

3. **Click a section of the area you want erased and hold the mouse button down briefly before dragging.**

   In our example, you would want to click that ugly wallpaper. Holding the button down briefly gives Paint Shop Pro time to do the calculations to figure out what wallpaper looks like so that it can erase it.

   If you're erasing on a background layer, Paint Shop Pro may pop up an Auto Actions dialog box which suggests that you let it promote the background to a full layer. Click OK. Your image background layer is now transparent, and the former background layer is now a layer.

4. **Drag the point of the tool across the background, to allow the outer radius of the tool to overlap the edge of the area you want isolated (Charlie).**

Don't drag the point of the tool across Charlie, or else he is taken as background. Dragging quickly may go too fast for Paint Shop Pro to keep up, and as a result it may start erasing bits you want to keep. Drag at a slow, sure pace along the edge.

 Using the Background Eraser is great for removing the bits around edges, but it's very slow (and not efficient) at removing large areas. If you're trying to erase everything except Cousin Charlie, we suggest that you use the Background Eraser to clear a "moat" of transparent space around Charlie and then switch to the regular Eraser tool to mop up the rest of the image.

Tweaking the Background Eraser

Mostly, the settings that Paint Shop Pro picks for special options (like Sampling) work pretty darned well. (You may have to click the tiny right arrow at the right end of the Tool Options palette to see all options.) If they don't work well for you, you may need to tweak them. Here's what you need to know to tweak:

Sampling: The Background Eraser works by looking at *(sampling)* the pixels directly under its black tip and calling that the background. It then erases matching pixels that it finds under the full radius of the tool.

Continuous: As you drag, the Background Eraser continually checks the image to discern a difference between the foreground and the background. This setting generally provides the best results.

Once: The eraser looks only at the place where you first clicked to determine background. Generally, this setting does very little erasing.

Foreswatch and Backswatch: The Background Eraser attempts to erase colors that are similar to what is in the Foreground or Background boxes, respectively, of the Materials palette. Use this setting if what you want to erase is one color and the Continuous setting isn't getting it right.

Limits:

Contiguous: Paint Shop Pro erases only background pixels that are contiguous. This option is often good for removing up to the edge of Cousin Charlie.

Discontiguous: The tool erases pixels that match the background even if they're isolated from each other. If a little bit of the wallpaper's color is on Charlie's shirt, it may well erase that too when the eraser overlaps the shirt.

Find Edge: The tool erases pixels starting at the tool tip outward until the tool finds an edge within its radius. This setting is also good for isolating Charlie.

Sharpness:

Low values produce a fuzzy line between the background and Cousin Charlie; high values create a crisp, sharp line. (Low values in the 40s look more natural.)

Auto Tolerance:

You can clear this check box to set your tolerance manually in the Tolerance setting. Lower tolerance values mean that a pixel must be a pretty close match to the sampled pixels to be erased.

Controlling Strokes, Sizes, Shapes, and Spatters: Tool Options

The Painting and Eraser tools can do much more than just create a plain, boring spot or line. The Tool Options palette, as shown in Figure 9-4, is your key to variety, artistic success, fame and fortune, and probably good dental health. It's the key to making your paint tool work the way you want. The palette works the same — or nearly the same — for all painting and erasing tools, except for the Warp Brush.

Preview brush with your settings. ┌ Click for more brush shapes.

Drag line sideways to expose or hide controls.

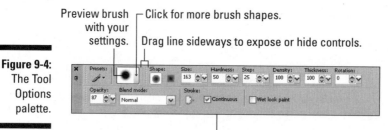

Figure 9-4:
The Tool Options palette.

Drag edge to make wider and display all controls.

One key role of the Tool Options palette is to show you what your brush looks like. As Figure 9-4 indicates, a preview area in the upper-left corner shows you the size, fuzziness (hardness), and speckliness (density) of the spot you make if you clicked your image. The Tool Options palette is so incredibly useful that it should almost always be open so that you can check your brush before you paint.

The Tool Options palette (or its title bar, labeled Tool Options) is probably already floating around somewhere on your PC screen. If you can't find the Tool Options palette, follow these steps:

1. **Press the F4 key on your keyboard a few times.**

   The palette appears and disappears. Leave it visible.

2. **If Tool Options appears as a floating window and you don't want it hovering over your painting, double-click its title bar to dock it.**

3. **If the Tool Options palette isn't where you want it (we prefer along the top), click the dark shaded bar at the far left and drag the palette to wherever you want.**

4. **If you don't see all the options on the Tool Options palette, you may need to slide the palette open to see everything.**

The Tool Options palette has three sections: the brush shape section, the opacity/blend section, and the shape/size/hardness section. Drag the small vertical row of faint dots shown in Figure 9-4 left and right (or up and down) until you can see all options clearly. Alternatively, you can drag the bottom edge of the palette down, as Figure 9-4 suggests, to widen the palette to display all sections.

(Of course, if you can see everything you intend to change, you don't *have* to open everything. Think of the three sections of the Tool Options palette as a chest of drawers: You can open them all at one time or close the ones you're not working on and keep open the ones you need.)

You don't need to put away the Tool Options palette before working on your image. Leave it up so that you can make adjustments as you go. Drag it out of the way, if necessary, like we just showed you.

Not all tools offer all the adjustments we discuss in the next few subsections.

Using convenient controls on the Tool Options palette

You can make adjustments on the Tool Options palette by using the dialog box gadgets you're familiar with from other programs. You can click the Size and other boxes and edit or type a new value or click either of the *spin dial* buttons (the pair of up and down arrows) to increase or decrease a value.

In addition to the usual ways of adjusting values, Paint Shop Pro has a nifty adjustment feature, as shown in Figure 9-5. Click the tiny down arrow at the far right edge of the box for any numerical value, such as the Size box. Hold the mouse button down, and a tiny ruler-like bar appears, with a pointer. Keep the mouse button down and drag the pointer left or right to adjust the value down or up, respectively.

Figure 9-5 shows a slider for the Paint Brush tool, although all or most of these same controls exist for the other painting tools. Clicking the far right down arrow for a given widget opens the adjustment slider, which gives you a rough preview of what your tool will look like.

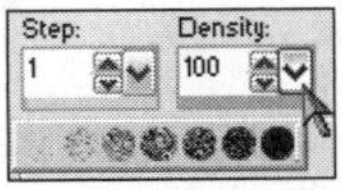

Figure 9-5:
The preview
adjustment
slider.

If you repeatedly use the same tool with the same tool options, you can save that tool's settings as a preset. *Presets* allow you to load a bunch of tool options in one click as opposed to entering them over and over again. Click the Presets icon, and in the Presets fly-out box that appears, click the disk (Save) icon. Type a memorable name for your settings in the Save Preset dialog box that appears and press Enter. Click the Presets icon to put away the fly-out. Thereafter, to choose your preset, click the Preset icon and choose your preset by clicking its name in the fly-out box.

Making lines wider or narrower: Size

You most frequently adjust *size*. One size of tool definitely does not fit all. Even Phil, Dave's house painter, uses different sizes of brushes. (What an *artiste!*) On the Tool Options palette, adjust the Size value to any value from 1 through 500 (from 1 to 500 pixels).

You can see just how big your tool is at any time by moving the cursor over the image. Big brushes may need smaller step values (the number in the box labeled Step) to avoid painting dotted lines.

Shaping clicks, lines, and line ends: Shape

Shape changes the way the painted (or erased) line looks when it ends or bends. Shape also lets you stamp a shape by clicking the image, as though you had a rubber stamp or were spraying paint through a template.

On the Tool Options palette, you have two options: You can go with a generic round or square brush or with brushes that simulate chalk or watercolor, or you can even select a variety of strange and unearthly brushes (like cherries, comets, or fuzzy circles) to paint with, as shown in Figure 9-6.

Selecting a round or square brush couldn't be simpler: Click the round or square box on the Tool Options palette. If you want something a little more esoteric, however, you can select a brush tip from the brush tip drop-down menu, next to the Presets menu. As shown in Figure 9-6, you're presented with a gallery of brushes, called the *Resource Manager,* that you can scroll through; double-click a brush tip to load it.

Using the various brush tips, you can make your lines look as though you have drawn them with a calligraphic pen. Figure 9-7 shows you, from top to bottom, the square, round, hard rake, and twirly spike brush shapes. The twirly spike uses the background color as well as the foreground color from the Materials palette. See Chapter 10 for more about the background color.

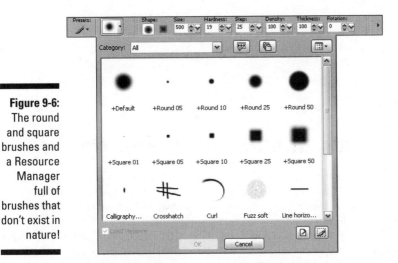

Figure 9-6:
The round
and square
brushes and
a Resource
Manager
full of
brushes that
don't exist in
nature!

As you make strokes, you see repeated stampings of this shape. The Step control (which we discuss in the section "Making lines more or less dotty: Step," later in this chapter) helps you change the separation between stampings.

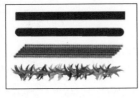

Figure 9-7:
Different
brush
shapes
make
different
strokes.

Painting with a softer or harder edge: Hardness

Hardness determines how sharp the edges of your tool are. Maximum hardness (100) gives your tool a sharp edge; lower hardness applies a gradual fade to the edge. Zero hardness gradually fades the edge all the way to the center of the brush shape. At low hardness, you may need to decrease the step to avoid creating a dotted line. Figure 9-8 shows you a single spot that shows a hardness of 100, 80, 60, 40, and 20 (from left to right).

Reduce hardness to minimize jaggies (a staircase effect also called *aliasing*) where your line bends.

Figure 9-8:
The effect of
changing
hardness.

Making paint thinner or thicker: Opacity

Opacity is how thick (opaque or solid) your paint is. A value of 100 means that your paint is completely opaque. Reduce opacity to make a more transparent paint. A value of 50, for example, means that an individual spot of paint (caused by clicking once with your mouse) is 50 percent transparent. Overlapping spots cause each stroke, or click of the mouse, to add paint and make the area more opaque. Figure 9-9 shows spots with an opacity of 100, 80, 60, 40, and 20 (from left to right).

Figure 9-9:
Out,
damned
spot! Single
spots with
decreasing
opacity.

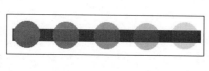

A brush stroke (*dragging* with your mouse) is more opaque than a single spot (*clicking* with your mouse) because strokes are simply repeated, overlapping spots. If you increase the values of the step variable (which controls the spacing of those spots), you make the stroke more transparent.

For the Eraser tool, opacity refers to how completely you erase. If you use maximum opacity (100), you erase the line entirely. Use repeated strokes or clicks with values less than 100 to shave the paint thickness and reduce opacity.

Getting speckles of spray: Density

The word *density* doesn't accurately describe this adjustment. The words speckly-ness or speckle-osity are more accurate, but still confusing. Density works like this: When density is at its maximum (100), you get nice, solid paint coverage (or *eraserage,* if you're using the eraser). At lower settings of density, you get random speckles, as though you were spattering or spraying. Figure 9-10 shows you a single spot, at densities of 100, 80, 60, 40, and 20 (from left to right).

Figure 9-10:
The effect of
different
density
settings.

For the Airbrush tool to do its job (which is spraying paint), you must set the density to less than 100. Yet, you can set density less than 100 for the Paint Brush or Eraser tools too, and they also give a speckly result, similar to the results you would get with the Airbrush tool.

Making lines more or less dotty: Step

It's time you knew the truth: The Paint Shop Pro paint tools don't apply paint continuously as you drag. (Gasp!) No, they apply repeated stampings of the brush's shape. (Imagine a jackhammer tipped with a rubber stamp.) The *Step control* determines the distance between those stampings.

If you set the step value at its maximum (100, or 100 percent), the shapes don't overlap; the step is 100 percent of the tool size, so you get a dotted line. At 50, the shapes overlap halfway, and at 25 they overlap three-quarters (25 is often a good choice). Figure 9-11 shows you step values of 20, 40, 60, and 100 (from top to bottom). The larger the step values, the more dotted the line.

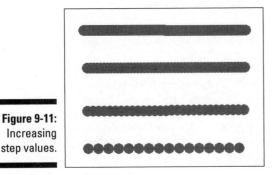

Figure 9-11:
Increasing
step values.

Very low step values use up lots of processor power because the computer has to draw a new stamp every time the mouse moves. If you're drawing and the computer hesitates a moment before it renders the line on the screen, you may consider raising the step value 10 or 20 percent.

Coloring within the Lines By Using Selection

When you're using painting tools in Paint Shop Pro and have selected an area, those painting tools work only within that selection. This feature is great for keeping you "within the lines" as you paint.

First, select the area you want to paint. (Refer to Chapter 3 to find out how to make selections.) If you have chosen to use multiple layers in your image, make sure that you're on the layer that contains the object you want to paint. (See Chapter 11 or the Cheat Sheet for help with layers.) Then, choose a painting tool and paint! Feel free to scribble or spray paint over the edges; the paint falls only within the selection.

Feathered selections work too, for blending the edges of your painting efforts into the rest of the image. Paint Shop Pro applies less paint in the feathered zone. Feathering expands the marquee to include feathered pixels outside the selection, however. If the selection has Swiss-cheese-like holes in it (as the Magic Wand tool selections often do), you may not notice the holes because the feathered expansion covers them. As you paint, because the holes are feathered areas, they reappear as fuzzy spots that resist being painted. If you don't want that effect, eliminate the holes in your selection before you apply feathering. Refer to Chapter 3 for help.

Replacing Colors

Here's your chance to fix that purple cow — the one that people always prefer to see, rather than be. The Color Replacer tool is your companion in reconstructive cow coloring.

The Color Replacer isn't a great tool for photographs. It tends to skip pixels, and it also replaces, with a single color, the natural range of color values that result from sun and shadow. Use this tool for cartoon cows with blocks of color or the text *COWs* and you will be fine. For photographic cows, you're better off selecting a colored area and using the Colorize tool, as described in Chapter 7. You'll get a far more realistic result.

Color replacement, like most Paint Shop Pro actions, works on only the active layer and within any selection you may have made. If you have chosen to use layers in your image, make sure that you're working on the correct layer during the following steps, or else replacement may not work.

Don't be cowed. Here's how to put new hue in your purple moo:

1. **Click the Color Replacer from the color selection tool group, six buttons from the top of the Tools toolbar, as shown in Figure 9-12.**

   The cursor takes on a brush shape. As with the Paint Brush and other painting tools, the brush size, shape, and other properties are controlled by the Tool Options palette. Refer to "Controlling Strokes, Sizes, Shapes, and Spatters: Tool Options," earlier in this chapter.

Figure 9-12: The Color Replacer hides in the color selection tool group.

2. **Hold down the Ctrl key and *right*-click in your image the color you want to *replace*.**

   The Background Material box takes on this color.

3. **Again, hold down the Ctrl key and *left*-click your new, replacement color, either in the image or in the Available Colors area of the Color palette.**

   The Foreground Material box takes on this color. Alternatively, you can use any technique we describe in Chapter 10 to set a new foreground material, complete with textures and gradients and whatnot.

4. **To replace the color in specific areas, drag across those areas. Double-click anywhere to replace the color everywhere.**

   Like most tools, the Color Replacer tool's action is constrained by layers and selections. If you have used layers in your image, color is replaced only throughout the active layer. If you have a current selection, replacement happens only within that selection.

The Color Replacer tool replaces a range of colors that are close to the one you picked to be replaced. Adjust the Tolerance setting on the Tool Options palette to control closeness. (Press F4 if you don't see the Tool Options palette.) The larger the Tolerance setting, the broader the range of colors the Color Replacer tool replaces. If you're replacing a single, uniform color, set the tolerance to zero. If you're purpling a cow in a photograph, you need to replace a range of browns (or blacks or whites, depending on the cow). Set the tolerance higher in that event; try 25 or so, to start. In short, select one of these methods:

- ✔ If the Color Replacer tool replaces more than you want, decrease the tolerance. Press Ctrl+Z to undo the overenthusiastic replacement, and then drag or double-click again.

- ✔ If the Color Replacer tool doesn't replace enough, increase tolerance and then drag or double-click again.

Filling Areas

For flooding an area with nice, even color, nothing beats the Flood Fill tool, except possibly spilling a glass of red wine on a white sweater. (Fortunately, unlike with the wine spill, you can undo the Flood Fill tool's actions by pressing Ctrl+Z.)

 Using the Flood Fill tool, shown in the margin, you can fill an area with solid color. You can not only fill with a simple color, but also fill areas with complex gradients, patterns, or textures. You only have to choose a foreground material in the Material Properties dialog box, as Chapter 10 relates.

Filling a selected area with solid color

The most basic kind of fill you can perform is filling a selected area with a uniform color (the sort of work that Phil, Dave's house painter, does). For example, the sky in your photograph may be gray — perhaps with clouds and power lines running through it — and you want to make it solid, cloudless blue with no power lines. Here's how to fill like Phil:

1. **Use any of the selection tools to select the area you want to fill.**

   For example, click the sky in your picture with the Magic Wand tool. Refer to Chapter 3 for help with getting exactly the selection you want. The selection marquee indicates your selected area.

   If you have chosen to use layers in your image, you must also select the layer that contains the portion of the image you want to fill. See Chapter 11 for more help with layers. If you don't use layers in your image, just make your selection and move on to Step 2.

2. **Click the Flood Fill tool on the Tools toolbar.**

   Your cursor icon changes to the paint can, the Flood Fill tool icon.

3. **Choose a foreground material to fill with.**

   For simple unpatterned, untextured fills, make sure that the Foreground and Stroke Properties box is set to a solid color. Refer to Figure 9-2, near the beginning of this chapter, to see how to choose just a plain color.

4. **Open the Tool Options palette.**

   If the Tool Options palette isn't visible on your screen, press the F4 key on your keyboard to display the palette.

5. **Make the following choices from the drop-down lists there:**

   - **Blend mode:** Normal
   - **Match mode:** None
   - **Opacity:** 100 percent for a fill that nothing shows through, or lower for a more transparent fill

6. **Click your selection in the image.**

   The color completely fills the selected area (in your chosen layer, if you use layers). If you choose an opacity lower than 100, the color just tints the selected area and increases in thickness if you click again.

Figure 9-13 shows the effect of a solid fill in a selection of the sky, using deep blue to fill the sky uniformly. (The edge of the selection is feathered a bit, causing the white band to appear along the skyline.)

Figure 9-13: A solid fill of the sky. In this image, a solid fill doesn't look natural.

If you're modifying a drawing, a solid color may be exactly what you want. In our photo, however, a solid color doesn't look natural as sky. Sky is never a uniform color in real life; it changes in color gradually as it approaches the horizon. For a more natural look, you need a gradient, or shaded, fill.

Filling with a gradient, pattern, or texture

In real life, you rarely see a uniform color (even if you think you do). Changes in lighting or the angles at which light strikes an object cause a gradual change across the object from one color to another, lighter color. The surface of your desk, for example, is probably a lighter color nearer your source of light.

If you need a realistic shading like that, or if for any other reason you want colors in an area to make a smooth transition from one color to another, try a shaded, or *gradient,* fill. Figure 9-14 shows the effect of a gradient fill on the sky area of the photograph.

For some fills, like filling a rectangle to look like a brick wall or a tree trunk, use a pattern rather than a solid color. To use gradients or patterns, you must first set your foreground material to be a gradient or pattern; see Chapter 10 for instructions on choosing the gradient or pattern you need.

Figure 9-14: Gradient fills make filled areas (the sky, in this photo) more realistic.

Or, you may want to apply color with a textured appearance. Just like the other painting tools, if the Material box has a texture, such as canvas or asphalt, the Flood Fill tool applies it. Again, see Chapter 10 for more details

TECHNICAL STUFF

What about tolerance?

Technical types may be wondering what the Tolerance control, on the Flood Fill tool's Tool Options palette, is good for. In this chapter, we bypass the need to use that control by instructing you to select the area you want to fill and then use a Match mode of None. We think that that's the easiest way to fill a specific area.

An alternative to selecting an area beforehand with a selection tool is to use the Flood Fill tool itself to determine which pixels are to be filled, according to their color or other qualities. Choose a Match mode other than None, and then set tolerance. The Flood Fill tool determines what pixels to fill based on those settings, exactly as the Magic Wand tool does to determine what pixels to select.

Blend modes

Sometimes, you don't want to overpaint the underlying image; you want to just tint or infuse the image with a color or increase or decrease color saturation or apply some other quality. The Flood Fill tool has some fancy features, called *blend modes,* that combine attributes of your chosen fill, such as hue and saturation, with the underlying image in complex and subtle ways. In general, these blend modes are too obscure to be useful for any except the most dedicated graphics professional. For the rest of us, two of the modes, Color and Hue, can be occasionally useful because they can infuse an area with color, although the Colorize command, which we describe in Chapter 7, does that job quite nicely.

To experiment with blend modes, click the Blend Mode drop-down list on the Flood Fill tool's Tool Options palette and choose a mode. Then try filling a selected area of your image.

Painting an Example: A Halo for Alex

As an example of all this brushing and filling hoo-hah, we have decided that Dave's dog Alex is the best-behaved dog in the world. We're attempting to convince the *Weekly World News* tabloid that Alex is *such* a good dog that he has a halo. (The *Weekly World News* may be naïve, but it pays well.)

Two problems show up in the current picture of Alex, though, as shown in Figure 9-15:

- ✔ One, he has no halo — but we draw that.

- ✔ Two, the *Weekly World News* uses only black-and-white photos, and that light slatted background behind Alex isn't dark enough to make the halo stand out. We rectify that in eight easy steps!

Figure 9-15: Alex, unedited dog about town.

If you're reading ahead in this chapter, you may notice that the doorbell directly above Alex's head, as shown in all the other pictures of Alex in this book, isn't present here. We got rid of that using the Clone Brush; refer to Chapter 8 to find out how to remove unsightly doorbells from your pictures.

1. **Select the slatted background behind Alex.**

   As we discuss earlier in this chapter, in "Coloring within the Lines By Using Selection," you want to select the background to make sure that you don't accidentally draw over Alex's head while you're changing the slats. Refer to Chapter 3 for help with getting exactly the selection you want.

   (For the record, we used the Magic Wand Tool set to a Match mode of Color, a tolerance of 17, a feather of 1, and a large amount of judicious Shift+clicking to clean up the small patches of unselected areas.)

2. **Select the Paint Brush tool from the brush tool group.**

3. **Change the material (as we discuss in Chapter 3), and then do a test paint along the edges to make sure that the edges look good.**

   We selected a dark red material for our paint, but we set the opacity for our Paint Brush to 50 (half-transparent) so that the slatting still appears through the paint. As you can see in Figure 9-16, our brush strokes have stopped at the marquee edge of the selection, right above Alex's Buddha-like gaze.

   If you don't see the Tool Options palette, press F4.

Figure 9-16:
Testing a
small patch
of the new,
transparent
paint color
for the wall.

4. **Paint the entire selected area.**

   You could also use the Flood Fill tool with a Match set to none. The Flood Fill tool is at its best, though, on fairly even areas that are mostly the same color, like the sky in the Fill example earlier in this chapter — not areas with dark vertical streaks through it, like this one. Besides, you're already using the Paint Brush tool, so why switch? The final results are just as good, as shown in Figure 9-17.

Figure 9-17:
The now
repainted
wall forms a
darker
background.

5. **Deselect the area.**

   Alex's halo needs to be big and impressive. *So* big and impressive, in fact, that it sticks out of the current selection — and as long as we have the background selected, we can't paint outside the lines. If you don't feel like skipping to Chapter 12, where we tell you how to deselect, you can either press Ctrl+D or choose Selections➪Select None.

6. **Select the Airbrush tool from the brush tool group.**

   A halo is supposed to be fuzzy, so we airbrushed it in. The airbrush also makes it easy to build up the halo from repeated loops so that we don't have to be so careful about shape.

7. **Set the Airbrush options on the Tool Options palette and choose your color (texture, pattern) from the Materials palette.**

   A halo is supposed to be fuzzy and bright white, so we picked a pure white color from the Materials palette. We wanted a reasonably small line for our halo, so a size of 11 seemed about right — and a halo is supposed to be bright, so we cranked up the Opacity to 100 so that the background doesn't bleed through.

   This process still doesn't address the "fuzziness" issue — but the Hardness and Step settings do. We reduced the Hardness to 0 to provide maximum fuzziness, and we set the Step to 35 to produce a slightly spottier line.

8. **Draw a halo.**

   Keep a steady hand, here! Alex's reputation is at stake! (see Figure 9-18).

Figure 9-18:
Beatific
Alex.

What's that, you say? It looks *fake*? Have you ever *seen* the *Weekly World News?*

You may be asking "Isn't Alex's halo a little shaky there? Doesn't Paint Shop Pro have a tool for drawing perfect shapes, like circles, squares, and elliptic halos?" Of course, it does — and we show you how to draw better halos in Chapter 12.

Chapter 10

Advanced Painting for the *Artiste*

· ·

In This Chapter

▶ Understanding foreground and background

▶ Convenient ways to choose materials

▶ Precise ways to choose colors

▶ Painting with gradients, patterns, and textures

▶ Storing swatches of materials for reuse

▶ Painting with picture tubes

▶ Mimicking real art materials with Art Media

· ·

*I*f you do lots of painting, this chapter is the one to check out before you go flinging your paint brush around with wild abandon. Among other things, an *artiste* like you needs the fastest and best ways to choose a color.

Moreover, because you're so talented, you don't just paint with color. How boring and pedestrian! No, you paint with *materials* in Paint Shop Pro!

Material, in this case, is the Paint Shop Pro term for anything from plain old solid colors to textured colors, gradients (shaded areas with transitions from one color to another), or even multihued geometric patterns. You can even save your carefully designed materials as *swatches* for future use.

All this excitement springs from the Materials palette, which in Paint Shop Pro 9 hides more secrets than a black dog hides ticks. Figure 10-1 shows the palette and some of its more important features.

If the Materials palette isn't on your screen, press F6 or choose View⇨Palettes⇨Materials. *Palettes* are lumps of useful tools and settings in Paint Shop Pro; the Materials palette is one of them. You can drag the palettes around to different places in your Paint Shop Pro window; they stick *(dock)* to various edges.

Here's a quick review of picking color: As we note in Chapter 9, the simplest way to choose a color is with the Rainbow tab in the Materials dialog box. (Press F6 to display the Materials palette if it's not showing already.) Click the center, or Rainbow, tab on that palette to display that tab, as shown in Figure 10-1. On the multihued Rainbow tab, just click the color you want. (Right-click for background color — we tell you more about background color later in this chapter.)

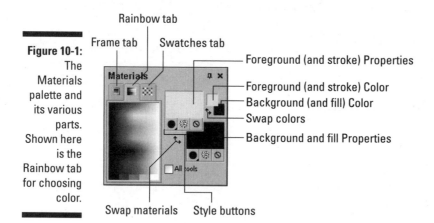

Figure 10-1:
The Materials palette and its various parts. Shown here is the Rainbow tab for choosing color.

The cursor is a Dropper icon while it's over the color selection area, to indicate that you pick up a color if you click. As you move the cursor, you see an enlarged sample of the color your cursor is over. (The numbers are primary color values that give you the exact numerical color you're using. We tell you more about this subject later in this chapter.)

Choosing paint for each tool separately or all tools together

In real life, if you paint with your brush dipped in red paint and then switch to spray-painting with a can of green paint, your brush remains red. It doesn't switch to green. Of course, in real life you can't insert your dog into a picture of Elvis and then spray-paint him purple, so you have to assume that Paint Shop Pro is a little stranger than the world outside your door.

Unless you tell Paint Shop Pro otherwise, it applies the same style and texture to all the tools you're using; if you use the Spray Paint tool with red paint and a rough texture and then switch to the Paint Brush tool, the paint brush is red with a rough texture. You can, however, choose to change this rather odd behavior by unchecking the All Tools box on the Materials palette. Checking All Tools applies your current paint choice to all tools; deselecting All Tools means that you choose paint individually for each tool.

Choosing a Background Color

Paint Shop Pro has two painting colors, called foreground and background. *Foreground* just means the color you normally paint with. *Background* is a secondary color used for certain operations, or just for convenience when you switch often between two colors.

To choose a foreground color, you left-click a color on the Materials palette; to choose background, you right-click. How do you know whether you need or want a secondary color? It depends on the tool you're using and how you intend to use it:

- ✔ If you want to be able to switch quickly between painting with one color and another, you can paint the foreground color by pressing the left mouse button and the background color by pressing the right mouse button.

- ✔ The Shapes tools require a background color if you want solid shapes. If you plan to draw filled-in squares (as opposed to just the outline of a square), you need to choose a background color to fill the shape in with.

- ✔ If you're using the Eraser tool, you can choose what the eraser leaves behind: a transparent streak (useful if you're using layers) or the background color.

- ✔ If you're using a tool that involves two colors — for example, the Color Replacer tool to replace one color with another, you need a second color — and the background color is that second color. Background color also provides the fill of filled shapes and text.

To swap the background and foreground materials, click the Material Switcher (the larger, double-headed arrow), as shown in Figure 10-1. The background material becomes the foreground, and vice versa. If you want to swap colors and keep textures or gradients the same, click the smaller arrow.

Choosing Color More Conveniently

Paint Shop Pro offers conveniences for the artist on the go who is in a rush to choose the correct color. You can choose a recently used material or pick up a color from the image.

Choosing a basic color or a recently used material

You may want to use your everyday, smiley-face yellow — but locating exactly that same color in the Available Colors area is often next to impossible: Your eyes and fingers can't be that precise. Likewise, you may have developed a cool gradient that slid from cool blue to a sea green, but do you think that you can do that again?

Fortunately, Paint Shop Pro gives you another way to choose a recently used material: the Recent Materials dialog box. The Recent Materials dialog box also gives you basic black, totally white, and a variety of other basic colors you can return to again and again.

Here's how to see this helpful box of recently used materials and basic colors:

1. *Right*-click the Foreground (or Background) Material Properties box, whichever one you want to set.

   The Recent Materials dialog box appears, as shown in Figure 10-2. The ten most recent materials you have used appear along the top two rows; ten standard colors appear along the bottom rows (including black, white, and two shades of gray). If the colors have circles with slashes, you're using an image that has its own palette of colors, and those colors aren't part of its palette.

   Colors in the bottom two basic-color rows are *pure* colors — except for the grays — that is, they're the reddest red, bluest blue, magenta-est magenta, and so on.

   Technically speaking, the top row contains the pure red, green, and blue primary colors of radiant light. The second row contains the pure cyan, magenta, and yellow primary colors of printed ink.

2. Click any color or material to choose it (or press the Esc key if you see nothing you like).

   The Recent Materials dialog box disappears immediately. The color you clicked is now chosen and appears in the color sample on the Materials palette.

   You may think that right-clicking in the Recent Materials dialog box would choose the background color, as it does on the Materials palette. You would be wrong. Right-clicking does nothing here.

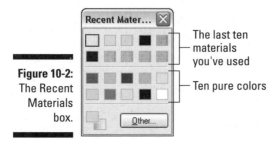

Figure 10-2:
The Recent
Materials
box.

The last ten materials you've used

Ten pure colors

Fix Photo Lighting Flaws

Color Plate C-1a: Dave's lovely wife, Katy, looks a little blue. Fortunately, the Manual Color Correction tool can take this Smurfish cast off her cheeks.

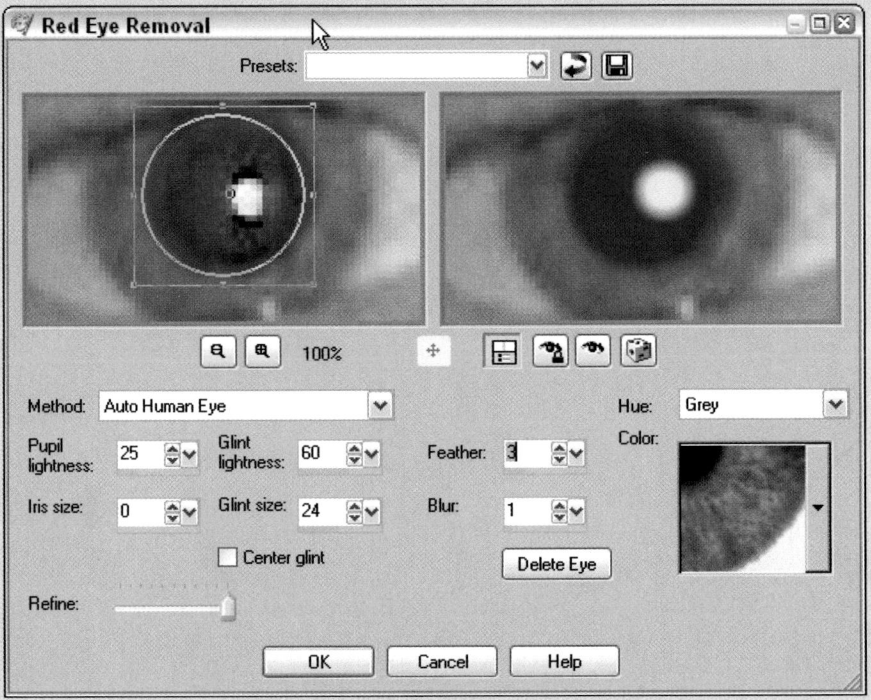

Color Plate C-1b: The Paint Shop Pro Red Eye Removal feature takes the devilish glint from Dave's eye.

Remedy Photo Flops

Color Plate C-2a: This picture of William's wife, Gini, is taken straight off William's digital camera, and it's not bad. Chances are, you wouldn't even think twice about it. But the white walls look grayish, the glare off the door is a little overpowering, and Gini's fair Irish skin appears darker than it really is.

Color Plate C-2b: After a slight Backlighting adjustment and a One-Step Photo Fix, you can see a clear difference. The walls are whiter, Gini's skin looks much more natural, and, overall, the picture is much sharper and clearer.

Color Plate C-2c: For a bonus round, we used the Clone Brush to fill in some of that ugly white glare behind Gini's right shoulder, pushed some color into the door frame by using the Smudge tool, and selectively used the Backlighting Photo Fix to darken some of the other sections.

Choose Plain Paint or Fancy

Color Plate C-3a: For simple text without separate fill and outline materials, disable the foreground material on the Materials palette. The background material does the job.

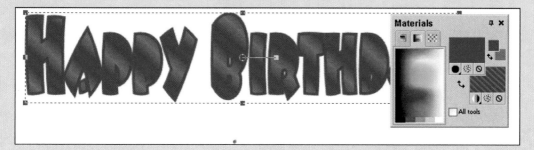

Color Plate C-3b: For fancier text with different fill and outline materials, enable the foreground material on the Materials palette. Here, we've used a patterned fill and solid outline.

Create Image Collisions with Layers

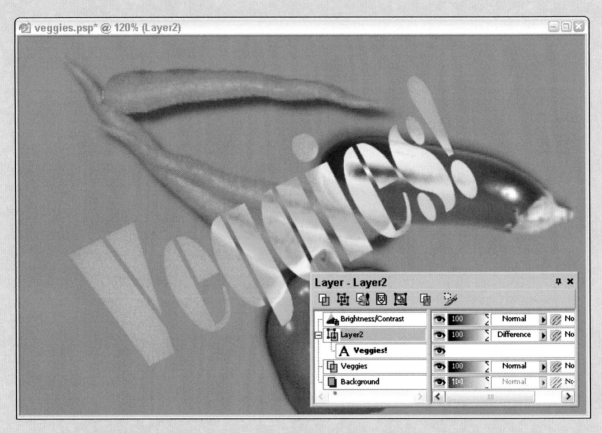

Color Plate C-4: Plain text is added as a separate layer (Layer 2) and rotated, and then a "blend mode" of "difference" causes its color to interact with the background.

Throw Text a Curve

Color Plate C-5: Text is bent to fit a hidden curved line. Text can follow the shape of any vector object if you click with the Text tool on that object.

Stitch Together Panoramas

Color Plates C-6a, C-6b: Two 640 x 480-pixel photographs of Dave's town need to be joined to make a panorama. We opened both photographs in Paint Shop Pro and zoomed out to get working room.

Color Plate C-6c: We created a new image with a white background, wide enough to fit both pictures (1280 x 480). Then we copied each image (Ctrl+C) and pasted it as a new layer (Ctrl+L) in the new image. The images can be dragged around for position.

Stitch Together Panoramas

Color Plate C-6d: Some mismatch is inevitable at the edges because of lens distortions. In this case, having the left image on top of the right one worked better. You can drag layers into different orders by using the Layer palette.

Color Plate C-6e: If you're finicky, you can fine-tune the edges. Useful tools are Mesh Warp, to fix distortion; retouch tools, like Lighten/Darken; and the Eraser. Set tools to low Hardness for a soft edge. Here, the Eraser let parts of the underlying image show through.

Straighten Up

Color Plate C-8a: Paint Shop Pro has several tools to straighten out images, deform them, take out or introduce perspective into them, or rotate them. Here, we take out the perspective in a tall statue.

Color Plate C-8b: The Perspective Correction tool displays a bounding box, and we drag its corners to align its sides with edges of the statue that should be horizontal and vertical.

Color Plate C-8c: Double-clicking the image adjusts the entire image so that the statue is now straight. Unfortunately, some distortion is introduced to the statue's head.

Color Plate C-8d: Switching to another tool, the Mesh Warp tool, and dragging a point in the mesh downward removes the distortion from the head.

Color Plate C-8e: The result.

Change Cardinals to Canaries

Color Plate C-9a: This cardinal's distinctive color makes selecting it easy. Clicking the Magic Wand tool on the red cardinal selects other red pixels. Sometimes, additions to or subtractions from the selection have to be made using other tools.

Color Plate C-9b: After an area is selected, you can do darned near anything to it. In this case, it was "colorized" a bright canary yellow!

Create a Hand-Drawn or Painted Look

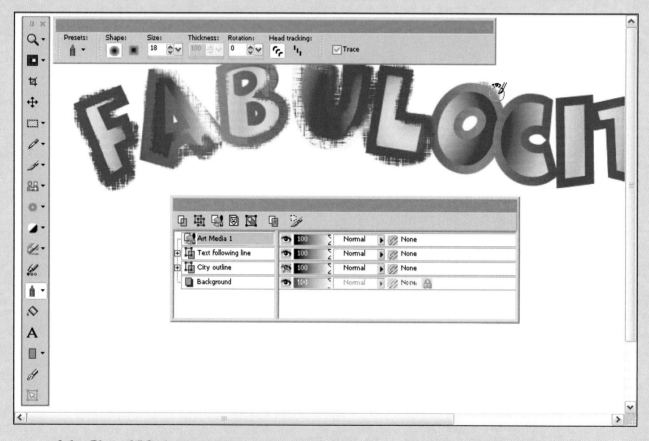

Color Plate C-10: Add an Art Media layer to any image, turn on the Trace feature, and your Art Media tool (here, Crayon on a coarse canvas layer) draws or paints using the underlying color. A skilled hand can turn a photo into a painting. (If your hand is less skilled, see Color Plate C-11.)

Create Paintings from Photos

Color Plate C-11: Other tricks for artistic effect: Using the Edge-Preserving Smooth effect, set high, removes fine detail, and then Posterizing reduces colors (here, to 17) and blends, for a watercolor effect.

Put Distant Friends Together

Color Plate C-12a: Alex the golden retriever looks dignified on the front stoop. But he misses his distant friend, Amy. Paint Shop Pro can help put them together.

Color Plate C-12b: With the Paint Shop Pro smart-selection tools, Alex can be separated from his favorite front stoop.

Color Plate C-12c: Alex is copied and pasted as a new layer with his pal. He can be scaled up or down as necessary with the Deform tool. A little touch-up with retouching tools and color adjustments, and they're picture-perfect.

Turn Farmscapes into Fabscapes

Color Plate C-13:
You won't be able to keep 'em down on the farm after they've seen some Paint Shop Pro effects. Here, you see the original, the Colored Foil effect, and the Brush Strokes effect.

Design Your Logo

Color Plate C-14: Layering and fill tricks help make a logo. A photograph of leaves makes a background. Text with an outline only (stroke, no fill) is created in raster form. A new layer is created to contain the white surround. The blank area around the text is selected with the Magic Wand in match mode None. The Fill tool fills the selection with white on the new layer, and the layer is made semitransparent using the Layer palette.

Print Photo Collages and Albums

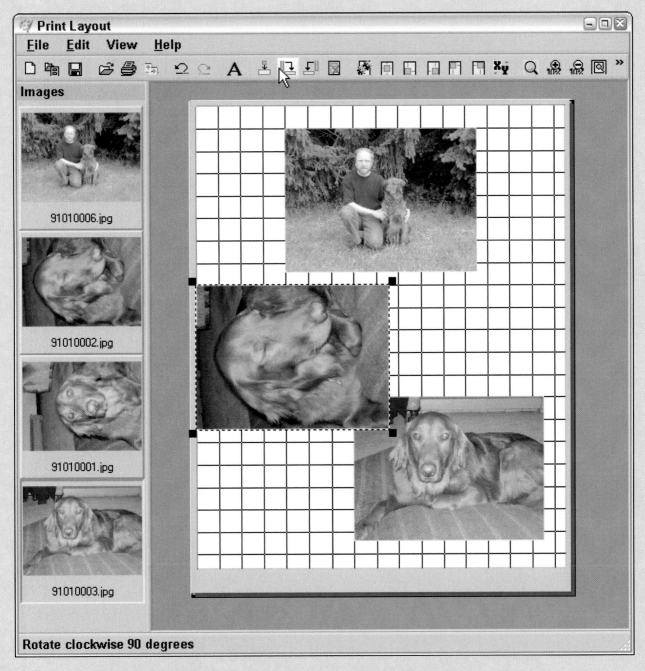

Color Plate C-15: The Paint Shop Pro Print Layout feature lets you lay out, size, and rotate images to create pages for photo albums, simple collages, multiphoto panoramas, and other collections of images.

Smudging and Retouching

Color Plate C-16a: The Paint Shop Pro Smudge Brush substitutes for your finger in doing artistic smudging and blending. A straight line smudges through the center, and swirls smudge the tops of these colors.

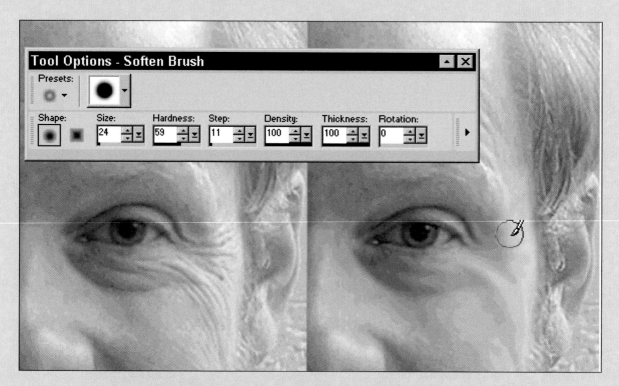

Color Plate C-16b: The Soften Brush makes quick work of the wrinkles this author acquired while writing this book. Balance reasserts itself in the universe.

To get shades of color other than the ones you see in the Recent Materials dialog box, click the Other button. This button takes you to the Material Properties dialog box. See the upcoming section "Choosing a Color for the Very Picky," for details.

Choosing a recently used color

If it's simply color you're interested in, not material with all its textures and gradients and stuff, follow this approach — it remembers more colors than the Recent Materials dialog box does:

1. ***Right*-click the small Foreground or Background Color box — whichever one you want to set.**

   The Recent Colors dialog box appears, as shown in Figure 10-3. The ten most recent colors you have used are in the top two rows of the dialog box, and the ten pure colors — exactly the same colors from the Recent Materials box — are in the bottom two rows. If the colors have circles with slashes, you're using a palette image, and those colors aren't available.

2. **Click any color to choose it (or press the Esc key if you see nothing you like).**

   The Recent Colors dialog box disappears immediately. The color you clicked is now chosen and appears in the color sample in both the Color and Materials boxes.

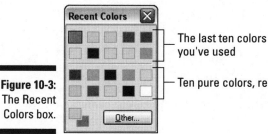

Figure 10-3: The Recent Colors box.

The last ten colors you've used

Ten pure colors, redux

Choosing a color from your picture

Sometimes, the easiest way to choose a color is to pick up that color from your picture. You have two ways to pick up color. Choose the one that makes your life easier:

✔ When using any tool that applies paint (for example, the Paint Brush tool), hold down the Ctrl button and the cursor turns into a Dropper icon. Left-click to pick up foreground color, and right-click for background color.

✔ On the Tools toolbar, click the Dropper tool icon, as shown in the margin. (If you see no Dropper icon, you may have been using the Color Replacer tool — click the Color Replacer tool and select the Dropper icon from the drop-down menu.) The cursor turns into a Dropper icon. Left-click to pick up foreground color, and right-click for background color.

If you have deselected the All Tools check box, colors you select for one tool don't apply to other tools.

Choosing Color for the Slightly Picky

If you need a slightly more precise way to choose color, try the Frame tab in the Material Properties dialog box, as shown in Figure 10-4. The Frame tab lets you choose the basic color (hue) by clicking a frame, and then lightness by clicking in the center.

Figure 10-4:
The Frame tab. Choose the basic hue and then adjust the light-ness or darkness.

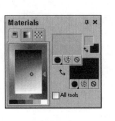

To choose a hue (yellow, for example), first click the hue in the frame. The center of the frame becomes shades of that hue.

Then, click in the center of the frame to choose how light or dark you want that hue to be. The foreground color box reflects your choice. To access a bigger version of the same color-picking technique, see the next section.

Choosing a Color for the Very Picky

Choosing a color from one of the Materials palette's tabs area is all well and good, but the palette is so small that you can't be precise. What if you're very picky?

To choose a color more precisely, *left*-click the Foreground or Background properties box (whichever color you want to set). Those are the big squares on the Materials palette.

The amazingly colorful Material Properties dialog box appears, as shown in Figure 10-5. (If the foreground or background material has a gradient or pattern, their respective dialog boxes are displayed. Don't worry: A row of tabs is at the top. Click the Color tab.)

Precise color using the color wheel

The color wheel works just like the Frame tab, as described in the preceding section — it's just bigger, and round rather than rectangular. The callouts shown in Figure 10-5 give the details. You need to follow only three steps:

1. **Drag the little circle on the color wheel to the basic hue you want.**

2. **Drag the little circle on the square to the precise shade you want.**

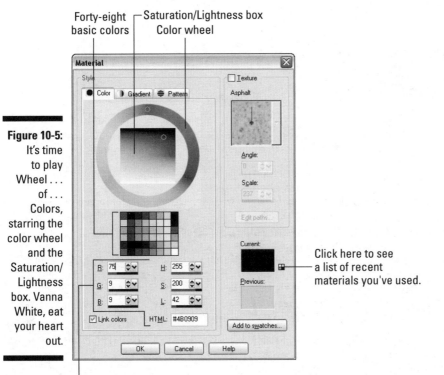

Forty-eight basic colors — Saturation/Lightness box — Color wheel

Figure 10-5: It's time to play Wheel . . . of . . . Colors, starring the color wheel and the Saturation/ Lightness box. Vanna White, eat your heart out.

Click here to see a list of recent materials you've used.

RGB, HSL, and HTML values

The Current swatch, in the lower-right corner of the dialog box, shows exactly which color you're choosing, overlaid with any textures you have selected. (The Previous swatch shows the color you started with.)

3. Click OK.

Your color has been changed.

Additional shades of basic colors

The Color tab in the Material Properties dialog box (as shown in Figure 10-5) is also home to 48 basic colors. These colors are shades of 6 primary colors (red, yellow, green, cyan, blue, and magenta) plus 6 shades of gray (including white and black).

Open the Color dialog box as usual by clicking either the Foreground or Background Material Properties box and selecting the Color tab.

Choose a basic color by clicking it in the Basic Colors area, in the middle-left corner of the dialog box. Click OK and your foreground or background color is changed to your chosen color.

Precise color adjustments — by the numbers

Just as saying "1 foot, 3 inches" is much more precise than saying "a little bigger than my shoe," choosing a color by using numbers is much more precise than clicking it on a palette or color wheel. But, how can you do color by the numbers?

TIP

Creating shadows and highlights

For brushing highlights or shadows onto an object, you often want a color that's the same hue as an existing one — just a little lighter or darker. Pick up the existing color from your picture and make it the foreground color by clicking it with the Dropper tool.

Click the Foreground and Stroke Properties square on the Materials palette to bring up the Material Properties dialog box, and then click the Color tab, if it isn't already selected. In the Saturation/Lightness box, drag the tiny circle up to make a shadow color, or down to make a highlight color.

As it turns out, you can specify any color by using just three values. Adjusting these values independently gives you more control. For example, you can change just the *lightness* of a color and be certain that you haven't changed the *hue*.

The situation is like measuring distance, where you can use either the English (feet, inches) or metric (meters) systems. In Paint Shop Pro you can use one of three alternative systems to specify colors: Hue/Saturation/Lightness (HSL, to its friends) or Red/Green/Blue (known as RGB) or HTML.

The Color tab in the Material Properties dialog box, as shown in Figure 10-5, shows the three values that describe your chosen color in all three systems (RGB, HSL, and HTML). The area displays values for Red, Green, and Blue (on the left) and Hue, Saturation, and Lightness (on the right). When you choose a new color using any control in this dialog box, those numbers change. In value, the numbers range from 0 to 255. An optional visual control appears when you click and hold the down arrow at the far right end of a value box (see Figure 10-6). The easiest way to adjust this value is with the slider control at the bottom.

Figure 10-6:
Achieving a
numerically
precise
color.

To adjust a color precisely, you can change the numbers in either the RGB or HSL value boxes (your choice). For example, do you want more red? Use the RGB controls and increase the value in the Red box. More yellow? To use the RGB controls, you would have to know that red and green make yellow in the RGB system and then increase the values in Red and Green (perhaps decreasing the value in Blue).

The HTML value is a numerical representation of the three RGB values, rendered into one hexadecimal code that Web browsers like Internet Explorer can understand. You should never try to adjust a color by using the HTML value. If you're designing for the Web, though, the only way to tell a browser that a sidebar should be precisely *this* shade of red is to use hexadecimals. If you're a Web designer, you know that you can use the HTML value within the color attributes of HTML; if you're not, you can safely ignore this section and go in peace.

Using the HSL values is sometimes a more intuitive alternative to using the RGB values. HSL values are connected to the controls on the color wheel and the Saturation/Lightness box. Here's how they work:

- **Hue:** The Hue value connects to your chosen position on the Color wheel, beginning at zero at the top (red) and increasing as you go around the circle counterclockwise. As you increase the number, the hue passes through red, yellow, green, cyan, blue, violet, and magenta.

- **Saturation:** The Saturation value connects to horizontal motion in the Saturation/Lightness box: left (for a lower value) or right (for a higher value). Use a higher value for a more intense (saturated) color.

- **Lightness:** The Lightness value connects to vertical motion in the Saturation/Lightness box: up (for a lower value) or down (for a higher value). Use a higher value for a lighter color.

As with any value box in a Windows program, you can change the values by either typing new numbers or clicking the tiny up and down arrows to gradually increase or decrease the value.

A more visual way to fiddle with the RGB or HSL values is to click the down arrow at the far right end of any of the RGB or HSL value boxes. As Figure 10-6 demonstrates, a multicolored bar appears, showing the range of colors you can achieve by dragging left or right. While holding the mouse button down, drag left or right to choose a color. Release the button when you're done.

Working with 256 Colors or Fewer

Images that have 256 colors or fewer are *palette* images: They use only a specific set of colors — the image's palette of available colors. You can change any of those colors individually, but you can't have any more colors than the palette size (color depth) allows.

You don't have to continue to live with this limitation. Press Ctrl+Shift+0 to increase the image to 16 million colors (full color) and then you can skip all the following stuff.

To choose colors in a palette image, click one of the Material Property boxes and select the Color tab from the Material Properties dialog box. You see a somewhat larger view of the palette. To reorder the colors, click the Sort Order drop-down list box and choose either Palette Order (an arbitrary, numbered order), By Luminance (ordered from light to dark), or By Hue (ordered by color). To choose a color, click it; then click OK.

To change any color on the image's palette (or change a black square to some other color), choose Image⇨Palette⇨Edit Palette. The Edit Palette dialog box that appears is identical to the Select Color from Palette dialog box, with one exception: If you double-click any color on the palette, the Color tab in the Material Properties dialog box is displayed. See the section "Choosing a Color for the Very Picky," earlier in this chapter, for instructions on choosing a color in this dialog box.

Going Beyond Plain Paint

Going beyond plain paint to something fancier means getting something straight in your head, first. Here's what to remember:

Paint Shop Pro can paint with any of three *styles* of paint:

- **Color:** Plain, solid color
- **Gradient:** Smooth transitions between two colors
- **Pattern:** Any pattern of multiple colors, or even an image

To any of these three types of paint, you can add *texture*. Texture is an effect similar to what you would create by doing a "rubbing" over some textured surface. (Place paper over a coin and then rub the paper with a pencil tip — you're doing a rubbing. Oh, come on — you must have done this.)

A quick way to choose style is with one tiny button, under the Foreground Properties (and Background Properties) box. Click one to choose plain paint, gradient paint, or pattern. Figure 10-7 shows you how the button works.

A tiny menu flies out and displays icons for the three styles (color, gradient, and pattern, in order). Any icons that are grayed out aren't available in your chosen tool.

You don't have to use these buttons. The alternative is just to click the Foreground or Background Properties box and then click the tab for Color, Gradient, or Pattern. Details follow!

Pattern

Gradient paint

Plain paint

Figure 10-7:
Clicking the Style button (pointed out by the cursor) gives you these three choices.

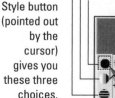
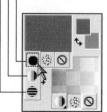

Choosing gradients

Click the Foreground (or Background) Properties box on the Color palette. The Material Properties dialog box appears. Click the Gradient (center) tab in this dialog box and you see what's shown in Figure 10-8.

Here's what to do:

1. **Choose a gradient style by clicking one of the buttons in the Style area that appears on the right side of the Gradient dialog box (refer to Figure 10-8).**

   Each button depicts a different kind of gradient: from side to side, from center to edges in a rectangular or circular fashion, or proceeding radially around in a circle. The Preview box on the left then displays a gradient in your chosen style.

2. **Click the down-arrow button to the right of the Preview box and choose from the ultrafabulous gallery of gradients that appears.**

   The colors of all choices are prechosen, except for those that use the terms foreground and background. Those choices make use of whatever foreground or background colors are current at the time you paint with this gradient. Click your choice.

3. **Customize the angle or center of the gradient by dragging the control in the Preview window.**

Figure 10-8:
Making the grade with gradients. Click the down arrow adjoining the preview box to open a gallery of gradients you can use.

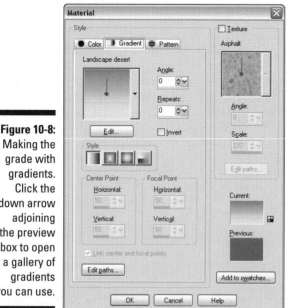

Gradients in the linear style (Linear is the leftmost button in the Style column) have an angle setting. In the preview window, drag the gadget that looks like the hand on a clock to set the angle.

Gradients in other styles have a center point. In the Preview window, drag the crosshairs to set the center point.

4. **Make the gradient pattern repeat several times, if you want.**

   Increase the number in the Repeats value box.

5. **Click OK.**

   Your chosen gradient appears in the Properties box that you originally clicked (Foreground or Background) on the Materials palette.

Creating gradients in your choice of colors is easy, although not many patterns are available for that purpose. Choose a foreground or background color or both as the one or two colors for your gradient. In the gradient gallery, choose any gradient you like that uses the term foreground or background.

Creating your own gradient patterns is possible, as is altering the existing ones, but — wow! It's definitely not a _Dummies_ kind of project. If you want to fool around with the controls, click the Edit button on the Gradient tab in the Material Properties dialog box to access the Gradient Editor dialog box. Whoa! Have fun; try dragging the little pointers around, and good luck.

Painting with gradients

Gradients fill a painted area with a series of colors. When you paint with a gradient by using the Text, Draw, or Preset Shapes tools, or fill with a selection by using the Flood Fill tool, Paint Shop Pro scales the gradient to fit within the object you have created or area you have selected. For example, to apply to the sky in your photo a sunset-like gradient from blue to orange, select the sky and use the Flood Fill tool. Paint Shop Pro ensures that the full range of colors (blue to orange) fills the sky area. Or, if you create text and use a gradient style, the text displays the full range of colors.

If you paint with the Paint Brush or Air Brush tool, however, the gradient is scaled to the _entire image._ If you paint with a sunset-like blue-to-orange gradient, anything painted near the top of the image is blue and anything near the bottom is orange.

Choosing patterns

Patterns are interesting surface images, like brick or wood, or other more exotic or creative patterns not found in nature. Their colors are fixed, like those in a photograph, and are unaffected by your choice of foreground or background color. The patterns that come with Paint Shop Pro are *seamless,* which means that they can maintain an unbroken pattern and fill any area without appearing like tiles (with distinct edges). The process of choosing a pattern is much like choosing a gradient.

Click the Foreground (or Background) Properties box on the Color palette, and in the Material Properties dialog box that appears, select the Pattern tab. The Pattern tab slightly resembles the Gradient tab, as shown in Figure 10-8, but it's not as complicated. A box on the Gradient tab shows a preview of the selected pattern.

With the pattern tab of the Material Properties dialog box displayed, follow these steps:

1. **Click the down-arrow button to the right of the preview box and choose from the boffo gallery of patterns that appears.**

   The preview box now shows your choice.

2. **Customize the angle of the pattern by dragging the clock-hand Angle control to point in any direction.**

3. **Click OK.**

   Your chosen pattern appears in the Material box.

To apply a pattern to an existing image, try the Sculpture effect and set its Depth control to 1. We describe artistic effects and how to use them in Chapter 13.

Applying a Texture

Textures give a result like rubbing chalk on concrete, or like spraying ink on your body and rolling on the floor. (Let us know if you try this latter activity — and send us a copy.) Paint Shop Pro supplies a variety of textures, such as concrete, construction paper, and bricks. When you use one, anything you do with the Paint Brush, Erase, Airbrush, Fill, Text, Draw, or Preset Shapes tools displays that texture. Textures don't change your choice of color and they work with any style: solid color, gradients, or patterns.

You can apply texture to either the foreground material, the background material, or both; you can turn textures on or off by clicking the texture button on the Materials palette (the middle of three tiny buttons under the Foreground or Background Properties box.)

Or, you can use the Material Properties dialog box that pops up whenever you click the Foreground (or Background) Properties box. Texture is normally turned off (disabled). To use a texture, follow these steps:

1. **On the Materials palette, click the Foreground (or Background) Properties box.**

   Figure 10-9 shows the dialog box that appears. Regardless of whether the Material Properties dialog box is asking for color, gradient, or pattern, the texture information is always on the right side.

Figure 10-9:
The Texture controls are always on the right side of the Material Properties dialog box.

2. **If the Texture check box isn't checked, check it.**

   Or, alternatively, if you don't want texture right now, uncheck it.

3. **Click the down-arrow button to the right of the texture sample.**

   A gallery of textures appears, as shown in Figure 10-10. Scroll down the gallery to find a texture you like.

4. **Click the texture you want in the gallery.**

   The gallery disappears and the sample area of the Texture dialog box shows your chosen texture.

5. **Customize the angle or scale of the texture by dragging the controls in the Preview window.**

   Textures have an angle setting that allows you to spin it around to point in any direction you want them to face. In the Preview window, drag the gadget that looks like the hand on a clock to set the angle.

   You can also make the texture larger or smaller by typing different percentages in the Scale box; you can shrink the texture to a tiny 10 percent of its normal size or swell it to a massive 250 percent.

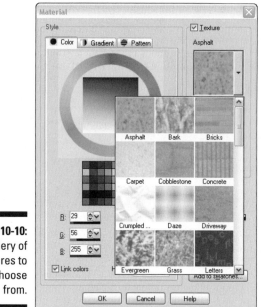

Figure 10-10:
A gallery of
textures to
choose
from.

6. Click OK in the Material Properties dialog box.

The Foreground or Background Properties box you originally clicked displays your chosen texture, laid over the top of any colors, gradients, or patterns you have selected.

Now, anything you create or erase appears textured.

Paint Shop Pro remembers the last texture you used — so even if you stop using a texture, all you have to do click the appropriate Material box to bring up this dialog box again and then click the check box to reenable it.

Texture thins your paint

When you use texture, paint goes on thin (with low opacity) with each click or stroke. Make repeated strokes or scribble with your paint tool to build up the thickness.

Do likewise for the eraser: Only a thin layer of paint comes off with each pass. Disable the Texture option and, on the Tool Options palette, set the Opacity option to 100 to erase fully in a single stroke.

When you use texture with the Fill tool, make repeated clicks if you need to increase the opacity.

Storing Swatches to Use Again

After you have done all your texturing and gradienting and coloring, some-times you don't want to have to re-create it all again the next day. The Swatches tab in the Materials box also provides a place to store swatches of material to save the colors and patterns you want to use repeatedly.

To see these swatches, click the Swatch tab on the Materials palette. It's the third tab, with the checkerboard icon, and looks like Figure 10-11.

A *swatch* is a combination of a color and any effects, like textures or patterns, that you have applied to them. It's still a material even if you *haven't* applied any textures or patterns to the color.

To save a swatch, follow these steps:

1. **Click the Properties box of the material you want to save — fore-ground or background.**

   The Material Properties dialog box appears.

2. **Click the Add to Swatches button.**

   This step displays a dialog box in which you're asked to name your col-orful creation. Name it as you like, and then click OK.

Your material is now stored on the Swatches tab, ready to be accessed when-ever you want. Click OK if you're done using the Material Properties dialog box.

Alternatively, if you're not as nearsighted as we are, you can click the tiny Create New Swatch button instead. It's the second button on the Swatches tab of the Materials palette, just under all the swatches. We would reproduce it here, but it would look just as blobby as it does in real life.

Figure 10-11: The Swatches tab — swatch this space for further details!

Using a Stored Material

Using a stored material is so easy that you can do it in two clicks. Of course, if you have a number of swatches, sorting through them all can be cumbersome. Follow these steps:

1. **Select the Swatches tab on the Materials palette, as shown in Figure 10-11, in the preceding section.**

2. **If you need to narrow the number of available swatches in order to find one, left-click the View button of the Swatches tab and hold the button down.**

   A drop-down menu appears, where you can choose one of four options: all swatches, colors only, gradients only, or patterns only. Choosing one hides all others until you change the view.

   To find out more about each swatch, hover the cursor over the swatch; a small, informational pop-up message appears, giving you the name of the swatch in question, the RGB numbers, the types of textures in the swatch, and the names of the gradients and patterns used.

3. **Click the swatch you want to use.**

   Left-click it if you want it to be in the Foreground Properties; right-click if you want it to be in the Background Material box. Whatever tool you use next is now loaded up with that swatch's material.

Deleting a Stored Material

Deleting a swatch is *so* easy that it's scandalous we're getting paid to tell you how to do it (don't worry — writing the rest of this chapter was darned hard work):

1. **Select the swatch you want to delete.**

   Remember that you can sort through the swatches if you need to hunt one down, as discussed in the preceding section.

2. **Click the Delete button on the Swatches tab.**

Using Pastiches of Pictures

Imagine a paint tube that, rather than contain paint, is crammed with images that pour out as you squeeze the tube. You now have a good mental image of the Paint Shop Pro *Picture Tube tool.* Paint Shop Pro comes with a gallery of tubes to use.

Each tube contains a set of images on a particular theme. For example, you can squeeze out a set of airplanes, butterflies, billiard balls, or coins. Each individual image in a tube is different. Figure 10-12 shows an illustration that uses two tubes: various blades of grass and many raindrops.

Picture tubes have several purposes. They can serve as

- ✔ A source of clip art on various themes
- ✔ Brushes for interesting textures and shapes, such as grass, fire, or 3-dimensional tubes
- ✔ Creative painting tools that are sensitive to your brush strokes

Basic tubing

Picture tubing is fundamentally easy. You choose what kind of pictures you want and click or drag the picture tube across the image. Here are the details:

1. **Click the Picture Tube tool (as shown in the margin) on the toolbar.**

   You may have to wait when you first choose this tool because Paint Shop Pro loads its cache with pictures. A Cache Status box may briefly appear.

Figure 10-12: Grazing in a marsh on a foggy dawn. It's five minutes of work, thanks to the Picture Tube's lawn, grass, and animal images.

2. **Choose which picture set you want from the Tool Options palette.**

   A sample image from the selected picture tube appears next to the Presets menu. Click the down arrow to the right of that sample to reveal a gallery of picture tubes of different types. Some picture tube pictures aren't much to look at individually, like the 3-D items, but they create cool effects when you drag your brush. Scroll through those images to review them, and then click the one you want.

3. **Click in the image window to deposit one picture at a time or drag to paint a line of pictures.**

   As you click or drag, various pictures similar to the sample you chose appear at intervals on the image. (If the image isn't much bigger than an individual picture, few pictures may appear. See the following section for instructions on reducing the picture size.)

One common way to use picture tubes is as a sort of randomly chosen clip art to ornament an illustration. Figure 10-12, for example, uses a single animal from the Animals image set. Choose a tube and then click the illustration in various places to drop in some art; press Ctrl+Z if you don't like one and want to try the next image. Other tubes are meant to be dragged to create a banner, like Filmstrip, Rope, and Neon Pink. In Figure 10-12, we used the Lawn tube to create the basic marsh and the Grass tube to create the tall vegetation.

Adjusting basic tube behavior

If the Picture Tube tool doesn't deliver images in quite the way you want, you can change its behavior. Behaviors you can modify include

- ✔ **Picture size:** Reduce the number in the Scale value box if the pictures are too large. Scale is initially set to 100 (percent), the largest setting.

- ✔ **Spacing between pictures:** Pictures initially flow off the brush at a certain preset spacing. Increase the step value on the Tool Options palette to separate pictures. To jam them together, decrease the value.

- ✔ **Regular or random spacing:** The Picture Tube tool is initially set to randomly vary the spacing between pictures as you drag. To make it deliver an evenly spaced stream of pictures, choose Continuous from the Placement Mode drop-down menu, on the Tool Options palette.

- ✔ **Picture sequence:** The tool is initially set to choose pictures randomly from its set of images. To have it select images in sequence, choose Incremental from the Selection Mode drop-down menu, on the Tool Options palette.

   The artist who created the tube determined the sequence. For each stroke you make, the sequence picks up where you last left off. The tube doesn't repeat the initial picture until it has delivered the last picture.

> ✔ **Angling to follow your brush stroke:** Some images, like butterflies, are ordered so that they angle themselves to follow your brush stroke; choose Angular under Selection Mode on the Tool Options palette.

Art Media: For Those Who Miss Real Paint

Those of us who were born while the earth was still cooling remember a primitive art medium involving suspensions of minerals in oil called *paint* and surfaces made of plant fiber called *canvas*. If you're nostalgic for the smell of turpentine, well, go sniff a cleaning rag because Art Media can't help you there.

But, if you long to be able to create brush-like strokes, blend colors on a palette or on your canvas, work with wet paint, brush over dried paint, and still have all the digital whoop-te-doo of Paint Shop Pro's digital features, expose yourself to Art Media!

Art Media is really a separate world in Paint Shop Pro. Art Media uses a special tool group on the Tools toolbar, as shown in Figure 10-13. You can use Art Media tools only on Art Media layers or backgrounds (canvases). This restriction is consistent: You can use only vector tools (like Rectangle) on vector layers and only bitmap tools (like the regular paint brush) on bitmap layers. If you try to use regular tools on an Art Media layer, Paint Shop Pro asks permission to convert the layer to raster. The good news is that you can add Art Media layers to an image with regular bitmap layers or vector layers. To use layers, see Chapter 11.

Art Media would be a great stage name for a TV art instructor. We ask only 1 percent of your royalties. Thank you.

Creating an Art Media canvas or layer

To paint with Art Media, you need an Art Media layer. You can start a new image by using an Art Media background layer or add an Art Media layer to an existing image.

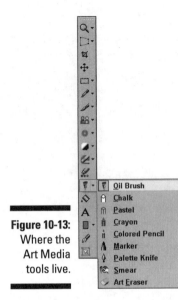

Figure 10-13:
Where the
Art Media
tools live.

Starting a fresh Art Media canvas

To start a new image where Art Media is the background layer (that is, a new Art Media canvas), follow these steps:

1. **Choose File⇨New or press Ctrl+N.**

   The New Image dialog box appears. Determine the settings for image dimensions. For help, see the section "Starting a Fresh Canvas," in Chapter 9.

2. **Choose Art Media Background in the Image Characteristics section of the dialog box.**

3. **Click the sample square in the Select the Canvas Texture area.**

   A flyout panel displays different Art Media canvas textures.

4. **Click whatever canvas you like.**

   If you want the canvas to have a color, click the Enable Fill Color check box; then click the sample square under the check box to bring up the Color dialog box. See the section "Precise color using the color wheel," earlier in this chapter, for help in using the color wheel in this dialog box.

5. **Click OK.**

   Your new canvas appears.

Creating an Art Media layer

Art media layers can add "hand-painted" elements to raster and vector layers. See Color Plate C-10 in the color section of this book for an example.

1. **Choose Layers⇨New Art Media Layer.**

2. **In the Art Media layer dialog box that appears, enter a name for your layer in the Name field.**

   If you don't see the Name field, click the General tab in this dialog box.

3. **Click the Canvas Texture tab.**

4. **Click the sample square in the Select the Canvas Texture area.**

   A flyout panel displays different Art Media canvas textures.

5. **Click whatever canvas texture you like.**

   If you want the layer to have a color, click the Enable Fill Color check box; then click the sample square under the check box to bring up the Color dialog box. See the section "Precise color using the color wheel," earlier in this chapter, for help in using the color wheel in this dialog box.

6. **Click OK in the New Art Media Layer dialog box.**

   Your new layer appears.

Pretending that you have real media

Art Media tools, like computer book authors, live in their own, special world that is as close to reality as technology can achieve. Figure 10-13 shows you where Art Media hang out on the Tools toolbar. You get a nifty toolbox of oil-paint brushes, chalk, crayons, pencils, markers, a palette knife, a smearing tool to keep your fingers clean, and a special eraser that you cannot chew on.

What is it about real paint, chalk, crayon, canvas, and the like that make them different from digital media? Here are a few characteristics:

- Surfaces have texture.
- Brushes run out of paint — how fast depends on how heavily you "load" the brush. They also can be cleaned between colors — or not.
- Brushes mix paint as you drag them through it.
- Brushes have bristles of different firmness and bristle size.
- Some tools (like brushes and markers) have thin tips that can give an effect like a calligraphy tool, depending on how much you rotate the head as you make a stroke.

✔ Some tools, like pencils, can mark more heavily on one side of the stroke than the other if you tilt them. Others, like crayons, may mark more heavily in the middle.

These are the effects that Art Media tools duplicate — and pretty well, too. You set these effects on the Tool Options palette, as you discover in the following sections.

Figure 10-14 shows a little of what you can achieve with Art Media. On the left is Oil Paint, which shows the natural blending that takes place on wet paint. The other marks are dry media: chalk, pastel, crayon, colored pencil, and marker (from left to right).

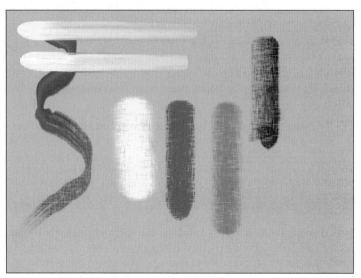

Figure 10-14:
Some of the
Art Media
media.

For the easiest adjustment of various controls on the Options palette and elsewhere in Paint Shop Pro, use the slider control where it appears. To the right of any numerical adjustment is a button with the downward-pointing V. With your cursor on this V, hold down the left mouse button. A slider appears with a visual representation of what you're adjusting (brush size or color, for example). Drag to the setting you want.

Setting up the basics of your Art Media tool

Before you make a stroke, you at least want to set the tool size on the Tool Options palette. Press F4 to pop up the Tool Options palette, and adjust the following settings to your liking:

✔ **Size:** Adjust the size as you would for any tool: Adjust the Size value up or down.

- **Shape:** Shape is also pretty obvious; choose round or square. When you make a stroke, you don't see much difference unless, for a square shape, you choose fixed head tracking (see the bullet in the following section).

- **Trace:** Enabling the Trace check box makes the tool pick up color from the underlying layer.

If your Art Media tool seems to switch color as soon as you click the canvas, you may have Trace accidentally selected. Click the check box to clear it and deselect Trace.

Getting calligraphy-like strokes

If you want calligraphic strokes that get wider and narrower as you go vertically or horizontally, set the following options on the Tool Options palette:

- **Thickness:** Some tools don't appear to let you set thickness (the control is grayed out), but, if you set a tool's head tracking to Fixed Angle, it allows a thickness adjustment.

- **Rotation:** This control sets the rotation of the tool's head in degrees. (Use the slider control to set rotation visually.)

- **Head tracking:** Computer book authors often lose their heads and wish for head tracking, but, we digress. Head tracking has to do with whether the tool rotates to give you a constant width as you make a curving stroke — or not. For constant width, choose Track Path; for calligraphic-style work, choose Fixed angle. If you choose Fixed Angle, set the angle by using the Rotation control.

Controlling colored pencil strokes

Colored pencils make variable-weight strokes depending on how you hold them. The Tool Options palette offers two styles to "hold" your brush:

- **Style:** Choose Point for a line that is heavier in the center. Choose Tilt for a line weighted to one side, and Edge for a similar effect, but broader. Control which side of the line is weighted by stroking up versus down on a vertical line and left versus right on a horizontal line.

- **Softness:** A higher Softness value produces a line that is denser in the center than a low Softness value does.

Controlling paint with the Oil Brush and Palette Knife

The Oil Brush (and, to some extent, the Palette Knife) have special controls that you want to set up on the Tool Options palette:

- **Paint Loading:** A high value means lots of paint on the brush; a low value means that the brush runs out more quickly.

- **Viscosity:** *Viscosity* measures how gooey the paint is (as opposed to runny). High viscosity paint starts out dense but runs dry quickly. Low viscosity paint goes on thinner at first but lasts longer on the brush stroke.

✔ **Auto Clean:** This option vacuums your automobile. No, sorry — if this check box is enabled, it means that your brush is cleaned of color between strokes and then dipped in pure foreground color. If you clear this check box, your brush retains a certain amount of color from the last stroke.

✔ **Clean:** Whenever you click Clean, Paint Shop Pro cleans existing color from your brush and then dips the brush afresh into the foreground color.

Brush firmness doesn't make much difference if you're using a mouse. A pressure-sensitive pad would allow it to make a difference. The bristle size is also a bit too subtle for us to care about it. You may find a reason to care.

Erasing and smearing

To erase Art Media, use the Art Eraser. You need several strokes of the eraser to totally erase Art Media.

The edge is somewhat indistinct. No controls exist to modify the sharpness of the eraser's edge or how fast it erases. But, if you click Presets on the Tool Options palette, you can choose various shapes from the menu that appears.

Sometimes you just want to run your finger through the paint. Paint Shop Pro gives you the digital finger you need, in the Smear tool. Unlike what you could achieve with your fingertip, which is pretty round, you can do calligraphic smearing by choosing any of various tip shapes from the Presets menu. See the section "Getting calligraphy-like strokes," earlier in this chapter, for other controls, like head tracking, that affect artistic use of the Art Eraser or Smear tool.

Mixing colors on the mixer

Ha! Software vendors have been calling their color-selector thingies "palettes" for so long that the folks at Jasc got stuck using the term *mixer* when technology finally allowed them to provide a *real* palette. A real palette is a place where you can mush colors together with a palette knife to get the color (or band of colors) you want to use. The Paint Shop Pro version of this feature is the Mixer.

You can use the mixer with any coloring tool in the art media tool group. To use the mixer, follow these steps:

1. Choose View➪Palettes➪Mixer or press Shift+F6.

(F6 is the Materials palette, so Shift+F6 makes sense for the Mixer.) The Mixer palette appears, as shown in Figure 10-15. Use the tube icon to pick up and place colors on the Mixer, use the Mixer Knife to mix colors, and then click the Mixer Dropper on the color you want.

The Mixer palette is misshapen and ugly if it appears docked to the top of the window. Drag it by its title bar at the left end until it floats.

2. **Click the tube icon in the upper-left corner of the Mixer to pick up some color.**

Mixer Tube

Mixer Knife

Mixer Dropper

Figure 10-15: The Mixer.

3. **To pick up color from the Materials palette (press F6 to see that palette), click any of the colors displayed there.**

If you're in the middle of painting with an Art Media tool, you can pick up color from the canvas by Ctrl+clicking that color.

4. **Click the Mixer to place a spot of color there.**

Repeat Steps 3 and 4 to place additional colors in the Mixer. You can start smearing on the Mixer even while the tube tool is selected.

5. **Click the Mixer Knife icon at the top of the Mixer.**

6. **Smear the paint samples together to create the blend you like.**

If you want stripey paint, it's okay not to thoroughly mix the colors. To undo a mix, click the Unmix button, at the bottom of the Mixer. To start with a clean Mixer page, click the New Page button, in the lower-left corner.

7. **Click the Mixer Dropper, at the top of the Mixer.**

8. **Click the Mixer where you like the paint blend.**

Notice that the foreground material on the Materials palette reflects whatever you click — including stripes! When you use dry media, like chalk, you can set the pixel size.

Now, you're ready to paint with your own unique blend of paint.

The Mixer is larger than you think. To get more room to work, drag the lower-right corner of the Mixer palette to expand the palette. To see hidden areas of the Mixer, click the cross-arrow Navigate icon, under the Mixer window and on the large-scale view of the Mixer that pops up.

Drying and wetting paint

Paint that has been applied to a layer normally smears (very artistically) when you drag your brush through it. If you don't want that smearing, dry the current layer:

Choose Layers➪Dry Art Media Layer. Now, your existing paint doesn't smear. New paint that you apply, however, is wet!

If you want to make old paint wet again, choose Layers➪Wet Art Media Layer.

Chapter 11

Layering Images

*T*he old masters of oil painting used layers of paint to give their paintings great depth and radiance. Now, artistic masters (who all work in Paint Shop Pro, of course) use layers for another reason: It makes changing stuff lots easier. It also lets you combine images more easily.

Layers are like transparent sheets of plastic that are laid over an opaque (nontransparent) background. You can put stuff on the background layer or on the other, transparent layers.

As simple as this basic idea is, Paint Shop Pro uses it to give you lots of flexibility and power in creating stunning images. To see what using layers can do for you, read on!

Putting Layers to Work for You

With layers, you can paint, erase, or move things around without worrying about ruining the underlying image. You can erase a line, for example, without erasing the background. You can move an entire object or see how something looks without permanently committing yourself to it. You can also combine images in various clever ways.

Because Paint Shop Pro layers are electronic, not physical, they can make your life easier in other ways, too. Here are just a few special tricks you can do, besides simply painting, moving, combining, or erasing images:

- Select an object painted on a layer without accidentally selecting other areas of the same color or that underlie that object.

- Make an image partly transparent, a sort of ghost on the background.

- Switch image objects into or out of the picture, as needed, or quickly change their stacking order.

- Combine layers into one layer, if you're certain that no more changes are needed, or lock several layers together temporarily to form a moveable group of objects.

- Make vector layers, which enable you to create basic shapes, text, and other objects in a special form that lets you easily change their shape.

- Make an adjustment layer (a brightening layer, for example) that affects only the underlying layers and which effect you can vary.

- Create the frames of an animation by simply moving one or more layers.

- Make layers interact, for special effects. For example, you can subtract one layer from another — a way to reveal changes between photographs.

Getting Layers

Your parents probably never explained where layers come from — unless, of course, you grew up on an egg ranch. Here's the real story.

You always have at least one layer: the background layer. That's the layer where nearly everything happens until you add more layers. If you download a digital photo from your camera, for example, the image is on the background layer. If you happily paint away, ignorant of all knowledge of layers, all your painting is on the background layer.

You can get images with additional layers in a variety of ways:

- Make a new, blank layer by using the various New commands on the Layers menu (on the menu bar) or by using the Layer palette.

- Turn a selection into a layer (*promote* it, in Paint Shop Pro terms).

- Incidentally, make a new vector layer by drawing lines or shapes or by adding text.

✔ Make a new raster layer by using a tool, like the Deformation tool, that requires a layer to work on, and Paint Shop Pro creates one automatically for you.

✔ Paste an image from the Windows Clipboard by choosing Edit➪Paste➪ As New Layer.

✔ Open an image file that already has multiple layers, such as many Paint Shop Pro or Photoshop files have.

✔ Add a picture frame with the Image➪Picture Frame command.

Calling a Pal for Help: The Layer Palette

The first thing you should do when you're working with layers is to call a friend for help. The Layer palette, as shown in Figure 11-1, is your best pal. It's a small pal; hence, the name *palette*. See how things make sense, after they're explained?

Figure 11-1:
Your pal,
the Layer
palette, is at
your side to
help you
with layer
stuff.

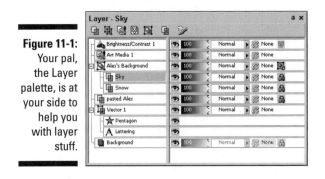

If your little pal isn't on your screen already, call it by pressing F8 on the keyboard or click the Toggle Layers button on the toolbar. Do the same thing to hide the palette again.

One of the not-so-adorable Paint Shop Pro quirks is that sometimes it opens the Layer palette so that the names of the layers (and, hence, the only way to *select* a layer) are hidden. Your Layer palette should look like ours, with at least the Background layer visible on the far left side; if it doesn't, right-click and drag the vertical bar immediately to the left of the Visibility toggle (the little eye) and drag it rightward to reveal all.

Here are a few basic factoids to help you get along with your new and complex-looking pal:

✔ **Each row of the palette represents a layer.** Your view of the image in the image window is down through the layers, from top to bottom (background). The layers' names are on the left side of the palette. You assign names when you create the layers, or else you allow Paint Shop Pro to create a boring but adequate name, like Layer3. Paint Shop Pro automatically calls the initial, background layer (the one that every image starts with) Background.

✔ **To work on a layer, click its name.** Clicking its name makes that layer the active one. Nearly everything you can do to an image in Paint Shop Pro, such as paint, erase, or fiddle with the colors, affects only the active layer. The palette helps you remember which one is active.

✔ **The icon to the left of each row tells you what kind of layer that row represents.** Four kinds of layers exist: raster, vector, grouped, and adjustment. You use raster layers most often. See the section after next, "Choosing a Layer That's Just Your Type," for details. In Figure 11-1, the row named Pasted Alex, Sky, and Snow show you a raster icon, the Lettering and Pentagon layers show the vector icon, the Brightness/Contrast layer displays an adjustment icon, and Alex's Background shows the group icon.

Don't bother trying to understand the palette all at once. We tell you how to use the rest of the palette's features as we go along.

Creating a New, Blank Layer

To create a new, blank layer, follow these steps by using the Layer palette:

1. **Choose where, in your stack of layers, you want the new layer to appear.**

   (If this is the first layer you have added to an image, you can skip this step. The new layer appears just above the background layer.)

   Otherwise, on the Layer palette, click the layer that you want the new layer to appear above. In Figure 11-1, for example, we have clicked the layer labeled Sky, to make that layer the active one.

2. **For a raster layer (the most commonly used type of layer), click the New Raster Layer button or choose Layers⇨New Raster Layer from the menu bar.**

   The New Layer button is in the upper-left corner of the Layer palette, as shown in Figure 11-1.

   If you're savvy about the various types of layer and know that you want a specific type, you can choose other types of layers from the Layer palette button bar or Paint Shop Pro menu bar. You can choose Raster, Vector, Art Media, Mask, or Adjustment layer. For more information about types of layer, see the next section.

3. **Type a name for the layer.**

   The Name field of the Layer Properties dialog box is already highlighted, so you don't have to click there before typing. Whatever you type replaces the descriptive but rather boring name (like Raster1) that Paint Shop Pro suggests. Enter a name in that field that describes what you will put on this layer. If you're not feeling creative, just skip this step and Paint Shop Pro uses the boring name.

4. **Click OK.**

   Get the heck out of this dialog box and get on with the fun!

Your image doesn't look any different, so maybe you're wondering "Just what have I accomplished?" Fear not! You have indeed added a layer. The image doesn't look any different because your new layer is transparent and blank. It's just like a sheet of clear plastic placed over a painting.

Look at the Layer palette. You see your new layer, with the name you gave it, highlighted. That means that it's the active layer, and any painting, erasing, selection, or color adjustment you perform now takes place on that layer.

When you float a selection, it appears on the Layer palette like a layer and is named *Floating Selection* (in italics). It's not really a full-fledged layer, but you can use Layer menu commands on it, like moving it down in the stack. You can turn a selection into its own layer, as we show you later in this chapter.

Choosing a Layer That's Just Your Type

To make life a bit more complicated, Paint Shop Pro has four different types of layers for different kinds of stuff. Four of those types of layers appear in Figure 11-1, where you can see that they're distinguished by special icons. Here's more about those layers:

 Raster: You use this plain-vanilla type of layer most of the time. A raster layer handles normal images — the kind made of dots, called raster, or bitmap, images. Raster layers are marked with the icon shown here.

Vector: This special type of layer comes into play mostly when you use the Paint Shop Pro text, preset shapes, or line-drawing tools. Vector images are made up of lines or curves connected in a connect-the-dot fashion. Paint Shop Pro normally creates text, preset shapes, and lines as vector images, although you can alternatively create them as raster images. Vector images can't appear on a raster layer, and raster images can't appear on a vector layer. Vector images are marked with the icon that appears here.

Art Media: Art Media layers are for artwork made using the special Art Media tools described in Chapter 10. These are paintings or drawings with an appearance of being done with real paint, chalk, crayon, and so on. Be sure to choose what type of texture you want when you create a new layer. Click the Canvas Texture tab when the Layer Properties dialog box appears, and then click the sample texture that's shown to choose from a fly-out menu of textures.

 Adjustment: This special type of layer doesn't contain any images! It's like a magical coating that imparts a particular image quality to the layers under it. It works almost exactly like color adjustments. The advantage of adjustment layers is that the enhancement is separated from the image, so changing your mind is easier. Adjustment layers are named according to the kind of adjustment they perform, and each of them has its own snazzy color icon; the one shown next to this paragraph is Contrast.

 Group: Many times, you want to apply an effect to the same two or three layers while leaving the other layers untouched. You can group the layers so that Paint Shop Pro treats them like a single layer, which is awfully handy; we show you how to do this later in this chapter.

 Mask: *Masking* is used to hide certain areas of an overlaying layer's image while letting other areas remain visible. It's a little like masking tape except that rather than cover parts of an image, like masking tape does, masking makes areas transparent — just as erasing on a layer does in Paint Shop Pro. That allows the underlying image to show through. This handy trick for advanced Paint Shop Pro users allows you to cut shapes out with little effort or create transparent areas on the background layer.

Working on Layers

To work on a layer, click its name on the Layer palette to select it (make it active). You can now paint, erase, adjust color, cut, copy, paste, and make image transformations, such as flipping, filtering, or deforming, and the results appear on only your selected layer. How tidy and organized!

 As an artist who is using multiple layers, you're like a doctor who is seeing multiple patients. To avoid mistakes, you must know which one you're operating on. You can't tell what image is on which layer by simply looking at the image. The transparency of layers prevents you. So, instead, keep an eye on the Layer palette to see which layer is active. The active layer is highlighted there. Pause your cursor over a layer's name to see a tiny thumbnail image of the layer's contents. If a tool doesn't seem to be working, you're probably trying to work on something that isn't *on* the active layer. Try turning various layers on and off to find the object you want.

Here are a few peculiarities of working with layers:

✔ **Moving:** You can use the Move tool (the four-headed arrow) to slide an entire layer around (but not the background layer). Click the Move tool on the Tool palette. Then, in the image window, drag the entire layer by dragging any object on that layer. To move an individual object independently of the others on that layer, select the object before you use the Move tool. (If the object still doesn't move independently, make sure that the object's layer is the active one, reselect the object, and try again.)

✔ **Selecting:** When you make a selection on a layer, the selection marquee penetrates to all layers. That means that you can select an object on one layer, switch to another layer, and then, for example, fill that selected area (within the selection marquee) with paint on that other layer.

✔ **Copying:** When you copy, you copy only from the active layer — unless you choose Edit⇨Copy Merged. A merged copy includes all the layers.

✔ **Erasing:** When you erase or delete on a (nonbackground) layer, you restore the layer's transparency. (On the background layer, you leave behind background color when you erase, or transparency if the image was originally created with transparent background — and for the record, photos are *not* created with transparent backgrounds.)

✔ **Using raster, Art Media, and vector tools:** Paint Shop Pro uses the three distinct image types raster, vector, and Art Media, and has three distinct sets of tools for these image types. (Refer to the section in Chapter 10 about Art Media and those who miss real Paint, and Chapter 12 for information about vector objects, like text and shapes.) These tools work only on layers of the same type (except that raster tools are also used on mask layers). As a result, if you're working on a raster layer, for example, and try to apply a vector or Art Media tool, Paint Shop Pro offers to create a new layer of the appropriate type.

Managing Layers

When you view a multilayer image, you look down through all the layers just as you would look down through a stack of plastic sheets with stuff painted on them. To control which layers you see and also adjust the order in which they're stacked, use these techniques:

✔ **To see just the active layer:** Choose Layers⇨View⇨Current Only.

✔ **To see all layers:** Choose Layers⇨View⇨All.

✔ **To see specific layers:** On the Layer palette, click a layer's Layer Visibility toggle, known to its friends as the eyeglasses icon. Each layer has this icon, to the right of the layer name. Click it once to turn the layer off (make it invisible) and click again to turn it on. When a layer is off, an X appears through the eyeglasses icon.

✔ **To move a layer up or down in the stack:** Drag it up or down in the left column of the Layer palette. While you're dragging, the layer itself doesn't move; instead, a black line follows your cursor to tell you where the layer will go when you release the mouse button. An alternative to dragging is to click a layer and then choose Layers⇨Arrange⇨Bring to Top, Move Up, Move Down, Send to Bottom, Move Into Group, and Move Out of Group.

✔ **Renaming a layer:** To change a layer's name, double-click the layer's current name on the Layer palette. When the Layer Properties box appears, type a new name in the Name field (already selected, for your convenience) and click OK. Or, right-click the name once and choose Rename from the context menu that appears, and you can edit the name right on the Layer palette.

✔ **Removing a layer:** To delete a layer on the Layer palette, click that layer's name and then click the Delete Layer button. Everything on that layer goes away with the layer.

Pinning Layers Together: Grouping

After you have carefully positioned objects on different layers, it's nice to pin those layers together so they can't reposition themselves. If you have painstakingly put Uncle Tobias's head on the neck of a giraffe, for example, you want to keep them together while you get creative with other layers.

The first thing to do is to select the first layer you want to add to your group and then click the New Layer Group button near the upper-right corner of the palette. This action brings you to the ever-so-titillating New Layer Group dialog box, which looks almost exactly like the New Layer dialog box, and you should do the same thing you did there: Ignore all those options and just type a friendly name for your group. Then click OK. (As with the New Layer dialog box, if you leave it to Paint Shop Pro, it chooses something delightfully nondescriptive, like Group 1.)

As you can see in the Alex's Background group, as shown in Figure 11-1, you now have a group on your Layers palette, complete with the layer you selected neatly tucked under it. (You also should see a tiny box with a – next to it; if you don't want to see all the layers contained in this group, click the – to hide them. Click the + sign next to the group to reveal them again.) To add another layer to your group, click the name of the layer, drag it back up to just underneath the name of the layer (it turns into a small black bar), and let go. Your layer is now a part of the group! (If only high school had been this easy.) To remove a layer from a group, simply drag it above the group name.

Layers with the same group name behave as though they were pinned together: When you move one layer with the Move tool (the 4-headed arrow thingy), you move the entire group. Members of a group keep their independence in other ways, though. If you change the appearance of a layer (make it brighter, for example), its fellow group members don't change.

Gone but not forgotten: Layer links

In the old days of Paint Shop Pro, you didn't have the handy-dandy Layer Groups command; instead, you used *layer links,* which were clumsier and harder to remember, and you could have only 12 of them. In a nod to older Paint Shop Pro .psp files that may not support layer groups, Paint Shop Pro 9 allows you to use layer links in addition to groups.

Click the layer link toggle to assign a layer link number to your layer; layers that share the same layer link number act exactly like groups. Click the Layer Link toggle button to assign a given layer to Layer Link 1, and click it again to raise the number by one each time, all the way up to the number of layers you have within your image — at which point it goes back to having no layer link. You can tell whether a layer is assigned to a layer link

because it has a small number next to the tiny chain image.

Honestly, the new Group Layer feature is so handy that we're only letting you know about this ratty ol' layer link feature in case you open a Paint Shop Pro 7 (or earlier) file that uses it. You don't want to *know* what happens if you start mixing layer links and layer groups. (It's much like mixing tequila and rum.)

The upshot is that if you have a layer that you could *swear* you have grouped properly but just doesn't seem to be affected by something that changed the rest of the group, check to see that it doesn't have a layer link number. If it does, click the toggle enough times to set the layer link to None and then group those layers. You can thank us in the morning.

Using Layers to Separate or Combine Images

The main reasons for using layers are either to break an image apart into several layers for more flexible editing or to combine multiple images into one. This section describes how to do both.

Combining entire images

Do you have two entire images to combine? To combine an entire image file with the image you're working on, follow these steps:

1. **On the Layer palette of the image you're working on, click the name of the layer above which you want to insert your new image.**

   If the image doesn't have multiple layers, skip to Step 2.

2. **Choose File⇨Browse and open the image browser to the folder containing the image file.**

Thumbnail pictures of the images in that folder appear. (For more information about how to use the image browser, refer to the section in Chapter 1 about opening, managing, and sorting files with the browser.)

3. **Drag the thumbnail picture of the image file to the image you're working on.**

   Paint Shop Pro inserts the new image as a layer, above the layer you selected in Step 1. (If the image you're dragging contains multiple layers, all its layers are grouped together.) The cursor turns into a 4-headed arrow to indicate that Paint Shop Pro has selected the Move tool for you.

4. **Drag the new image to position it where you want it.**

After dragging, we often click the Arrow tool (at the top of the Tool palette) or some other tool to avoid accidentally dragging the selection when we move the mouse again.

Separating image parts into layers

How do you get an object separated out and on its own layer? One answer is that you can select the object and turn it into a new layer, called *promoting a selection*. Take these steps:

1. **Select the desired chunk of any existing layer (the background layer, for example) by using any of the Paint Shop Pro selection tools.**

   We cover selection tools for normal (raster) images in Chapter 9. To select an object on a vector layer, click the object with the Object Selector tool (at the bottom of the Tools toolbar).

   Is your selection tool not selecting on the object you want? Remember that selection works within only one layer at a time. Your object may be on a different layer than the active one. On the Layer palette, click the layer where that object lives to make that layer active. Then try selecting again. If you're not sure where that object lives, pause your cursor over each layer's name, one at a time, and look for your object in the thumbnail image of the layer's contents.

2. **On the Layer palette, click the layer that you want the new layer to appear above.**

3. **Choose Selections⇨Promote to Layer from the Paint Shop Pro menu bar.**

   A new layer, cleverly named Promoted Selection, appears on the Layer palette. Although nothing appears to change in your image, your selection is now on that Promoted Selection layer.

Your object is now on its own layer. A copy of that object remains on the original layer. You can now deselect the object; press Ctrl+D or choose Selections⇨Select None.

If you would prefer that no copy be left behind when you promote a selection, drag the selection slightly after Step 1. On the background layer, this action leaves behind an area filled with the background color. On other layers, the area becomes transparent.

Another way to separate image chunks into layers is to select the chunks and then cut and paste the chunk as a new layer (see the following section).

Copying, cutting, and pasting with layers

A good way to get an image or chunk of an image onto a layer is to copy (or cut) it and then paste it as a new layer. This approach uses the same, familiar Windows Clipboard system that other applications use, which is a great way to combine multiple images, even if the additional images come from a program other than Paint Shop Pro. In the following sections, we tell you how to copy, cut, and paste a selected image as a new layer.

Copying or cutting an image

You can copy or cut images from a variety of sources. Here's how to do it:

- ✔ **From a program other than Paint Shop Pro:** First, open that program and display the image you want. (You don't need to close Paint Shop Pro.) Exactly how to copy or cut an image from that program varies somewhat from program to program. By copying from a Web page in Internet Explorer, for example, you can right-click the image and then choose Copy from the menu that appears. In many programs, click the image to select it and choose Edit⇨Copy to put a copy on the hidden Windows Clipboard.

- ✔ **From another layer within your Paint Shop Pro image:** On the Layer palette, click the layer containing the object you want. Select the image chunk you want with any of the Paint Shop Pro selection tools. (Refer to Chapter 3 for help with selection tools. If the layer is a vector layer, use the Object Selector tool at the bottom of the Tools palette.) Then choose Edit⇨Copy (or Edit⇨Cut, if you want to remove the chunk from its current layer).

- ✔ **From another image file:** Open that file in Paint Shop Pro. A new window appears and displays that image. Use any of the Paint Shop Pro selection tools to select your chosen chunk. Choose Selections⇨Select All if you want to select the whole image. Choose Edit⇨Copy to copy from the active layer. To copy combined images from all layers, choose Edit⇨Copy Merged.

Pasting the image as, or on, a new layer

After you have copied (or cut) an image to the Windows Clipboard, you can paste it *as* a layer or *on* an existing layer. Here's how to paste it as a layer:

1. **Click the title bar of the window in Paint Shop Pro where you want to paste.**

   This step makes sure that you paste it in the right place.

2. **On the Layer palette, click the layer that you want the new layer to appear above.**

   To put a layer above the background layer, for example, click Background. If your image has only one layer, you can skip this step because Background is already selected.

3. **Choose Edit⇨Paste⇨As New Layer or press Ctrl+L.**

   Your image appears as a new layer, and the Paint Shop Pro cursor appears as a 4-headed arrow. That cursor tells you that Paint Shop Pro has automatically selected the Move tool for you.

   (If you copy a vector object from outside Paint Shop Pro, such as a Microsoft Draw object from Microsoft Word, Paint Shop Pro converts it to a raster layer when you paste it. First, however, Paint Shop Pro displays a dialog box labeled Meta Picture Import. In that dialog box, set Width in Pixels and Height in Pixels to the sizes you want for the pasted image and click OK.)

4. **Drag your newly pasted image where you want it.**

When you're done dragging, consider clicking the arrow tool (at the top of the tool palette) or some other tool to avoid accidentally dragging the selection with subsequent mouse motions.

You can also paste an image on an *existing* layer rather than paste it as its own *new* layer. After you have copied or cut the image to the Windows Clipboard, click the existing layer's name on the Layer palette and choose Edit⇨Paste As New Selection or press Ctrl+E. The image appears; drag it where you want it and then click to make it a floating selection. Press Ctrl+D to deselect the image.

Copying entire layers from one image to another

When you start using layered images, you may find that a layer you created in one image is useful in another image. To copy a layer (or layers) from one image to another, you drag the layer from the Layer palette of the source image to the destination image. To do so, take these detailed steps:

1. **Open both images in Paint Shop Pro.**

   Each image gets its own window. Arrange the windows so you can see at least part of both images. (For example, choose Window⇨Tile Vertically.)

2. **Click the title bar of the destination image.**

   By destination image, we mean the one where you want the layer to go.

3. **On the Layer palette, click the layer above which the new layer is to go.**

   Clicking makes that layer the active one.

4. **Click the title bar of the image containing the layer you want to copy.**

5. **On the Layer palette, click the name of the layer you want to copy and drag it to the destination image.**

   Drag the layer directly into the middle of the destination image, and not onto the title bar of its window. When you release the mouse button, the copied layer appears.

Blending images by making layers transparent

Double your pleasure, double your fun. One popular effect is a sort of double exposure, which you do by making an overlaying layer on which the image is partially transparent. For example, you may want to overlay a diagram on a photograph or add a faint image of a logo to a picture.

Figure 11-2 shows a few tasty vegetables overlaid with the word *Veggies,* perhaps to be used as a sign for a vegetarian buffet. (It looks much more appealing in color — see color plate C-4 in the color section of this book.)

To make a layer transparent, you merely adjust one little setting, Layer Opacity. Each layer has a Layer Opacity setting on the Layer palette (the shaded bar shown in Figure 11-2). Until you change it, the setting for every layer is 100 to indicate that the layer is 100 percent opaque (you can't see through the image on the layer).

At the far right end of each bar is a pair of pointers (triangles). Drag that pair to the left to make the layer more transparent. Drag the pair to the right to make the layer more opaque. The number on the bar changes as you drag, between 100 and 0. In Figure 11-2, the layer containing the text *Veggies!* is set to 52 percent (roughly half-transparent).

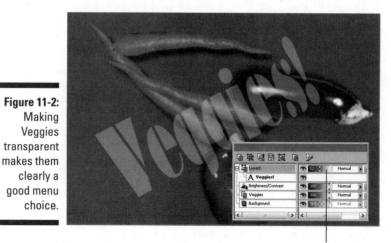

Figure 11-2: Making Veggies transparent makes them clearly a good menu choice.

Note that Layer2, which contains the text *Veggies!*, is at 52 percent opacity.

Blending images in creative ways

Sometimes, simply overlaying one image on the other doesn't give quite the effect you want. For example, if you overlay colored text on an image that has like-colored areas, you can't read the text in those areas.

In that case, the result may be better if the layer could, for example, lighten or darken the underlying image — or perhaps change the underlying color, no matter what color it is. With Paint Shop Pro, you can create those effects, and more, using *layer blending*. Layer blending is determined by two settings: *layer blend mode* and the *layer blend levels*.

To use blend modes with forethought and skill requires pondering all kinds of technical stuff about computer graphics. Do like we do: Use blend modes with reckless abandon rather than forethought and skill. Try one mode, and if you don't like the result, try another!

The right side of the Layer palette contains layer blend mode settings you can change for each layer. Until you change a layer's blend mode, it's normal, which means that the paint on that layer simply overlays the paint on lower layers, like paint on transparent plastic (see Figure 11-3).

Click the Blend Mode control for your chosen layer and choose a blend mode from the menu that appears. To restore the original appearance, choose Normal from the list of modes.

Figure 11-3:
To make
Veggies
tastier, try
another way
of blending.
Here, Blend
mode is
Exclusion,
which is
how some
kids prefer
their
veggies.

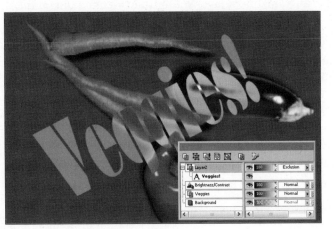

Here are a few tips:

- For maximum contrast between underlying and overlying images, try Difference mode.

- Try making the color of the overlying layer lighter or darker, if you can't get the results you want otherwise.

- Make a layer more transparent if you want to reduce the effect of any blend mode, producing a more subtle result.

- For a speckly, spray-painted look, try Dissolve mode and also make the layer partly transparent.

Using a blend mode on a group may or may not work, depending on what layers are in it; having a group with mixed raster and vector layers will almost certainly reject the attempt. If you're trying to blend a group and it's not "taking," try removing layers one by one from the group until it works.

Creating and Using Adjustment Layers

An adjustment layer is sort of like a perfect facial makeup. It doesn't cover anything up; rather, it magically changes the appearance of underlying layers. Changes include brightness or contrast, color, and other effects.

Many of these effects you can create in other ways — with commands on the Colors menu, for example. In fact, the dialog boxes for adjustment layers are *very* much like those for commands on the Colors menu, both of which we cover with one set of instructions in Chapter 7.

So, why use an adjustment layer rather than a command on the Colors menu? Here are a few good reasons:

- ✔ Adjustment layers can affect the entire, combined, multilayer image (if it's placed on top of all other layers). Most commands on the Colors menu, on the other hand, affect only the active layer.

- ✔ Adjustment layers are useful when you're using different layers to combine two images. One image may have lower contrast than the other, for example. You can put a contrast-adjustment layer above one image and put the second image above that adjustment layer so that it remains unaffected.

- ✔ An adjustment layer lets you make changes that are later easily reversible. You can simply delete the layer or change its settings if you later find that the adjustment is wrong. Otherwise, you need to counter your earlier adjustment — a trickier job than undoing or changing it.

- ✔ You can paint the layer to apply the effect in different strengths in different places! This process is admittedly a bit mind-boggling, but if you can imagine being able to paint brightness (rather than a color), for example, you have the idea. Rather than paint, you can copy an image to the layer, and the brightness of each pixel of the image determines the strength of the effect.

Adjustment layers change only the *appearance* of the underlying colors, not the *colors* of the layers. For example, when you use an adjustment layer, the colors that the Dropper tool picks up and displays on the Materials palette are the real colors — the color of the paint in the layer, not the apparent color caused by the adjustment layer.

Creating an adjustment layer

To create an adjustment layer, follow these steps:

1. **Open the Layer palette (press the F8 key) if it isn't already onscreen.**

2. **On the Layer palette, right-click the name of the layer above which you want to add the adjustment layer.**

3. **Choose Layers⇨New Adjustment Layers.**

4. **Choose the type of adjustment layer you want from the menu that appears.**

   (See the following section for information about choosing adjustment types.) The Layer Properties dialog box appears.

5. **Click the Adjustment tab, near the top of that dialog box.**

   The tab shows various sliders, and other adjustments appear, depending on your choice of layer type.

6. **Make your adjustments and click OK.**

   We describe how these adjustments work in Chapter 10.

You can delete or move adjustment layers just as you do other layers. See the section "Working on Layers," earlier in this chapter, for instructions. To rename an adjustment layer, double-click its name on the Layer palette; when the Layer Properties dialog box appears, click the General tab, enter a new name in the Name field there, and click OK.

To change these adjustments after you create a layer, double-click the layer's name on the Layer palette. You find these adjustments on the Adjustments tab of the Layer Properties dialog box that appears. It's the same dialog box that appears when you create a new adjustment layer (refer to Step 5 in the preceding list).

Choosing the type of adjustment layer you need

The Paint Shop Pro adjustment layers give you lots of different ways to fiddle with the color, contrast, and brightness of the underlying layers of your image. Here are some suggestions for what to use to achieve various results:

- ✔ To adjust brightness or contrast, use the Brightness/Contrast layer.

- ✔ The Brightness/Contrast layer affects *all* three major tonal ranges — shadows, highlights, and midtones — at one time. To independently adjust *any* of these three ranges — to just get darker shadows, for example — try a Levels layer.

- ✔ If shadows, highlights, and midtones aren't precise enough for your brightness and contrast adjustment — you need better contrast only within *specific* shadows, for example — you can adjust brightness or contrast within *any* range of tone by using a Curves layer.

- ✔ For richer/grayer or lighter/darker colors, try a Hue/Saturation layer. The Hue/Saturation layer also lets you colorize underlying layers (give them a monochrome tint).

- ✔ To make a negative image, choose an Invert layer, set the blend mode to Normal (if it isn't already), and set the opacity to 100.

- ✔ To reduce the number of colors, which results in a kind of paint-by-numbers effect, try a Posterize layer.

- ✔ To get a truly black-and-white (two colors, no shades of gray) effect, choose a Levels layer.

Applying adjustments to only certain areas

One cool feature of adjustment layers is that you can apply their effects selectively, to certain areas of your image. Paint Shop Pro uses paint on the adjustment layer to accomplish that result.

After you create the adjustment layer, you can, by using black paint, paint out the areas on that adjustment layer where you *don't* want the effect. Apply the paint to the adjustment layer with any painting tool, such as the Paint Brush tool. The paint doesn't show up as black — only as a masking-out of the effect. Use gray paint to screen out the effect. (You can also use a texture while you do this, to create some neat-looking effects.)

You can also paint in an area with white or gray, if that area is painted out. Notice that black, white, and shades of gray are the only colors the Materials palette gives you to paint with when you're working on an adjustment layer.

Using Vector Layers

Most people discover vector layers accidentally. They use the Text, Draw, or Preset Shapes tools to create vector objects, and Paint Shop Pro automatically (and without telling them) creates a vector layer to contain the vector objects these tools produce. (We explain the difference between vector and raster images and layers in the section "Choosing a Layer That's Just Your Type," earlier in this chapter.) See Chapter 12 for more information about using these tools.

You can also create vector layers intentionally, as we describe in the section "Creating a New, Blank Layer," earlier in this chapter. After you create a vector layer, you can use the Text, Draw, or Preset Shapes tool to add objects to that layer. You can also copy and paste to move these objects from one Paint Shop Pro vector layer or image to another.

You can convert a vector layer to a raster layer. The command to choose is Layers⇨Convert to Raster Layer. Converting an image to raster form allows you to apply any of the raster paint tools to your vector shape to get cool effects, such as graduated fills or airbrush spraying. The drawback is that you can then no longer edit the shape by adjusting the lines and points that make up a vector object. You can't convert a raster layer to a vector layer.

If you copy the vector layer before converting it, however, you have a backup copy of it. Simply hide it when it's not needed.

As you add vector objects to a vector layer, each object gets its own entry on the Layer palette. The left side of Figure 11-4 shows the Layer palette with two layers: the background layer and a vector layer, Vector1. To see each individual object in the vector layer, click the white box with the + sign to the left of the vector layer's icon. That action reveals the individual vector objects, indented under the layer. (To hide the objects, click that same white box again, which now holds a – symbol.)

Figure 11-4:
Clicking the + symbol next to Vector1 has revealed individual objects on the layer.

Paint Shop Pro has three kinds of vector objects: line objects, text objects, and groups of objects. Each kind of object has its own icon, as Figure 11-4 demonstrates. Vector1 contains a line object named Rectangle, a line object named Star 2, and a text object named It's Some Text. Star 2 is a single, multi-segment line that is part of the Preset Shapes object library (see Chapter 12).

Having objects listed on the Layer palette lets you select, delete, hide, or reposition them in the stack, just as you would a layer — the main difference is that each object is grouped within a vector layer, just like regular layers are grouped in layer groups.

Clicking an object on the palette selects it and displays its name in bold type. (Hold down the Shift key as you click to select multiple objects.) Pressing the Delete key deletes the selected object. Dragging it moves it up or down in the stack and enables you to place it over or under other objects. Double-clicking it reveals one of two things: If it's a text object, it displays the Text Entry dialog box; if it's a shape, it displays the Vector Property dialog box. See Chapter 12 for more information about managing vector objects.

Merging Layers

Using multiple layers usually makes working with images easier. Sometimes, however, you would rather have (or need to have) everything on one layer. For example, you may want to use one of the commands on the Colors menu on the entire image, but the command works on only a single layer. Or, if you try to save your image as something other than a Paint Shop Pro file, Paint Shop Pro may offer to merge all the layers for you. (Merging can sometimes be necessary because not many file types support multiple layers. Adobe Photoshop is the most popular format that supports layers.)

If Paint Shop Pro merges layers when you're saving a file, it merges layers only in the file you're creating on your disk drive. It doesn't merge the layers in the image you're working on in Paint Shop Pro.

Paint Shop Pro gives you two ways to merge layers into one layer. To merge all the layers (including those whose visibility is switched off), choose Layers⇨ Merge⇨Merge All. To merge only the visible layers (leaving the hidden ones as layers), choose Layers⇨Merge⇨Merge Visible. To merge a group into one handy layer, choose Layers⇨Merge⇨Merge Group. Choosing Layers⇨Merge⇨ Merge Down merges the selected layer with the one underneath it.

What happens when you merge? Nothing *visible* happens to your image when you merge. The merged layers, however, become one normal (raster) layer, named Merged, that you see listed on the Layer palette. Any vector layers (typically text, lines, or preset shapes) are converted into raster images, so you can't edit them any more with the text, drawing, or shape tools. When adjustment layers are merged, they no longer simply affect the image appearance; rather, they modify the underlying colors.

Chapter 12

Adding Layers of Text or Shapes

· ·

In This Chapter

▶ Not getting lost when you use objects and layers

▶ Vectorizing versus rasterizing

▶ Playing with text

▶ Modifying lines and shapes

▶ Changing colors, fills, and whatnot

▶ Positioning and arranging objects

· ·

Given a paintbrush, most of us would have trouble making nice, neat text, regular shapes like circles, or even straight lines. We would clamor for a typewriter, template, ruler, or some other special tool that gives nice straight edges and shapes.

Clamor not. Paint Shop Pro offers multiple tools for creating such stuff and one to help you manage the stuff you create. Figure 12-1 shows those tools as they appear at the bottom of the Tools toolbar.

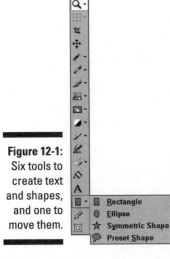

Figure 12-1:
Six tools to create text and shapes, and one to move them.

Unless you tell Paint Shop Pro otherwise, these tools create text, lines, and shapes in a special vector form that makes them easier to change. Images in this form are known as *vector objects*. Unlike the other things you can paint or otherwise create in Paint Shop Pro, vector objects aren't a collection of pixels (colored dots). Instead, they're shapes that have color, line width, and other properties. These easily modified shapes can exist only on special *vector layers*.

So, you ask in businesslike, Donald Trump fashion, "What's the upshot?" Here's the bottom line:

✔ **Creating stuff as vector objects:** If you use the Paint Shop Pro text, line, or shape tools in the normal, vector way, your creations are easier to modify — but you have to know how to deal with layers and the special features of vector objects. Refer to Chapter 11 for help with layers, and we explain vector features in this chapter.

✔ *Not* **creating stuff as vector objects:** If you don't want to bother with vector layers and special vector object features, you can create text, lines, and shapes as though they were painted with a brush. This form is called *raster* form. If you're such a dedicated, um, rasterfarian, you must do this: After you select your tool but *before you create the object,* go to the Tool Options palette (press F4 if it's not visible). For any object other than text (shapes or lines), click to clear the check mark in the Create As Vector check box. For text as a raster selection, choose Selection or Floating from the drop-down Create As menu on the Tool Options palette. Eh, but we talk about it in the next section. Your choice of raster remains unless you change it. No problem, *mon.*

If you need to work on vector objects with raster tools (like the Paint Brush or Eraser tools), you can convert a vector layer to a raster layer. Choose Layers➪Convert To Raster Layer. You can't convert back, however (though you can use the Undo function if you have done the conversion recently).

Keeping Track of Objects and Layers

Here's the most important thing to remember about adding text, lines, or shapes: If you try to add these types of vector objects to a normal, raster image (such as a digital photograph), Paint Shop Pro automatically, and quietly, creates a vector layer to hold the new object.

If you want to return to the rest of the image, you have to switch to the layer on which the image lives. For example, if you add text to a photograph (which usually appears on the background layer), in order to work on the image, you need to press F8 to see the Layer palette (if it's not visible already) and then select the background layer.

Antialiasing for smoother edges

Shapes with nice, sharp edges tend to look a bit ragged when those edges run in any direction other than perfectly horizontal or vertical. They develop an objectionable staircase look called *aliasing. Antialiasing* is a process of filling in those steps with a little bit of color, which gives the illusion of a straighter, if slightly fuzzier, edge. To antialias objects, place a check mark in the Antialias check box on the Tool Options palette.

To add text, lines, or shapes in a nice, controlled fashion, where you know exactly what layer every object is on, create or select a vector layer before you create or paste a vector object. Refer to Chapter 11 for help with creating and choosing layers. As you put vector objects on a vector layer, each object is listed separately, indented under the vector layer's name on the Layer palette. Click the + sign to the left of the layer's name to display these objects individually. From within the Layer palette, you can select, reorder, rename, or delete objects; refer to the discussion of using vector layers in Chapter 11.

Adding and Editing Text

Text in Paint Shop Pro isn't just your grandfather's plain old letters and numbers. Oh, my gracious, no. Although you can certainly have plain text in a straight line, you can also have it filled or outlined with colors and patterns, bend it around curves, or rotate it into a jaunty angle. It's truly the cat's pajamas!

Creating, placing, and editing text

Text has two parts: an outline, set by the Materials palette's foreground controls, and a fill, set by the background controls. You can have both or either.

If you already have a vector layer (one that has text, lines, or shapes on it), you can put your text on that same layer; just choose the layer now on the Layer palette. Or, you can create a new vector layer on which to put your text. If your active layer is a raster layer (background, for example), Paint Shop Pro creates a new vector layer for you in the following steps. If you're not familiar with layers, don't worry about all this layer stuff for now.

Begin with the Materials palette open. Press F6 if you don't see it, and refer to Chapter 10 for details about what's what on that palette.

Here's how to create basic text:

1. **Click the Text tool (as shown in the margin) on the toolbar.**

2. **If you want outlined text, do the following:**

   a. Choose the inside color by *right*-clicking any color on the Materials palette. This action sets the background color. (For a more sophisticated fill material, left-click the Background and Fill Properties box to open a Material Properties dialog box. For guidance, refer to the section in Chapter 10 about choosing a color for the very picky.

   If you want to have *just* an outline, leaving the middle of the letters completely see-through, click the Transparency button under the Background and Fill Properties box. (It's the rightmost button, and should have the international circle-with-a-slash No sign in it.) The box turns gray and contains an international No sign of its own, indicating that the background color is now set to no color. (If this confuses you, refer to Chapter 10 to understand these kooky Material boxes.)

   b. Choose a foreground color (the outline) by left-clicking the Foreground and Stroke Properties box. On the Tool Options palette, set the value in the Stroke Width dialog box to the width of the outline you want, in pixels. For example, for an outline 4 pixels wide, set it to 4.

3. **If you want solid (filled) text (no outline):**

   a. On the Materials palette, click the transparency button under the Foreground and Stroke Properties box. (It's the rightmost of the three tiny buttons there.) The box turns gray and contains an international No sign of its own.

   b. Choose a background color by left-clicking the Background and Fill Material box and selecting one from the Materials palette.

   In Paint Shop Pro, a material is a combination of a color, pattern, and texture. It's just as easy to use gradients and patterns as the foregrounds and backgrounds of text as it is to use colors, as we show you in Figure 12-2 — and it makes things look so much snazzier! Again, refer to Chapter 10 to unveil mysteries of the Material boxes.

4. **Click your image where you want the center of your text.**

   The text entry dialog box appears, as shown in Figure 12-2. Note that a preview of your text, as it appears when you click OK, appears on your image. You can change your choices here by changing what's in the Foreground and Background Property boxes.

   Figure 12-2 shows how the Tool Options palette controls the width (and style) of the text outline. If you don't see the Tool Options palette, press F4.

5. **Choose a font from the Font drop-down menu on the Tool Options palette.**

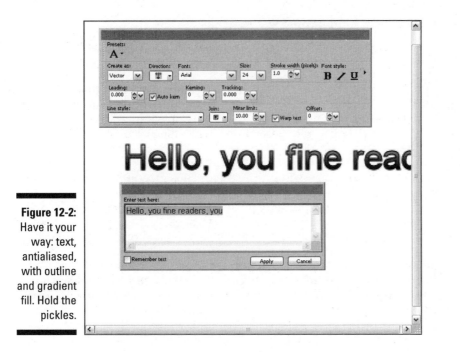

Figure 12-2:
Have it your
way: text,
antialiased,
with outline
and gradient
fill. Hold the
pickles.

6. **Choose a font size from the Size selection box or manually enter any other size you want, in points, on the Tool Options palette.**

7. **Enter your text in the big box labeled Enter Text Here.**

   The text appears in your chosen font and size. For long, multiline text, you can press the Enter key to start a new line. If you have multiple lines of text, decide how you want them aligned (left-justified, centered, or right-justified) by clicking the appropriate button in the upper-right corner of the Tool Options palette.

   If you know that you will use the same text the next time you use the Text tool, you can check the Remember Text check box, next to the OK button.

8. **To selectively apply any font style (bold, italic, underlined, or strikethrough), drag across the text you want styled to highlight it. Then click the B, *I*, U, or A (strikethrough) buttons on the Tool Options palette, just as you would in most word processors.**

   You can also selectively change the font or size of any text by highlighting the text and then choosing a new font or size.

9. **For vector text, remember to choose Vector from the Create As menu on the Tool Options palette.**

   If you prefer raster text, choose Selection to create a nonfloating selection (or Floating to create a floating selection). If you don't care, use Vector.

10. **Click the OK button when you're done.**

    While you're using the text entry dialog box, it displays a continuously updated preview of your work in the image window.

Your text appears attractively displayed in a rectangular frame that has squares *(handles)* around it. This *selection frame* means that your text object is selected. You can do several things to the text object now, including move, resize, rotate, or delete it. See the section "Controlling Your Objects," later in this chapter.

You can also edit your text. With the Text tool chosen, double-click directly on the body (outline or fill) of the text. The cursor turns into a 4-headed arrow when your cursor is properly positioned; clicking and dragging allows you to reposition it, whereas double-clicking brings up that darned text entry dialog box all over again, where you can change the text or its appearance.

You can turn text into shapes, if you like. For example, you may want to alter the shape, rotation, or other attributes of a text character in a creative way. Select the text you want to convert and then choose Objects➪Convert Text to Curves. Then, to make each character an individually selectable, movable, rotatable object, choose As Character Shapes. If you want the characters to remain part of a single object, choose As Single Shape.

Bending text to follow a line or shape

Is your theatre company performing *The Wizard of Oz*? Before you can click your heels together three times and say "There's no place like home," you can make the text on your advertising posters follow the yellow brick road — or any other (vector) shape or line in Paint Shop Pro. Figure 12-3 shows a before (top) and after (bottom) picture of fitting text to a line.

Here's how to do your own:

1. **Create your (vector) text.**

   See the preceding two sections for help with text.

2. **Create your shape or line.**

   See the rest of this chapter for help with lines or shapes. Bear in mind that if a line is created from left to right, text ends up on top of that line. If a closed shape is created clockwise, text ends up on the inside. In both instances, the opposite direction gives opposite results.

3. **Click the Object Selection tool.**

If you just want to shape the text — you don't really want the line (or shape) itself to appear — take one additional step before proceeding to Step 4. The selection frame is still around your shape or line from its creation, and you have chosen the Object Selection tool. Now, click the Properties button on the Tool Options palette. In the Properties dialog box that now appears, click to clear the Visible check box and click OK. Your chosen shape becomes invisible, and the selection frame remains.

4. **Hold down the Shift key and click the text, which places both the line and text within the selection frame.**

   The top illustration in Figure 12-3 shows this stage of the game.

5. **Choose Objects⇨Fit Text to Path.**

   Zap! Wanda the Good Witch puts your text safely on the yellow brick road to Oz. The bottom part of Figure 12-3 shows the result of fitting text to the path.

Don't use solid-color-filled shapes if you intend for your text to be on the inside of the shape — the fill hides your text! A gradient, textured, or patterned fill, however, usually allows your text to be seen.

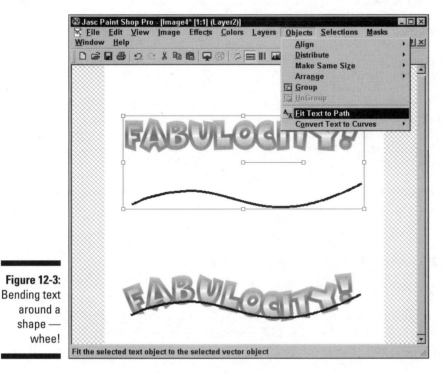

Figure 12-3:
Bending text around a shape — whee!

Drawing Lines and Shapes

Paint Shop Pro is a quirky little devil. It makes drawing lines and shapes so darned easy that it's not even funny, which allows you to draw point-to-point, like connect-the-dots, to draw freehand like a crayon, or even a combination of the two. And, if you want shapes, hoo-boy! You can select stars, diamonds, and lucky clovers (not really) from a drop-down menu. Simple!

What about *adjusting* those lines and shapes when you have drawn them? That's a bit trickier and involves adjusting things called nodes — but we walk you through that process in the next section — never fear. After all, we're professionals: professional dummies.

Setting line and fill color for lines and shapes

To determine how lines and outlines look, choose a foreground color, style, or texture (or all of them) on the Color palette before creating the line or shape. To determine how fills look (unless you're making a single straight-line segment, where fill doesn't apply), choose a *background* material from the Background Material box before creating the line or shape. (Remember that a *material* is a combination of a color, pattern, or gradient and any textures you choose to add to it.)

Note that for open shapes (a curvy line, for example), if you use fill, it fills the area between the starting and ending points of the shape. In many such cases, you may want to turn off background (fill) material altogether: Click the Transparent button on the right side, just underneath the Background Material box.

If you have already created a line or shape and want to change its appearance, see the section "Changing Colors and Other Properties," later in this chapter.

Drawing single lines and connected line segments

To draw a straight (vector) line or a series of connected straight lines, click the Pen tool on the Tools toolbar and then follow these steps:

1. **Choose a foreground color, style, or texture (or all three).**

   Left-click the Foreground Material box on the Color palette. Refer to Chapter 3 for more help.

2. Set the mode to Drawing, as shown in Figure 12-4.

Press F4 to bring up the Tool Options palette if you don't see it.

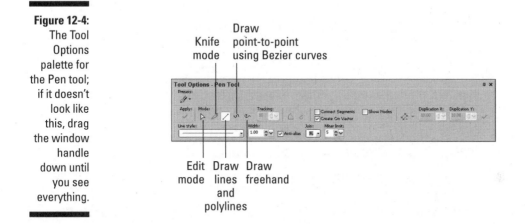

3. Click the Draw Lines button from the Tool Options palette, as shown in Figure 12-4.

4. Also on the Tool Options palette, set the Width value to the width (in pixels) of the line you want.

All the Paint Shop Pro value boxes offer a nifty way to adjust them: Click and hold the big down arrow on the right side of the value box and drag left or right in the slider that appears.

You can also choose a line style (like dashes or barbed wire) for your line at this time by choosing a style from the Line Style drop-down menu, also on the Tool Options palette.

5. Enable the Connect Segments check box if you want to play connect-the-dots: make multiple, connected straight lines.

Clear that check box to make separate lines.

6. Drag or click line end points.

If you want lines drawn at perfect 90-degree or 45-degree angles (perfect horizontal, vertical, or diagonal lines), hold down the Shift key before you drag or click, and Paint Shop Pro snaps your lines to the nine compass points.

To move individual line segments, or move the points where line segments connect, enable the Show Modes check box. Your line appears with square dots (handles) around the perimeter. Drag the dots to move them. For more flexibility in changing lines, see "Picking at Your Nodes," later in this chapter.

With all vector shapes, click the Apply button on the Tools toolbar after each shape if you want that shape to be an independent object. Otherwise, objects are all linked together even if they appear separate.

Drawing freehand lines or shapes

Freehand lines are basically any old scribble you want to make (or almost so). Here's how to scribble in high-technology land. Click the Pen tool on the Tool toolbar, choose your color (together with any textures, patterns, or gradients) from the material boxes, and then follow these steps:

1. **On the Materials palette (press F6 if it's not already visible), click the Transparent button in the Background and Fill Properties box.**

   This step ensures that whatever shape you draw doesn't get filled in like a closed blob. If you want a filled shape, choose a material instead.

2. **On the Tool Options palette (if the palette isn't onscreen, press F4), click the Draw Freehand button.**

3. **Also on the Tool Options palette, set the Width value to the width (in pixels) of the line you want; also, set the line style and other options.**

4. **Drag any old way on your image.**

5. **If you want to turn your line into a shape (with a closed line), click the Close Selected Open Contours button on the Tool Options palette when you're done.**

6. **If you want to start a new, unrelated line elsewhere on the canvas, click Apply on the Tool Options palette. Otherwise, your lines are visually separate but linked together.**

Paint Shop Pro has this *adorable* habit of keeping everything you draw with the Pen tool joined. Even if you draw a squiggle in one corner, start a new contour, and then draw a loop on the other side of the screen, Paint Shop Pro thinks of them as one big shape — even if they're not connected. If you want to draw two entirely separate shapes so that you can apply separate fills and strokes to them, make sure that you click the Apply button between shapes.

If you enable the Show Modes check box,, your line appears with square dots (handles) around the perimeter. Drag any handle around the outside of the rectangle to resize or reorient your line.

The line is a clever, automatically constructed, connect-the-dots line. If you want to drag a line that follows your tight turns more smoothly, you need dots that are closer together. For a line more obviously made up of line segments that connect dots, the dots need to be farther apart. On the Tool Options palette, you can set that closeness by adjusting the Curve Tracking value: smaller for closer dots and larger for more widely spaced dots.

Making curved lines

To make curved lines, you lay down a series of points where Paint Shop Pro makes the line bend. Click the Pen tool on the Tools toolbar and ensure that the Tool Options palette is visible (if it's not, press F4).

On the Tool Options palette, click the Draw Point-to-Point Bezier Curve button (which looks like a lumpy *S* on its side). To make just a single curve, make sure that the Connect Segments check box is clear; to make curve after curve, enable that check box.

You click to lay down the points, but don't just click when you place your dots — click where you want the dot, and then keep your mouse button down and drag a little. As you drag, you pull out an arrow by its tip. Your line no longer bends sharply at the dot. Here's how that arrow works for you:

 ✔ As you drag the arrow longer, the curve gets broader at the dot. If you make the arrow shorter again, the curve gets sharper at the dot.

 ✔ When the arrow appears, you can release the mouse button and make your adjustments by dragging either end of the arrow.

 ✔ If you drag either end of the arrow around the dot, your line rotates to stay parallel to the arrow where the line and arrow pass through the dot.

Figure 12-5 shows the effect of dragging the tip of the arrow. On the left, a curved line is created and the arrow appears for the latest dot. On the right, the arrow's tip is being extended and dragged upward a bit. You can see how the curve broadens and changes angle to follow the arrow's direction.

Figure 12-5: Making a curved line. On the right, dragging the arrow's tip to adjust the curve.

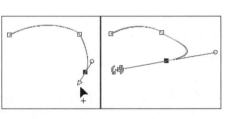

Adding shapes

Need a square? Need a star? The Paint Shop Pro shapes tool group lets you choose from a wide range of predetermined shapes, including circles, rectangles, stars, triangles, and cool icons.

 In the margin appears the one tool, Preset Shapes, that can deliver any shape known to Paint Shop Pro. The Preset Shapes tool lives with three of its more specialized cousins in the tool group that is third from the bottom on the Tools toolbar (refer to Figure 12-1). These other cousins (Rectangle, Ellipse, and Symmetrical Shape) are really just convenient shortcuts to access commonly used shapes. Use them if you like — they work similarly. We discuss only Preset Shapes here.

 Preset shapes are normally vector objects (as are text, lines, and arbitrary shapes). If you prefer them as raster (normal, bitmap) objects, make sure that the Vector option box is cleared on the Tool Options palette. If you create any vector object, it must be on a vector layer. If your active layer isn't a vector layer, Paint Shop Pro adds a vector layer for you and places the shape there.

If you like, you can edit the shapes of preset shapes after you have placed them in your image. Follow the instructions in the section "Picking at Your Nodes," later in this chapter.

When you're done adding preset shapes and you want to work on other parts of the image, you may need to change to another layer — probably the background layer. Otherwise, refer to Chapter 11 for the skinny.

Dragging a shape

The Preset Shapes tool can deliver a shape from its library of shapes in any size, proportion, color, gradient, pattern, or texture you like! Like text and drawn shapes in Paint Shop Pro, preset shapes have two parts: the outline and the fill. Follow these steps:

1. **Click the Preset Shapes tool on the Tools toolbar.**

2. **If you want your shape to have an outline, do the following:**

   On the Materials palette (press F6), click the Foreground *and* Stroke Properties box and choose a color from the dialog box that pops up. For a gradient or patterned outline, switch to the appropriate tab; refer to Chapter 10 for help on how to set gradients, patterns, or textures.

On the Tool Options palette, set the value in the Width dialog box to the width of the outline you want, in pixels. For example, for an outline 4 pixels wide, set it to 4.

If you want to use a styled outline (like arrows or dashes) to surround your shape rather than a solid line, choose a custom line from the drop-down Line Style menu, also on the Tool Options palette.

If you want no outline, click the Transparent button on the right side underneath the Background Material box.

3. **Select a fill for your shape.**

   Click the Background and *Fill* Properties box and choose a color from the dialog box that pops up. For a gradient or patterned outline, switch to the appropriate tab; refer to Chapter 3 for help on how to set gradients, patterns, or textures.

   If you don't want your shape filled (that is, you want just the outline of a shape), click the Transparent button on the right side underneath the Foreground and Stroke Properties box.

4. **On the Tool Options palette, click the down arrow next to the Shapes preview box and choose a shape in the gallery of preset shapes that appears.**

   The Tool Options palette and its gallery of shapes appear.

5. **If you want to use the colors, styles, and textures you chose in Steps 1 and 2, make sure that the Retain Style check box is unchecked on the Tool Options palette.**

   Otherwise, if that box is checked, Paint Shop Pro uses the colors, line width, and other properties of the original shape that is stored in the shape library.

6. **Drag diagonally on your image.**

   As you drag, your chosen shape appears and expands. (The colors and other style attributes don't appear until you release the mouse button.) If you drag more horizontally than vertically, the shape is flattened. Likewise, dragging more vertically gives you a skinny shape. Hold down the Shift key as you click and drag to create a shape with the original proportions that's not skinny or fat.

   When you release the mouse button, your shape appears fully colored and filled according to your choices. The shape appears within the usual Paint Shop Pro object selection frame, which means that you can redimension the shape by dragging any of the handles (squares) around the edge of that frame. To rotate your shape, drag the handle at the end of the arm that sticks out from the center of the frame. A star is born: Figure 12-6 shows the various elements we have discussed in the preceding steps.

Figure 12-6:
A star is born, using the Preset Shapes tool. Because the Retain Style check box is cleared on the Tool Options palette, the outline and fill chosen on the Materials palette apply.

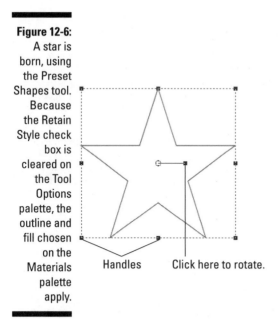

Handles   Click here to rotate.

Picking at Your Nodes

Paint Shop Pro users have an old saying: "You can pick your friends and you can pick your nodes, but you can't pick your friend's nodes." It's not true, of course, but that doesn't keep users from saying it. You can freely pick, or pick at, all your nodes — including your friend's nodes, if that person gives you a Paint Shop Pro file with vector lines or shapes in it.

If you want to alter a shape or a line after you have drawn it, you need to get down and dirty and start changing the nodes. *Nodes* are the dots that Paint Shop Pro plays connect-the-dots with to create lines and shapes; you can move nodes, remove them, or change how the line passes through them.

To start fiddling with nodes, you need to select the Pen tool and click the Edit Mode button on the Tool Options palette (right under the word *Mode*).

When you have the Pen tool selected, even if you're not in Node Edit mode, enable the Show Nodes check box and you still have node-editing options available. This redundancy is nice, but makes a fine distinction between Edit mode and Draw mode generally a little fuzzy to the casual user — or even to the writers of *Dummies* books, for that matter. You can tell that you can edit nodes if you can see the nodes (tiny squares) along the line. Also, your cursor turns solid black, and the nodes turn black when you click them.

To enter Node Edit mode, follow these steps:

1. **Select the Pen tool.**

2. **On the Tool Options palette, click the Edit mode button.**

After you're in Edit mode, you can manipulate your nodes all you want. Here are some changes you can make:

- ✔ To select a node for any action (like deleting, dragging, or changing its type), click it. You know that you can select it when a 4-headed arrow appears under the cursor; you know that a node is selected when it's solid black.

- ✔ To move a node, drag it. You can move multiple nodes at one time as long as they're all selected.

- ✔ To delete a node, press Delete.

- ✔ To select several nodes, hold down the Shift key while clicking them.

- ✔ To select several nodes at one time, make sure that you're in Node Edit mode (this action doesn't work if you're in Drawing or Knife mode) and draw a square around the nodes you want to select.

- ✔ To select *all* nodes, right-click a node and choose Edit⇨Select All from the context menu that pops up.

- ✔ To join two line segments that are part of the same object (for example, if they were created by cutting a line in half with the Pen tool in Knife mode), select the two ends you want to join by Shift+clicking both of them and then right-click your image and choose Edit⇨Join.

If your vector shape is the only vector layer in your image, you may be able to select nodes in it, regardless of which layer you're in — which is a direct reversal of everything we have told you in all the other layer sections. (Paint Shop Pro loves to make us look foolish.) However, if you have more than one vector layer in an image, you can select nodes from only the vector object you have selected. For more information on what these layers are, look to Chapter 11.

Note that a line has *direction,* based on the order in which you create the line. The control arrow that appears on a node in Node Edit mode points in the line's direction. The word *Start* or *End* that appears when you pause your mouse cursor over end nodes of a line also tells you the direction. A few things you do may be dependent on direction, such as aligning text to the line or shape.

Slicing Alongside Your Nodes

The Pen tool is mightier than the Sword tool — or would be, if a Sword tool existed. Ironically, though, Knife mode is a part of the Pen tool, and it's mightier than the *rest* of the Pen tool, by slicing in half the lines and shapes you have drawn.

Select Knife mode from the Tool Options palette and drag a line through your vector object. This action separates your object into two separate sets of nodes, cut cleanly where you drew through them with the knife. Be warned that even if you separate an image in two with the knife, both still count as one vector object.

Changing Colors and Other Properties

Don't like the color or some other look of your vector text, shape, or line? No problem. Put on colored glasses — or use the Vector Properties dialog box. Sound like fun? No? Well, it *is* fun. Follow these steps:

1. **Click the Object Selection tool at the bottom of the Tools toolbar.**

2. **Select the object or objects you want to modify.**

   The selection frame appears around your chosen object or group of objects. See the following section for different ways to select objects.

3. **Right-click the object and then choose Properties from the context menu that drops down.**

The Vector Property dialog box, as shown in Figure 12-7, makes the scene. With this puppy onscreen, you can change all kinds of features.

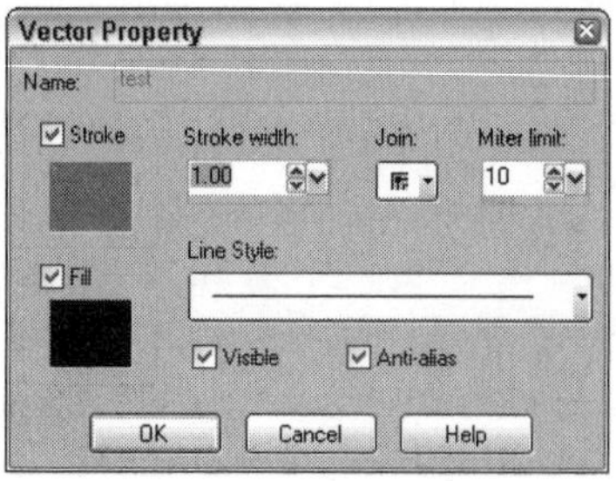

Figure 12-7:
Change
color, or
darned near
anything
else, in the
Vector
Property
dialog box.

Here's a list of what you can change:

- **Object name:** If you have lots of different objects in your image, you may find naming them useful. Enter a name in the Name text box, if you like.

- **(In)visibility:** Clear the Visible check box to make your object invisible. What good is an invisible object? It's useful mainly as a hidden curve for text to follow. Refer to the section "Bending text to follow a line or shape," earlier in this chapter, to find out how to make text follow a curve.

- **Aliasing (staircasing):** Place a check mark in the Anti-alias check box to avoid the jaggies (jagged edges) that afflict the edges of computer-generated shapes.

- **Color/gradient/pattern/texture:** The Styles and Textures swatches work just like the ones on the Material palette, except that you can't make them transparent from here.

- **Thickness of line or outline:** For a thicker line, adjust the Stroke Width value upward.

- **Dashed line or outline:** Click the Line Style drop-down list and choose something appropriately cool.

The rest of the controls have to do with joins. The term *join* refers to the point that forms where line segments meet. Paint Shop Pro offers three basic types of join, which you select by clicking the arrow next to the Join drop-down list box and then choosing one of these options:

- **Miter:** A miter join (what Paint Shop Pro normally creates) is one that ends in a point. It *tries* to end in a point, anyway. If the lines meet at an acute angle, Paint Shop Pro gives up in disgust and creates a flat (beveled) end. The point at which it gives up is controlled by the value in the Miter Limit value box. Fiddle with it this way:

  - If you want a point, increase the Miter Limit value.
  - If you want a flat end, decrease the Miter Limit value.

- **Round:** A round join is one that is, well, round at the point. Enough said.

- **Bevel:** A bevel join is one that is flat at the point, like a miter join that has reached its miter limit (or a computer user who has reached her limit and has been banging her head against the wall).

These join settings are available when you first create a line or shape, on the Tool Options palette.

Controlling Your Objects

Creating objects is one thing; getting them to do what you want is another — sort of like having kids. If the time has come to discipline your vector objects, Paint Shop Pro can make them straighten up and fly right.

Lots of illustrations need objects that are precisely centered, balanced, or distributed evenly. You can certainly arrange objects by dragging them and rotating them. For drill-team precision, however, you should also check out the Paint Shop Pro vector object positioning talents.

Selecting and grouping vector objects

To do anything to an existing object, you need to select it first. Vector objects (the usual Paint Shop Pro form of text, lines, and shapes) have their own selection tool — the Object Selection tool. The Other Paint Shop Pro selection tools (the Magic Wand, Freehand, and Selection tools) don't work on vector objects.

Click the Object Selection tool that appears on the Tools toolbar and then do one of the following:

- ✔ **Click your vector object to select it.** If the object has gaps in it (spaces between letters, for example), don't click the gaps. Even if the object isn't on your active layer, the tool selects the object. Your layer selection doesn't change.

- ✔ **Drag around one or more objects.** Whatever vector objects you drag around become selected. Selecting multiple objects lets you treat them as a group for many purposes: You can change their color, change other properties, or use the Paint Shop Pro automatic arrangement features.

- ✔ **Hold down the Shift key and click multiple objects to select a group.** To remove objects from that selection, hold down the Ctrl key and click them.

You don't need to use the Object Selection tool. With the Layer palette open, you can click the object's name on the list of layers.

A selection frame appears around your object or group of objects, with squares (handles) you can drag to move, resize, or rotate the object or group.

To create a single object out of multiple objects, select them all and choose Objects⇨Group. To ungroup them again, select the group and choose Objects⇨ UnGroup.

To deselect, press Ctrl+D or choose Selections⇨Select None from the menu bar. To select all objects, press Ctrl+A or choose Selections⇨Select All.

Paint Shop Pro selects an object automatically after you create it so that you can move, resize, or rotate the object. You can tell that the object is selected by the rectangular frame that appears around it. Even though the object is selected, however, you can't access the same context menu (the thing that pops up when you right-click) that you could access if you had selected the object with the Object Selection tool! For example, you can't change the object's color unless you first select the object with the Object Selection tool.

Deleting, copying, pasting, and editing

As with nearly any Windows program, you can delete, cut, copy, or paste selected objects in Paint Shop Pro by using the Windows Clipboard. First, select the object with the Object Selection tool. Next, do any of the following:

- ✔ **Copy, cut, or delete:** Use the conventional Windows keystrokes (Ctrl+X to cut, Ctrl+C to copy, and the Delete key to delete) or the familiar tool-bar buttons Cut (scissors icon) or Copy (2-documents icon).

- ✔ **Paste:** You can use the conventional Paste command (Ctrl+V) and Paste button (Clipboard-with-document icon). These conventional methods, however, create an entire, new image from the Clipboard contents. More likely, you want to paste the object as a new object on the current layer. For that, choose Edit⇨Paste⇨As New Vector Selection or press Ctrl+G on your keyboard. Your copied object appears and is selected so that you can position it; click to anchor it. Another alternative is to paste your object as a new layer: Choose Edit⇨Paste⇨As New Layer or press Ctrl+L.

Positioning, arranging, and sizing by hand

To move an object (or group of objects), select it with the Object Selection tool. You can then position it in the following ways:

- ✔ **Move it:** Click anywhere on an object (on the outline or fill, but not in gaps like the spaces between letters), and then you can drag it anywhere. Or, you can drag the object by the square handle in the center of the selection frame. You can tell when your cursor is properly positioned over the square handle because the cursor displays a 4-headed arrow.

- ✔ **Resize or reproportion it:** Drag any corner of the frame, or any side of the frame, by one of the square handles to resize the object or group. By default, Paint Shop Pro keeps the proportions constant; if you want to drag one corner away to skew your shape, hold down the Shift key as you drag, and if you want to change the perspective, hold down Ctrl. These work pretty much like the Deformation tool, described in Chapter 4.

✔ **Place it on top of or underneath another object:** Vector objects can overlay one another, so sometimes you need to control which object is on top of which. Envision them in a stack and the following menu choices on the Objects⇨Arrange menu make sense:

- Bring to Top (puts your selected object on top of all)

- Move Up (raises your object in the stack)

- Move Down (lowers your object in the stack)

- Send to Bottom (puts your object on the bottom of the stack)

Alternatively, you can see the stack of objects on the Layer palette and adjust an object's positioning by dragging it up or down. Refer to Chapter 11, where we discuss managing vector and other layers.

✔ **Rotate it:** Sticking out from the center square is an arm that ends in a square handle. Pause your mouse cursor over that handle so that the mouse cursor displays a pair of circling arrows. Drag the handle around the center square to rotate your object.

✔ **Delete it:** Press the Delete key on your keyboard.

Chapter 13

Adding Artsy Effects

*T*his chapter is, without a doubt, the most entertaining one in this book. Oh, we're not saying that the other chapters aren't useful — you need to know how to do the everyday tasks, like scanning photos, and we can make it painless. But we can't do much to make those everyday tasks *riveting*. Nobody's reading through Chapter 5 and giggling as they scan photo after photo and titter, "Look! The light on the platen is moving! How cool is *that?*"

Rest assured, you *will* giggle at some of the stuff you can do in this chapter. With a few mouse clicks, you can turn a photo of your back yard into a watercolor painting! You can make your image all wavy, like a Scooby Doo flashback! You can even twist your photo into a compact, reflective sphere! Now, *that's* cool.

Paint Shop Pro has enough wild and crazy effects to satisfy the most *avant garde artistes* (also known as psycho art geeks). The Effects menu in Paint Shop Pro 9 hides more than 70 different effects that you can apply to your images — and they can make some dramatic differences, by surrounding your image with a wooden picture frame, showering your picture with colored lights, or adding leather and fur textures. These gadgets are great fun, and incredible timesavers when you need a striking effect in a hurry.

Many of these effects use adjustment dialog boxes, which all have a set of common controls for zooming, previewing, proofing, and other functions. Refer to Chapter 7 for help in using these controls — specifically, the section about understanding the Paint Shop Pro dialog boxes. We don't repeat those instructions here.

Paint Shop Pro categorizes its creative effects into these ten major categories:

- **3D effects:** For turning selected areas into raised buttons or cutouts, dropping shadows, or doing anything else that looks like it's raised above or dropped below the page.

- **Art Media effects:** For simulating physical art media, like pencil, colored chalk, and paint brushing.

- **Artistic effects:** For changing your picture into another media entirely, like a big neon glow, a topographical map, or a tinfoil stamp.

- **Distortion effects:** For warping the surface of your image, by sending gentle ripples across the top of it, making it look like you're looking at it through a big lens, or pixelating parts of it just like they do whenever someone is exposing too much flesh on *Cops*.

- **Edge effects:** For finding the edges within a picture and bringing them into focus or softening those edges into a fine Silly Putty-ish blur.

- **Geometric effects:** For wrapping or distorting the image as a whole. In Distortion Effects, you change the surface, but the picture still stays the same size and shape; in Geometric Effects, you can wrap your picture around a can, or stre-e-e-tch it like it was a big rubber band.

- **Illumination effects:** For introducing a sunburst or placing one or more spotlights on parts of the image.

- **Image effects:** A catchall category for creating tiles, moving images slightly, or creating a page-curl effect.

- **Reflection effects:** For holding a mirror — or several mirrors — up to your fabulous image, creating a simple reverse image or a funhouse array of reflections.

- **Texture effects:** For giving your image the effect of being laid on different surfaces, like crinkled paper or leather, or seen through mosaic glass.

Effects, like most other features of Paint Shop Pro, are applied only to the active layer you're working on — and, if you have an area selected, only within that selection. This restriction is designed to let you modify just the portion of the image you want, but it can also be confusing if you forget that you have a selection or have changed layers: Your effect may not appear to work. If your image has multiple layers, make sure that you're on the layer you want the effect applied to.

If you're working with a photograph or scanned picture, your image probably has just a single layer. (Every image contains at least one layer, known as the background layer.) For more information on layers — which are *fantastically* handy things to know about — check out Chapter 11.

Also, effects don't work on Vector or Adjustment layers. If you use an Adjustment layer, you must merge it with your image if you want your effect to act on that adjustment.

Effects don't work on 256-color images. If your image has 256 or fewer colors, Paint Shop Pro asks whether it's okay to automatically increase the color depth to 16.7 million. Click OK, and then see Chapter 16 if you want it to stop asking these silly questions.

If you use a certain adjustment often, you can save its settings as *presets;* see Chapter 18 for more details on this timesaver.

Try 'Em On: Browsing the Effects

An easy way to try an effect on your image is to use the *Effect Browser.* Choose Effects⇨Effect Browser. The Effect Browser dialog box appears, as shown in Figure 13-1.

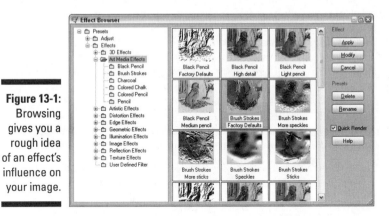

Figure 13-1:
Browsing gives you a rough idea of an effect's influence on your image.

Choose an effect on the left side; as you can see in Figure 13-1, each of the effects is grouped into ten subfolders stored in the Effects folder — conveniently enough, there's one subfolder for each of the ten categories we list in the preceding section.

You can expand a folder by clicking the plus box to the left of it, or you can collapse the folder by clicking the minus sign. Click in any of the folders to get samples of all the effects within each folder; the preview window on the right side gives you a tiny preview of what the effect does to your image. If you have a selected area (or if the active layer contains only one filled-in area), that area fills the preview window.

Note: A folder named Adjustments has a bunch of filters and corrections that you can apply in order to improve photo quality. We go over most of the relevant adjustments in Part II, but feel free to click the Adjustments folder if you want to see a constellation of color shifts, blurs, and focusings.

If your computer is taking a long time to render the effects, click the Quick Render check box on the right side, which creates a quick-and-dirty thumbnail version of the effects. If you want the full Monty in finely rendered glory, feel free to uncheck the box.

A given subfolder often holds several variations on a single effect. For example, an Artistic effect named Chrome makes your image look shiny and reflective. But, when you look in the Artistic Effects folder, you can see many different Chrome effects — Dark and Rough Chrome, Underwater Chrome, Toxic Chrome, and Smooth and Bright Chrome.

All those effects were created by entering different settings in the dialog box that appears when you choose Effects➪Artistic Effects➪Chrome. (The Effect Browser is where Jasc, the creator of Paint Shop Pro, likes to show off, so some truly spectacular effects are hidden in the browser.) If you want to tweak those settings, you can click the Modify button, which brings up the dialog box of whatever effect you're viewing. You can alter those settings and click OK to apply them to your image. If you want to rename an effect, click Rename and enter a new and snazzier moniker for your effect.

Technically speaking, these different effects are called *presets,* and you can create your own — which then show up in the Effect Browser. For details, see the section in Chapter 18 about saving tool and effect settings as presets.

Then again, if you like what you see, simply click the effect you want and click Apply. That effect is then applied to your image. If you don't like the results, press Ctrl+Z or click the Undo button on the toolbar.

3-D: Holes, Buttons, and Chisels

Except for the Buttonize effect, you must select an area before you apply any of the 3-D effects. The area you select is what is turned into a button, chiseled, cut out, or beveled inside or outside the selection marquee. Also, if you intend to use background color for the Buttonize, Chisel, or Inner Bevel effect, choose it now.

Choose Effects➪3D Effects. Then, choose one of these options from the menu that appears:

✔ **Buttonize:** Creates a raised appearance (inside your selection if you have made a selection). Because it's a Web thing, we discuss buttonization in Chapter 15, in the section about creating buttons.

✔ **Chisel:** Creates a raised appearance by making an edge *outside* your selection. In the Chisel dialog box that appears, increase the edge width by increasing the Size value. Choose Transparent Edge to see through the edge, or Solid Color otherwise. Choose a color for your chiseled edge by clicking the Color box.

✔ **Cutout:** Creates the illusion of cutting out your selected area and extending a shadow in two directions. Drag the Vertical and Horizontal sliders left or right to extend the shadow from different edges. Increase the Opacity setting to darken the shadow, or increase Blur to blur the shadow's edge. You can change the color of the shadow or the underlying surface by clicking the Shadow Color swatch or the Fill Interior with Color swatch, respectively. Then, choose a color from the Color dialog box that appears.

✔ **Drop Shadow:** Drops a shadow in any direction from your selected area, as though that area were floating over a surface. In the Drop Shadow dialog box that appears, drag Vertical and Horizontal sliders to change the shadow location — or, if you want something a little more intuitive, you can click the crosshairs in the left window and drag them around the central circle to indicate which way (and how far away) you want the shadow to fall. The Opacity, Blur, and Color settings work exactly the same way as they do in the Cutout section.

✔ **Inner Bevel or Outer Bevel:** Creates a framelike effect around the selected area by raising it up as though it were a pyramid. The pyramid's sloping sides (the bevel) appear within your selection area for Inner Bevel or outside the area for Outer Bevel. A rather complex-looking dialog box appears. Click the Bevel illustration to choose a bevel profile from a gallery. (Each profile is like the cross sections of wood moldings you see in a hardware store.)

Art and Artistic Effects: Simulating Traditional Art Media and Beyond

Welcome to Fun Central. The Art and Artistic effects are where you get to turn your casual snapshots into Monet-style paintings, transform your shot of London Bridge into a charcoal scribble, or turn your senior prom photo into an Andy Warhol–style halftone.

Paint Shop Pro offers *far* too many artistic effects for us to discuss them indi-vidually here. Besides, we don't want to rob you of the pleasure of squealing "Hey, look! It did that!" So, rather than explain every item on the two menus, we show you a couple of examples in this section and move on.

Choose Effects➪Artistic Effects or Effects➪Art Media Effects and Paint Shop Pro reveals a large menu of possibilities. (As we said earlier, Art Media effects tend to simulate things you can do in real life, like turning your picture into a pencil drawing, and Artistic effects transform your picture into another media entirely, like an old newspaper or hot chrome.) Choose one from the list.

Scripts as an alternative to effects

Not all Artistic effects are under the Artistic Effects and Art Media Effects menu selections! Paint Shop Pro 9 also includes several scripts designed to transform a picture into nice-looking watercolors, charcoals, and airbrush paintings. Because scripts can apply multiple commands to an image, the results are often *far* superior to a single effect. In the following figure, compare the simple Black Pencil effect, on the left, to the Black and White Sketch script on the right.

To run a script, select the Artistic category from the drop-down list on the Scripts toolbar, and then choose the effect you want to see. Next, click the Run Selected Script button, and watch in awe as Paint Shop Pro applies several care-fully tuned effects to your image.

For more information about scripts, see the section in Chapter 18 about using scripts to auto-mate repetitive tasks.

Nearly all these effects display an adjustment dialog box. See the section "Common Adjustments," later in this chapter, for help regarding more specialized controls. For the most part, your best approach is to fiddle with the controls for a while. A few effects take place immediately. If you don't like the result, press Ctrl+Z to undo it.

Here are a few more general tips for using artistic effects:

- ✔ If the result is too fuzzy, try decreasing various values, (especially density, if that adjustment exists). Most effects do some blurring, so if you turn it down a bit (decrease the effect), the image becomes clearer.

- ✔ If the result is too speckly or has too many lines, look for a detail adjustment and if you find one, turn it down.

- ✔ Some effects that do stuff with edges need a little help. Try running the Edge Enhance effect (choose Effects➪Edge Effects➪Enhance) or boosting contrast before applying your artistic effect. Or, in the adjustment box for your edge-fiddling effect, look for an intensity control and increase it.

Example 1: Topography

Topography is, for no particularly good reason, one of our favorite artistic effects. Its result is an image that looks like stacked, cut sheets of cardboard or foamboard (like the ones architects use in models to simulate sloping ground). Figure 13-2 shows the creation of Sir Topography.

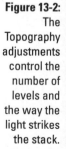

Figure 13-2:
The Topography adjustments control the number of levels and the way the light strikes the stack.

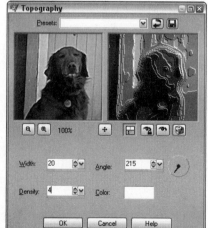

The controls do the following:

- **Width:** At low Width settings, contours follow the details of the picture more closely. At high Width settings, contours are broad and without sharp turns; detail is lost.

- **Density:** Density controls the number of layers in the virtual stack of layers. A higher density results in a surface that conforms more to the original detail. A lower density gives a more abstract result.

- **Angle:** The Angle control in the Lighting section determines the direction from which light is coming to illuminate the side of the stack. Drag its clock-hand-like control to point in the direction you want this light to shine.

- **Color:** Color determines the color of light that strikes the stack from the side. Originally, the Color control is set to white. To change it, you can left-click the swatch to bring up the Color palette.

Example 2: Brush Strokes

The Brush Strokes effect has lots of things to fiddle with, and you probably have to spend some time fiddling to get a result you like. It gives the appearance of applying thin or thick paint with a brush. In real life, the edges of paint strokes catch any incidental light, and in this effect you can simulate that appearance in varying degrees. Figure 13-3 shows a photograph of faithful Alex, who stays there forever as long as you keep stroking his fur.

The Brush Strokes controls work as follows:

- **Length:** Short lengths (low values of Length) create a stippled effect, like someone poking the end of a brush into the canvas. Longer lengths produce visible stroke directions.

- **Density:** Density determines the number of strokes. The greatest sensitivity of this control is at the very low end. A very low density (1 or 2) gives the appearance of a few strokes made over a photograph. Higher density makes a more abstract effect of many overlaid strokes.

- **Bristles:** A higher value of Bristles gives the distinct patch of paint that a nice, new, neatly trimmed brush, packed densely with bristles, lays down. A lower value simulates the scratchy result of a brush where the bristles are few or frazzled.

- **Width:** The Width control determines the width of the brush stroke. A higher value makes a wider brush.

- **Opacity:** The Opacity control sets the density of the paint. A low value gives a blurred effect that is more like looking through frosted glass than anything else. A high value makes paint look like it was applied thickly, as though with a palette knife.

✔ **Softness:** The Softness control gives a smoother look to the paint surface, with less speckling.

✔ **Angle:** The Angle control determines the direction of the incident light that glints off the edges of thick paint strokes. Drag the clock-hand-like control to point *toward the source* of the light.

✔ **Color:** To change the color of incident light striking the paint edges, click the Color swatch and choose from the Color dialog box. (Or, right-click to choose from the Recent Colors dialog box.) Black gives no incident light, a dark color (low lightness value) gives a little, and so on. High lightness values strongly emphasize the stroke edges.

As with many effects, if you return to this adjustment dialog box later, it normally resumes whatever settings you last used. This intelligent behavior saves you from lots of time spent returning to settings you like.

If you use this effect often, you may want to save any given combination of settings as a *preset* for later use. See the section in Chapter 18 about presets.

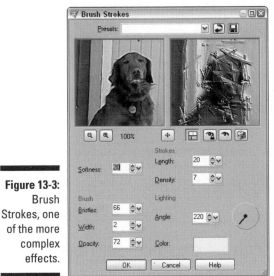

Figure 13-3:
Brush
Strokes, one
of the more
complex
effects.

Geometric, Distortion, and Image Effects: Curls, Squeezes, Wraps, and Waves

Paint Shop Pro has enough curls, squeezes, and waves to outfit an entire army of cute toddlers. If you want anything bent, distorted, or wrapped, Paint Shop Pro can tie it up in a knot.

Choose Effects⇨Geometric Effects, Effects⇨Distortion Effects, or Effects⇨ Image Effects and then choose from the large list that appears. As with the Artistic effects, Paint Shop Pro has too many effects for us to try to cover completely. Fortunately, most controls are either self evident or do something that you can easily figure out by playing with them. We give you a couple of examples, though.

Here are a few tips for using Geometric effects:

✔ Some effects are centered on a particular location. To move the center, adjust the Horizontal and Vertical controls. A setting of zero centers the effect horizontally or vertically. Negative horizontal values are to the left of center; negative vertical values are *above* center.

✔ Remember that you can apply any effect to a particular area by selecting that area first. Using a feathered edge on the selection feathers the modified image into the original image.

Need a thinner face? If you have a portrait on a plain background, Paint Shop Pro can help. First, carefully select the face. Then, equally carefully, remove areas around the eyes, nose, and mouth from the selection. (See Chapter 3 for help with removing areas from a selection.) Apply the Pinch effect from the Distortion Effects menu.

The Page Curl effect is, for some reason, one of the most enduringly popular image effects. It seems that we never tire of remarking, "Why, Martha, that photo looks like it's a-peelin' right off the page!" We guess that the Page Curl effect (easily accessible by choosing Effects⇨Image Effects⇨Page Curl) is just plain a-peelin'. Figure 13-4 shows this remarkable effect.

Here's how to control your curl, with the most important stuff listed first:

✔ **Corner:** Which corner do you want to curl? Click the button depicting your chosen corner.

✔ **Curl Bounding Rectangle Width and Height:** To set the position of the curl, drag the tiny gear-shaped widgets at either end of the black line that diagonally crosses the left preview window. As Figure 13-4 shows you, your cursor becomes a four-headed arrow when it's over the line's end. Alternatively, you can adjust the Width or Height values to move those points; watch the line as you do so, and see how the Width and Height values affect it.

✔ **Radius:** How broad do you want the curl to be? The smaller the Radius value, the tighter the corner is rolled up. The smaller the corner you're curling (that is, the lower the X and Y values), the smaller the Radius value usually needs to be.

✔ **Curl Settings Color:** This setting controls the color that appears on the highlight of the curl (the underside of the curled picture). Paint Shop Pro makes the rest of the curl, the shaded part, the same hue, but darker.

✔ **Edge Mode:** This setting controls the shade that appears on the flat page revealed by the lifted corner. Click the box to choose a different color from the Color dialog box, or right-click to choose from the Recent Colors dialog box, or select Transparent to do away with any nasty colors.

Bear in mind that besides curling the edge of the entire image, you can select a rectangle — a stamp on an envelope, for example — and curl that. (Other selection shapes don't usually work as well.)

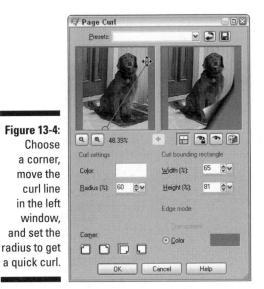

Figure 13-4:
Choose
a corner,
move the
curl line
in the left
window,
and set the
radius to get
a quick curl.

Illumination Effects: Sunbursts and Flares

If you need a sparkle of sunlight, unwrap the Paint Shop Pro Sunburst effect. It places a bright spot on your image, with rays of light and circles of lens flare. The adjustment dialog box appears, as shown in Figure 13-5, on top of the image that it's modifying, to better show the effects.

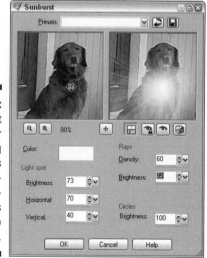

Figure 13-5:
A sunburst placed over Alex's dog tags catches him in mid-transformation into his superhero identity.

Each of the controls for the three different components has its own area: Light Spot, Rays, and Circle Brightness. All share the same color setting. Here's how to use these adjustments:

- **Color:** Click the Color sample to choose some color other than white from the Color dialog box.

- **Light Spot Brightness:** Increase to brighten the light spot.

- **Light Spot Horizontal/Vertical:** Adjust to position the spot. Or, if you can see a tiny set of crosshairs in the left preview window, drag that instead. When your cursor is over the crosshairs, the cursor becomes a four-headed arrow.

- **Rays Brightness:** Set this option higher to bring out the rays of light you can see in Figure 13-5.

- **Rays Density:** Adjust this setting lower to see fewer rays or higher to see more rays.

- **Circle Brightness:** Set this option higher to make the lens flare circles brighter. On light photos, these circles are barely visible, even at full brightness.

Reflection Effects: Mirrors and Patterns

The Reflection effects are a funhouse phenomenon. You can choose a single mirror, or multiple mirrors in various configurations, turning your image into a pattern. Choose Effects⇨Reflection Effects and then one of the four menu items that appear:

✔ **Feedback:** The mirror-reflecting-into-mirror effect you get in barbershops with mirrors on opposite walls. See "Common Adjustments," later in this chapter, for help with this effect's controls.

✔ **Kaleidoscope:** A humdinger of an effect, like looking at your image through a kaleidoscope.

✔ **Pattern:** Another way, besides Kaleidoscope, to turn your image into a pattern. See the following two sections.

✔ **Rotating Mirror:** Similar to putting a mirror edge-down on your image. You can rotate a reflection to any angle and position the mirror horizontally and vertically on the image.

REMEMBER

You can limit any of these effects to a particular area by making a selection first.

Texture Effects: Bumpy Surfaces from Asphalt to Weaves

Texture is the neglected third dimension of an image. *Texture,* the surface on which the image is constructed, is a quality that most of us don't think about when we think about images, but it's very much a part of the visual experience. An image made up of mosaic tiles, for example, feels very different from the same image painted on canvas.

To choose a Texture effect, choose Effects⇨Texture Effects and then choose from the extensive menu that appears. Paint Shop Pro has too many textures to cover in detail, but the next few sections should help you sort things out. All effects except one (the Emboss effect) open an adjustment dialog box, in which you should feel free to fiddle while watching the effect.

Relating texture effects to the Materials palette's textures

You may be a bit confused because Paint Shop Pro gives you two ways to use texture in your images. If you're *painting* an image, you can apply texture by using the Properties dialog box (as we show you in Chapter 9). If you already *have* an image, the Texture effects are the way to go.

Texture effects offer more variety and more powerful effects than the Properties box does. For example, you can't paint fur texture or leather crinkling over an image by using the Material box, but you *can* apply it as an effect. Also, unlike Texture effects, which offer scads of ways to change each effect, with Properties box textures you're stuck with three options: the texture, the angle, and the size. That's it; take it or leave it.

If you find that this isn't nearly enough meddling, you can select a sort of superpowered Properties box texture from the Texture Effects menu by choosing — surprise — Texture. In that effect's dialog box, you can achieve all kinds of variations using the texture effects that you can't achieve within the Properties box itself.

(Why didn't Jasc just provide a separate tab for textures in the Properties box that had all this stuff in one place, the way it does for gradients and colors? Heck if we know.)

Just as the Texture effect gives you more leverage over the Material box's textures, the Sculpture effect lets you leverage the Color palette's *patterns*. The effect's main job is to turn your image into a sort of etching or embossing, but it also applies patterns. Patterns are sort of like textures, but come with their own colors. The Sculpture effect applies a Paint Shop Pro pattern, which allows you to set a number of variables that are unavailable on the Properties box palette. In the Sculpture effect, for example, you can give a pattern a (uniform) color or change its size (scale).

Using Texture effect controls

Texture adjustments have, in general, two main types of controls:

- Those for the virtual substance that puts ridges and valleys in the image
- Those for the light that strikes at some oblique angle and reveals that unevenness

In addition, the virtual substances that make up some textures have optical qualities you can adjust, like transparency and blurring.

If a texture or pattern is unclear at some settings, try zooming out in the adjustment dialog box. (Click the magnifier-with-a-minus-sign button.)

The best way to understand most texture controls is to fiddle with them while watching the right preview window in the adjustment dialog box. (Only the Emboss effect goes to work immediately, without displaying a dialog box.) Some of the more common controls you find in the adjustment dialog boxes are shown in this list:

- **Length (and occasionally Width) or Size:** The dimensions of the ridges and valleys that make up the texture.
- **Blur:** The overall fuzziness imparted to the original image.
- **Detail:** How much detail the lines of texture inherit from the edges of the original image.
- **Density:** The degree to which ridges and valleys are packed closely together.

✔ **Transparency:** The ability to let the original image show clearly through the virtual substance that overlays the image.

✔ **Angle:** The direction from which incident light strikes the surface.

✔ **Elevation:** The height of the light source above the image. Low elevations show the ridges and valleys more strongly. High elevations make a brighter image. Some textures allow you to set the intensity or luminance and color of the incident light as well.

✔ **Ambience:** The overall brightness (ambient light) of the image.

Example 1: The Fur texture effect

A simple texture effect is Fur, excessively applied to Alex in Figure 13-6. The Fur effect causes fibers to radiate from clusters throughout your image, giving a result not unlike the fur of a cat engaged in discussion with a member of the canine profession.

Figure 13-6: From the Department of Redundancy Department — giving Alex more fur.

You can go "fur" with this effect if you interpret your controls in the following ways:

✔ **Blur:** A kind of fluffiness control. Increasing the blur minimizes the visibility of individual hairs and also makes the original image less clear.

✔ **Density:** Determines the number of hairs; very low settings give a cactuslike, whiskered appearance.

✔ **Length:** Sets the length of individual hairs. High length values tend to give more of a frosted-glass appearance than a furry one.

✔ **Transparency:** Determines the extent to which the original image shows through the hair, undisturbed. High transparency values give an effect like hair sprinkled on a photograph.

Example 2: The Texture texture effect

The Texture effect you see when you choose Effects⇨Texture Effects⇨Texture gives you access to the same textures you may use for painting with the Paint Shop Pro Color palette. Here, rather than paint with them, you apply them to an existing image. Figure 13-7 shows faithful Alex, this time receiving a cobblestone texture.

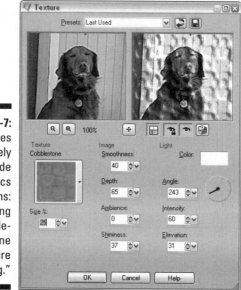

Figure 13-7: Sentences you rarely use outside of graphics programs: "I'm adding a cobblestone texture to a dog."

The controls of this dialog box provide enough fiddles to outfit a symphony orchestra. Here's how to make them play in tune:

- ✔ **Texture:** Click here and choose a texture from the Paint Shop Pro gallery of textures that appears.

- ✔ **Size (%):** Make the texture pattern larger by increasing this value above zero. Decrease the value (to make the value negative) for a smaller pattern.

- ✔ **Smoothness:** To blunt the sharp edges of your texture, increase this value.

- ✔ **Depth:** To have deeper valleys and higher hills in your pattern, increase this value. This action usually makes the pattern more visible, so you can also think of it as a kind of strength control.

- ✔ **Ambience:** Adjust this control for a brighter or darker image.

✔ **Shininess:** A higher value of shininess puts a bright glint on the edges and corners of your texture pattern.

✔ **Color:** Click this swatch to choose a different color of incident light from the Colors dialog box.

✔ **Angle:** Drag the clock-hand-like control to point toward the imaginary light source that illuminates the texture.

✔ **Intensity:** Higher intensity increases the incident light that reveals the contrast.

✔ **Elevation:** Lower values emphasize the hills and valleys; higher values brighten the flat hilltops and valley bottoms. (Reduce the Ambience value to avoid washout at high elevations.)

Common Adjustments

Effects use a wide range of adjustments to set their various variables. In most cases, the function of a control becomes apparent as soon as you fiddle with it, but in complex dialog boxes, you may need to understand what does what. This list helps you distinguish one variable from another:

✔ **Ambience:** General illumination. Determines the image brightness with the incident light source's intensity and elevation.

✔ **Amplitude:** The degree to which the effect is applied.

✔ **Angle:** The direction of incident light in the plane of the image. Drag the clock-hand-like control to point toward the source.

✔ **Blur:** A fuzziness that affects mostly the original image showing through the texture. It makes the texture fuzzier in some textures.

✔ **Color:** A swatch showing the color of light that glints off the texture's hills and valleys. Click the swatch to choose a new color from the Color dialog box. (To find out how to adjust color, refer to Chapter 9.) Right-click the swatch to choose from the Recent Colors dialog box.

✔ **Density:** The closeness and number of hills and valleys in the texture.

✔ **Detail:** The degree to which the texture picks out the detail in the original image.

✔ **% Effect:** The degree to which the effect is applied.

✔ **Elevation:** The height of the incident light above the plane of the image. Low elevations show the ridges and valleys more strongly. High elevations make a brighter image.

- **Height:** The height of the hills in the texture.

- **Horizontal/Vertical Center:** The position of the center of the effect.

- **Horizontal/Vertical Offset:** The position of the overall resulting pattern.

- **Intensity:** The strength of the incident light that reveals the texture.

- **Length:** The length of the ridges and valleys that make up the texture.

- **Opacity:** The degree to which the blobs of virtual substance pick up color from the underlying image, as opposed to letting the image's original pixels show through.

- **Presets:** A drop-down list that lets you choose from among any named collection of settings you have saved or your Last Used settings. After you change any setting, the Presets selection says Custom.

- **Radius:** The broadness of any curve or curl; smaller radius values make curves or curls tighter.

- **Save As:** A button leading to the Preset Save dialog box, in which you enter a name to label your current collection of settings. Choose the name from the Presets list box to recall the setting.

- **Shininess:** The glare off the sloping sides of the hills and valleys of the texture.

- **Size:** The overall size of the elements of the texture.

- **Smoothness:** How rounded the bumps are that make up the texture.

- **Symmetric:** A check box that makes an effect work the same way in all directions.

- **Transparent/Background color:** Options that either make an edge reveal the underlying image color (Transparent) or color the edge with the current Paint Shop Pro background color.

Framing Your Art

So, you may have transformed a picture of Fido into an oil painting, complete with sweeping strokes and a little bit of texture to flesh it out. But, you still feel unsatisfied. That's only natural — after all, what masterpiece is complete without an elegant frame?

Choose Image➪Picture Frame to display the Picture Frame dialog box, as shown in Figure 13-8. Clicking the arrow next to the Picture Frame drop-down list displays a gallery of frames to choose from, including modern art frames, edge brushings, filmstrip frames, or the ever-popular masking-tape-on-the-corners look. Select a frame to see a preview of your framed image on the right side.

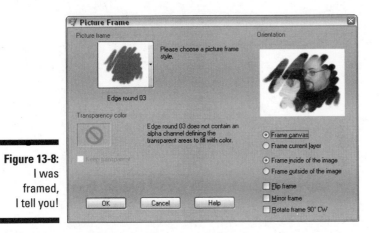

Figure 13-8:
I was
framed,
I tell you!

Two radio buttons give you the option to have your frame placed on the out-side of your image or to have the frame jutting into the inside (and potentially obscuring something on the edges of your picture, just like a real frame). Two other radio buttons give you the option to frame just the current layer, or your image as a whole. (*We* can't see a reason that you would want to frame just a single layer, but *somebody* must have asked for it.)

Only a few frames have transparent edges. You can opt to keep them trans-parent by clicking the Keep Transparent check box, or you can click the check box to choose a color to fill in the gaps.

Three check boxes allow you to flip, mirror, and rotate the frame, exactly the same as you would flip, rotate, or mirror an image (we show you how in Chapter 2). When you're ready to frame, click OK.

Part IV
Taking It to the Street

The 5th Wave   By Rich Tennant

"My God! I've gained 9 pixels!"

In this part . . .

Having an image in a Paint Shop Pro window on a PC monitor is very nice, but not particularly useful in the big, bad world. Unless that image can make its way successfully to paper or the Web, only you and your fellow Paint Shop Pro *aficionados* will get much of a thrill from it. In this part we take you through the process of letting go of your baby, giving it wings, and watching it soar without you! How beautiful! Sob!

Chapter 14

Printing

*A*ll this electronic image stuff is just fine, but in the end, many of us want our images printed on dead, flattened, bleached trees — paper. As a good friend once said, "The paperless office of the future is just down the hall from the paperless bathroom of the future." Paper will be around for a little while yet.

Paint Shop Pro has some great features for making the printing job easier: It automatically fits the image to the page, prints a collection or album page of images, prints browser thumbnails, and more. Read on for ways to make paper printing work better and faster for you.

Fitting Your Print to the Paper

"Let the punishment fit the crime," said Gilbert and Sullivan's Mikado, who prescribed the death penalty for flirting. With the help of the few hints in this section, your image should fit your page with far less pain.

If you have multiple images open in Paint Shop Pro, click the title bar on the window of the image you want to print. That makes it the active window.

You can find all the controls for sizing and positioning your print on paper by choosing File⇨Print to bring up the Print dialog box and then clicking the Placement tab if it's not already shown. You can see the handy-dandy Placement tab, as shown in Figure 14-1, and then consult the following bulleted list for help.

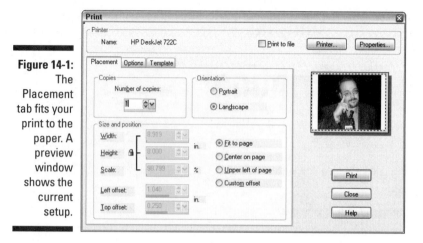

Figure 14-1:
The
Placement
tab fits your
print to the
paper. A
preview
window
shows the
current
setup.

Keep in mind that when Paint Shop Pro changes the size of your *print,* it's not changing your *image.* It's only resizing the printed output; the image itself isn't changed in any way. If your image is 500 pixels across, it remains 500 pixels across. Stretching a small image to fill a page may result in quite a grainy printed copy!

Use these options in the Placement dialog box to fit your print to your paper:

- ✔ **Number of copies:** This option is self-explanatory. You can print as many as a hundred copies at a time, but we wouldn't advise it unless you have *lots* of ink hanging around.

- ✔ **Printing sideways (orientation):** Paint Shop Pro initially sets you up to print in *portrait* orientation on the paper, in which the paper's long dimension runs vertically. For prints that are wider than they are high, however, you may want to print sideways, or in *landscape* orientation. Click either Portrait or Landscape to choose orientation.

- ✔ **Centering:** Often, you want your print centered on the page. Click the Center on Page radio button to do just that.

- ✔ **Filling the page:** To fill the page with your image (to the maximum extent possible), click the Fit To Page radio button, and your print is enlarged until it fills either the width or height of the paper, within the allowable margins of your printer.

- ✔ **Upper left of page:** What else can we say? It's in the upper-left corner.

- ✔ **Offset:** If having your image in the middle or the upper-left corner isn't good enough for you, selecting the Custom Offset value allows you to position your image on the paper wherever you want it. The Left and Top Offset values — which are grayed out unless you specifically choose Custom Offset — control how far your image is placed from the left or top margin. Enter however many inches you want your image to be shoved away from either side, and the result is shown in the preview window.

✔ **Making the image larger or smaller:** You can print your image as small as .025 percent of its original size or scale it up to a Godzilla-sized 1,000 percent (ten times larger). Adjust the Scale value in the Size and position area to whatever percentage you want. A setting of 100 percent means that the image's resolution, assigned at its creation, is observed. An image that's 144 pixels wide, for example, at a typical resolution of 72 pixels per inch, is printed 2 inches wide. (This option is grayed out in the Fit to Page feature, which scales your image automatically.)

Another method of scaling your printed image is to specify a specific size, in inches, at which the image is printed. Enter a value for either the width or the height; the image scales proportionately, so if you double the width, the height is also doubled. (If for some reason you *want* to print a squashed image, we refer you to the Distortion tool — described in Chapter 4, in the section about doing the deformation — where you can presquash it.)

When you print an image at a scale much greater than 100 percent, your pixels may begin to show. Scandalous! Rather than scale your print, try closing the Print dialog box (click Close), scaling your *image* by that same percentage, and resampling it via Smart Size. Refer to Chapter 2 for help with resizing. Your image may be a bit blurred, but it doesn't look as pixelated.

Printing in Greyscale and Other Options

If you're looking to save some colored ink, you can choose File➪Print to bring up the Print dialog box and then click the Options tab. It gives you a choice of three colors in which to print: Color, Greyscale (black and white), and CMYK separations. (Don't worry about printing CMYK separations unless you're a professional artist — if you are, you'll know what to do when you see it.)

If you're going to print lots of images, you may want the filename of the image on the print. If so, enable the Image Name check box. (If you have entered a title on the Creator Information tab in the Current Image Information dialog box, that title appears in place of the filename.)

In some instances, you may want to trim the margins off the print when you're done. If your image has a white background, however, finding those margins may be hard. To solve that problem, enable the Print Corner Crop Marks and Print Center Crop Marks check boxes.

Printing an Image

After you have set everything to your liking, it's time to get printin'!

1. **If you haven't done so already, choose File⇨Print, press Ctrl+P, or click the Print button on the toolbar.**

   The Print dialog box appears.

2. **If necessary, choose your printing options.**

   By clicking the Properties button, you can adjust the usual controls that come with any Windows program: the printer you're using, the number of copies you want, and a Properties button that takes you to the printer's driver software. (That's where you can set the print quality, speed, paper type, and other variables. Refer to the section "Printing at Different Speeds or Qualities," later in this chapter.)

3. **Click Print after you have set all the options you want.**

Shortly, you'll have a hard copy of your hard work.

Printing Collections or Album Pages

One of the most popular Paint Shop Pro features is its ability to print multiple images. It's a great way to create album pages or make collages of photos to celebrate an event.

You can use one of two ways to choose the pictures you want to add to a collection, which allows you to print several images on a single page:

- ✔ Use the image browser to select the pictures you want to add. Hold down the Ctrl key as you click each picture.

- ✔ Open all the images that you want to add to your collection. Paint Shop Pro automatically adds any open images to the Print Layout screen.

Next, choose File⇨Print Layout. Your entire Paint Shop Pro window changes to the multi-image printing tool shown in Figure 14-2.

The multi-image printing tool occupies the entire Paint Shop Pro window. To close it and return to the normal window, choose File⇨Close Print Layout. Unless you have saved your layout (see the section "Saving and reusing your template," later in this chapter), closing the tool discards your layout.

With the multi-image printing tool onscreen, here's the basic procedure:

1. **Choose the page orientation.**

   Paint Shop Pro initially gives you a portrait-oriented page (with the long dimension vertically). If you want a landscape- (sideways-) oriented page, choose File⇨Print Setup and then click Landscape in the Print Setup dialog box that appears. Click OK.

Rotate Counterclockwise 90°   Zoom in or out

Rotate Clockwise 90°   Positioning buttons

Figure 14-2:
Composing
a multi-
image page.

2. **If you want to use a template for your images, choose File⇨ Open Template.**

   A *template* is a prefab layout you can use to arrange your photos to save time. As a bonus, templates look nicer than dragging pictures helter-skelter onto the page (well, better than the way *we* drag them, anyway). Paint Shop Pro gives you a dialog box with three categories of templates you can choose from: Avery, Combinations, and Standard Sizes. Click a category to bring up the following gallery of templates, as shown in Figure 14-3:

   • **Avery and Avery International templates:** Intended for the industry standard Avery labels — sheets of precut stickers you can use in your printer. Yes, you can print stickers with your baby's picture on them! Each Avery template has a number underneath it, like Avery 8386; this number refers to the product number of a specific Avery label sheet, which you can buy at your local office supply store. Use the right sheet with the right template, and you have perfect stickers.

   • **Standard sizes:** Templates in which all the images are one size: 5x7, wallet-size photos, miniwallets, and the like.

   • **Combination sizes:** Templates with mixtures of sizes, generally one or two larger photos at the top and a bunch of smaller ones at the bottom.

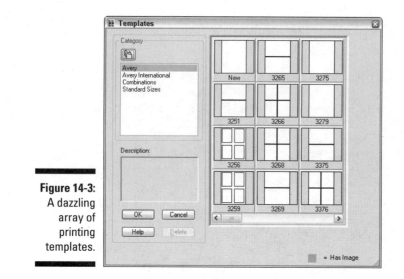

Each template has a small thumbnail that shows you what its layout is like; click a template and click OK to apply it or click Cancel to escape.

3. Drag images, one at a time, from the left column to the page.

If you have a template applied, drag the photo into each of the boxes; Paint Shop Pro automatically resizes the photo so that it fits as best it can into the box.

If you don't have a template applied, you have to resize the photos manually. If the images are too large for the page, Paint Shop Pro asks whether you want to scale it. If you click Yes, your image appears with *handles* (square dots) at the corners that you can drag to resize the image. Choose No if you want to use the Paint Shop Pro autoarrange feature (see Step 4) to place and size the image for you.

If an image is rotated 90 degrees the wrong way, drag it to the page and click the Rotate Clockwise 90° or Rotate Counterclockwise 90° button on the toolbar to rotate the image.

4. If you haven't applied a template and want to position the images yourself, drag them into position.

If you don't want to use a template and still want everything lined up neatly, you can choose View⇨Auto Arrange, which lines up your images for you sans template.

5. To print your page, click the Print icon on the toolbar or choose File⇨ Print.

Neither choice gives you a Print dialog box, but immediately sends the page to your printer. If you need to change any printer settings, do so *before* sending the page to the printer. Choose File⇨Print Setup and click the Printer button in the Print Setup dialog box that appears.

If you're done, return to the normal Paint Shop Pro window by choosing File⇨ Close Print or click the Close button on the toolbar (the door-with-arrow icon).

If you're using a pregenerated template and Paint Shop Pro asks "The current template has changed, do you wish to change it?" when you exit, *do not accept the default name if you choose to save it.* (Avery templates in particular don't like being fiddled with — and, by just clicking OK, you're overwriting the template and potentially changing vital placement information.)

Instead, if you want to save both pictures *and* layout, flip ahead to the section "Saving and reusing your template."

Fooling with the pictures and layout

You can fiddle with the pictures and their arrangement all you want, after they're on the page. Most controls for fiddling are duplicated on the menu bar (the toolbar across the top of the window) or, if you right-click an image, on the context menu that appears. Nearly everything can be done fastest by using the right-clicking approach, so that's mainly what's in the following list. Here are some basic fiddlings you may want to do:

- To select a picture so that you can do something with it, click it. (Handles appear at its corners.)

- To move a picture, drag it.

- To position a picture in the center or at any of the four corners of the page, click any of the five positioning buttons in the center of the toolbar. The icon indicates the position the button delivers. Pause your cursor over the button for a text indication of its positioning (such as Place Lower Right).

- To resize a picture, drag any of its handles.

- To remove a picture from the layout, either click it and press the Delete button on your keyboard or right-click it and choose Remove from the context menu.

- To rotate a picture, right-click it and choose Rotate Clockwise 90 Degrees or Rotate Counterclockwise 90 Degrees from the context menu that appears.

- To see an alignment grid, right-click the white page background and choose Show Grid from the context menu. (Repeat to turn the grid off; this action doesn't work if you have a template loaded.)

- To make photos snap to the grid when you move them, right-click the white page background and choose Snap to Grid from the context menu. (The grid must be on first, or else this command is grayed out.)

Saving and reusing your template

To save this attractive arrangement of photos, choose File➪Save Template. In the Save dialog box that appears, enter a name for your layout in the filename text box. Unless you tell Paint Shop Pro otherwise, it saves the layout as a set of empty boxes, forgetting which photos were there; you can tell it to remember the photos by checking the Save with Images check box.

To reuse this layout, reopen the Print Layout screen and then choose File➪ Open Template. Select your template in the Open dialog box that appears.

 When you open a template, it brings up the image in its current condition, whatever that may be. For that reason, be sure not to move any images to other folders or rename them because the multi-image print tool won't be able to find them.

Printing at Different Speeds or Qualities

Paint Shop Pro itself doesn't have much to do with choosing the quality or speed of printing your printer delivers. That falls in the province of the software that runs your printer, known as its *driver.* To access that piece of software, click the Properties button in the Print dialog box. Because what happens next depends on your printer, we can't tell you exactly what you will see from then on.

Speed, size, and ink

Quality comes at the cost of speed and of ink. Most printers have *draft* and *quality* settings. If you want just a general idea of how your image will look and want to save time and ink, choose Draft. Your image is printed lighter and fuzzier than if you choose the quality (or nondraft) setting, but is printed more quickly.

The size of your printed image also costs you time and ink. Doubling the size increases by four the amount of ink you need.

Many inkjet printers do a much better job on special photograph-quality paper. In that case, the printer driver generally has a setting where you can tell it that you're going to use special paper.

Printer and image resolution

One aspect of print quality is *resolution,* or dots per inch. A higher resolution generally gives a better-quality image. That resolution number is often confusing because your image has resolution too, in pixels per inch. The two don't match, either. The printer resolution is always a higher number than image resolution.

What's going on? Your printer creates its range of colors by putting out tiny dots in four colors: cyan, magenta, yellow, and black. It needs many tiny dots to make a pixel of a particular color, so your printer needs many more dots per inch (dpi) than your image has pixels per inch. Dave's printer, for example, can print 1440 dpi. So, each pixel of a 72-pixel-per-inch image covers an area of 20 x 20 dots of ink. For an image twice that resolution, Dave gets an area of only 10 x 10 dots, giving him one-forth the number of possible colors.

The bottom line? Although using a higher image resolution when you create your image gives you more detail in your prints, don't push it too high and don't try to match your printer's resolution. If you use a higher image resolution (pixels per inch), each pixel uses fewer printer dots, so color accuracy may suffer. Although your printer driver does a few tricks to keep things accurate, the laws of physics eventually win.

Chapter 15

Creating Web-Friendly Images

. . . .

In This Chapter

▶ Improving download times

▶ Choosing the best file type

▶ Creating GIF and JPEG images

. . . .

The Web makes special demands on graphics. Images have to be stored as particular file types, and they can't take too long to download or else people get bored. In this chapter, we show you how to make your Web images look their best while downloading as fast as possible.

If you're a professional (or even semiprofessional) Web designer, Paint Shop Pro has automated Webtools that can quickly generate Web pages and rollover icons. Because that topic is a little advanced if you're just interested in creating snazzy Web graphics, we show you how to do that in Chapter 18.

Paint Shop Pro offers a special Web toolbar for the Web features we discuss here. With the Web toolbar enabled, you simply click a button for an effect rather than use the menu commands. To enable the toolbar, choose View⇨ Toolbars⇨Web.

Making Images Download Faster

The key trick with images on the Internet is to make sure that they don't take any longer to download than they have to. Web users are fickle: Why should they stick around and watch a blank screen when more amusement is simply a mouse click away? If you make your audience wait, they don't stay around. Images are downloaded faster when their files are smaller, which is especially handy when you're sending pictures via e-mail. The following list describes a few general tips for making sure that your images are downloaded as fast as possible — some you do when you're creating the Web page and others you do in Paint Shop Pro:

- ✔ **Reduce image size:** The main mistake beginners make is to use excessively large images on their Web pages. Web page authoring tools sometimes give the illusion of having made an image smaller, but in fact they just squeeze a large image into a small space. Size or resize your image in Paint Shop Pro to exactly the size you need on the Web page; refer to Chapter 2 for details.

- ✔ **Repeat images:** In your Web page authoring software, if your page uses the same image over and over again (for a bullet icon, for example), insert exactly the same image file each time. Don't use multiple files that are identical copies of the same image.

- ✔ **Use solid colors:** Gradient fills, dithered or airbrushed areas (hues made up of multicolored pixels), and scanned printed images (made up of visible dots) require larger files. Paint with solid colors wherever possible if you want to keep file sizes down. Noise effects, such as Edge Preserving Smooth on the Paint Shop Pro Effects menu, can help reduce dots to uniform colors.

Exporting Images for the Web

The images that appear on Web pages are almost always stored as one of two main types of file: GIF or JPEG. (Sometimes, they're stored as PNG files, a new and improved type of file, but that type is still rarely used.) To make your image viewable on a Web browser, all you have to do is make sure to save a copy of the image as one of these file types.

To create a Web file from your image, you can go either of two ways:

- ✔ Save the image as a particular type of file (choose File➪Save As or File➪ Save Copy As).
- ✔ *Export* the image to a particular type of file.

Exporting takes you immediately into an optimizer dialog box for that type of file, where you choose features and trade-offs.

Always store your image as a Paint Shop Pro file before you create Web image files from it. Paint Shop Pro files retain lots of features that are lost when you store an image as a Web image.

Choosing features and file types

Each file type has its own advantages and features. Table 15-1 lists attributes you may want and the file type or types that are generally best to use. *Best* considers both image quality and speed of downloading (file size).

Table 15-1	Images, Image Features, and Which File Types to Use	
Image Attributes	*File Type to Use*	*Notes*
Is (or is like) a photograph	JPEG	Color photographs are much smaller in JPEG than in GIF.
Uses patterns or textures	JPEG or GIF	More complex patterns or textures are better as JPEG.
Uses mainly solid colors	GIF or PNG	Solid-color images, like cartoons or text, often have thin or sharp edges, all pixels of which are entirely preserved in GIF or PNG.
Has transparent areas	GIF or PNG	Transparency lets the page background show through (see Figure 15-1).
Fades in during loading	GIF, JPEG, or PNG	Fade-in *(progression)* is an optional feature.

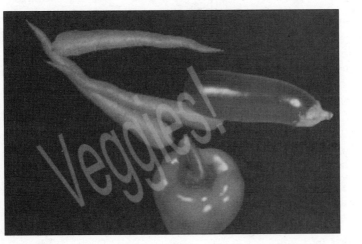

Figure 15-1: Transparency, a popular Web feature, allows this slanted-text image to float over a Web page's background image.

Creating GIF files

GIF files are the most widely used graphics files on the Web. They offer certain popular features, such as transparency (as shown in Figure 15-1), but are also limited to 256 colors. If you're displaying simple text or cartoony images, though, they're also *much* smaller than JPEG files; used properly, they save lots of downloading time. To export a GIF file from your image, follow these steps:

1. **Choose File⇨Export⇨GIF Optimizer.**

   The GIF Optimizer dialog box (the *optimizer*) appears and contains five tabs of settings that we cover throughout the next few sections. The optimizer has before and after preview windows (left and right, respectively) that show what effect your choices have. Click the magnifier with the + to zoom in or the one with the – to zoom out.

2. **Click the OK button.**

   The familiar Save As dialog box appears.

3. **Choose a filename and folder for the file and click OK.**

You can (and should) make image files smaller so that they're downloaded faster; see the section "Reducing download time," later in this chapter.

Creating transparent areas

To prepare an image to have transparent portions on the Web, first save your image as a Paint Shop Pro file. Then choose *any one* of the following alternative approaches to mark a transparent area — whichever approach seems easiest:

- ✔ **Color:** If all the pixels in the area you want to become transparent are roughly the same color (a white background, for example), you don't need to do much more in preparation. Just make sure that your chosen color does *not* appear in any pixels where you *don't* want transparency, such as the whites of people's eyes. If the color *does* appear elsewhere, try one of the two following approaches instead.

- ✔ **Selection:** Select either the object that you want to be visible (opaque) or the background that you want to be transparent. You have to make the selection before you begin to export.

- ✔ **Transparency:** If the object (your logo, for example) that you want to be visible (opaque) isn't already on its own layer or layers, select it and promote it to a layer. On the Layer palette, turn off the visibility of the background layer and any other unwanted layers, and the transparent portions of the logo layer are apparent (display a checkerboard pattern).

To have the edges of a selected area blend gradually into the Web page's background, contract the selection by a certain number of pixels (4, for example). Then, feather the selection by that same number of pixels. (Refer to Chapter 3 for help with contracting and feathering a selection.)

A tab in the GIF Optimizer dialog box lets you translate your chosen area into a transparency. In the GIF Optimizer dialog box, click the first tab, Transparency. This tab asks "What areas of the image would you like to be transparent?" Your choices are shown in this list:

- **None:** Choose this option if you want no transparent areas whatsoever.

- **Existing image or layer transparency:** Choose this option if your image already has transparent areas (appearing as a gray checkerboard pattern) that you want to remain transparent on the Web page. This is the Transparency approach, as described in the preceding bulleted list.

- **Inside the current selection:** Use this option if, using the Paint Shop Pro selection tools, you have selected the area (the background, for example) that you want to become transparent (the Selection approach in the preceding bulleted list). If you have selected instead the area that is to remain opaque, choose Outside the Current Selection.

- **Areas that match this color:** Choose this option (the Color approach in the preceding bulleted list) if the areas you want transparent are all the same color. If the color that is already displayed in the adjoining color swatch is *not* the one you want to make transparent, move the cursor outside the dialog box, over the image, and click any area of your chosen color. The result appears in the right preview window. Increase the Tolerance value to make a wider range of similar colors transparent or decrease it to narrow the range of colors made transparent.

Choosing image fade-in

As GIF images are downloaded, they build gradually onscreen. You can choose whether they build from top to bottom or fade in from fuzzy to increasingly detailed. For small images that are downloaded quickly, the choice doesn't matter much. To choose a method, click the Format tab.

On the Format tab, choose Non-Interlaced if you want the image to build from top to bottom. Choose Interlaced if you want the image to fade in. Leave the option labeled What version do you want the file to be? set to Version 89a unless someone specifically requests a file of Version 87a.

Reducing download time

For GIF files, you can reduce download time in two ways: Reduce the physical size of the image, and reduce the number of colors in it. (We tell you how to resize in Chapter 2.) Removing unused colors saves time, which makes sense — why send 256 colors across the Internet when you can send only 40?

Opening and using transparent GIF files

If you open a transparent GIF file in Paint Shop Pro, you may be surprised at what you see: Areas that appear transparent in a Web browser are filled in with a color. That result occurs because GIF transparency is a special trick used mainly in Web browsers. Paint Shop Pro shows the reality behind the trick.

GIF files achieve transparency by designating as transparent a particular color on the palette. Web browsers pay attention to that designation and show the underlying Web page background where that color occurs. Paint Shop Pro, however, shows the color itself — unless you tell it otherwise.

To tell Paint Shop Pro to show the transparency, choose Image⇨Palette⇨View Palette Transparency. Repeat this command to return to viewing the color.

If you want another color on the file's palette to be displayed as transparent, choose Image⇨ Palette⇨Set Palette Transparency. In the Set Palette Transparency dialog box that appears,

click the option Set the Transparency Value to Palette Entry and then click your chosen color in the image window. To turn off transparency, choose the No Transparency option. Click OK when you're done.

Be careful when you're choosing a color. It may be used in places where you're not expecting it — white, for example, may appear in someone's eyes, giving a spooky result when the whites of that person's eyes become transparent! Likewise, you may find that the area you want transparent is composed of more than one color, which leaves an unseemly halo of not-quite-your-selected color around everything else in the image. To fix it, you have to select the area and tell Paint Shop Pro to make it transparent; refer to Chapter 3 for an example of this halo problem and how to select it properly.

Remember that GIF files are palette-type files, so many Paint Shop Pro features don't work unless you convert the file to 16.7 million colors first. (Press Ctrl+Shift+0.)

To reduce colors, select the Colors tab of the GIF Optimizer. You have several options:

- **How many colors do you want?** The lower the number of colors, the quicker the file is downloaded. Take out too many colors and the image may start to look grainy or choppy. Experiment with this value, by setting it as low as you can until you find something acceptable in the preview window.

- **How much dithering do you want?** It sounds like if you set this option high, Paint Shop Pro would just waste your time, saying "Oh, I don't know — what do *you* want?" In reality, though, if you have removed a bunch of colors, this setting controls how much Paint Shop Pro attempts to simulate those removed colors by filling them in with the colors it *does* have. That helps to make a low-color image look smoother, but at high values it may add weird moiré patterns or make it look spotty. Again, experiment to find the right value for you.

✔ **What method of color selection do you want to use?** You need to be concerned with only two options:

- **Existing Palette:** Uses the colors in the original image, although they may not look right on other computers.

- **Standard/Web-safe:** Ensures that the image looks the same on all computers, although it may not look quite like what you originally created.

When you're done selecting all these options, you can select the Download Times tab to see a chart of how quickly your image is loaded at various speeds. People with modems are generally running at 56 Kbps; unless you know for a fact that the people who will view these images have something other than a modem, *assume that they use a modem.* (High-speed connections are increasingly common these days, but at least 40 percent of all Internet users are still stuck with dial-up.)

Using the GIF Wizard

Alternatively, you can choose to click the Use Wizard button at the bottom of the GIF Optimizer dialog box. The GIF wizard asks you five questions dealing with palettes, backgrounds, and quality, all of which we detail in the preceding section.

Creating JPEG files

JPEG files tend to be smaller than GIF files for many kinds of images, so they're downloaded faster. The main trade-off is that JPEG files are *lossy.* They lose some detail in your original image, and the clean lines of text can look fuzzy. You can choose how much detail to trade off for a reduction in file size, however.

The second trade-off is that JPEG files can introduce *artifacts:* blurs, spots, and rectangular blocks that weren't present in the original image. Again, however, you can choose how many artifacts you're willing to live with to get a smaller file.

To export to JPEG, follow these steps:

1. **Choose File⇨Export⇨JPEG Optimizer.**

   The JPEG Optimizer dialog box appears. It has three tabs. It also has before-and-after preview windows (left and right, respectively) that show the effect of your choices. To zoom in or out, click the magnifier icons. Click the magnifier with the + to zoom in or the one with the – to zoom out. To view different parts of your image, drag in a window.

2. Click the Quality tab to trade off file size for quality.

Adjust the Set Compression Value To value box to a value from 1 to 99. Higher values make the file smaller, but give it lower quality. You can see changes in the file size under the right preview window, in the line that says Compressed bytes. As you can see in Figure 15-2, you can save *lots* of time with comparatively little loss in image quality.

A menu offers Chroma Subsampling options. This deep juju tells Paint Shop Pro when to average the color information for any given block of pixels, and the best subsampling approach is a subject of debate among graphics professionals. To make things simple, we just say that you should go with the default value (unless you feel like experimenting).

A check box on the quality tag also asks you whether you want to save EXIF data into the JPEG. Whether you even *have* EXIF data depends on what camera the image was taken with, as we explain in Chapter 5. If you leave this box unchecked and save the image, the camera settings and artist information aren't saved with the new image.

To see estimates of how fast your file is downloaded, depending on the viewer's Internet connection speed, click the Download Times tab. A table there gives estimated download times for various connection speeds. Unless you have specific knowledge that the people who will view this image have anything faster than a modem, *always assume that they're running at 56 Kbps.*

Figure 15-2:
The original image of William's lovely wife, Gini, took 2 1/2 minutes to download at modem speed; after some compression, it can be seen in 3 seconds, and she remains as cute as ever!

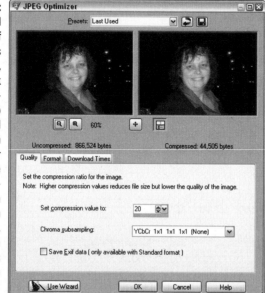

If you can't get your image to download fast enough, don't forget that resizing, as shown in Chapter 2, saves *lots* of time. Do people really need to see a poster-size picture of your baby?

3. **Click the Format tab to control how the image fades in.**

   JPEG files normally assemble themselves from top to bottom as they're downloaded to a Web browser. If you would rather have your image fade in from blurry to detailed, choose Progressive on this tab. Otherwise, leave the choice set to Standard.

4. **Click the OK button.**

   The familiar Save As dialog box appears.

5. **Choose a filename and folder for the file and click OK.**

Using the JPEG Wizard

Interestingly enough, the JPEG Wizard is available at the bottom of the JPEG Optimizer, but it involves clicking more times than the regular JPEG Optimizer. Our advice is to skip the wizard and just use the optimizer, which allows you to see your download time in one click, as opposed to three.

Doing Common Webbish Tricks

Unless you're Spider-Man, creating Web pages is a complex business. But Paint Shop Pro can make some aspects of Web design much easier! This section describes two tricks that Paint Shop Pro can help you with.

Creating buttons

Paint Shop Pro offers an effect that's great for creating graphical buttons for Web pages. The *buttonize* effect makes any image (or selected part of an image) look like a raised button by shading around the edges.

Choose Effects⇨3D Effects⇨Buttonize. The Buttonize adjustment dialog box that appears offers two styles of button. Click the Solid radio button for a button that has flat sides (and then choose your color in the palette box), or choose Transparent Edge for a button with rounded sides. The Buttonize dialog box also offers three adjustments:

✔ **Height and Width:** These controls adjust the vertical and horizontal dimensions, respectively, of the top surface of the button.

✔ **Opacity:** Increasing opacity makes the edges of the button darker and obscures the underlying image more.

The right preview window in the Buttonize dialog box shows the result of your choices.

Matching image colors to HTML colors

You may want to match colors used in your image to colors used in the text of your Web page — or vice versa. Text colors are often given in cryptic, geekish codes called *hexadecimal* in the HTML code used to write Web pages. They're written like this: #FFC0FA. These codes always begin with a # symbol, followed by six characters — digits or the letters *A* through *F.*

If you're creating a Web page and want to match the text color to a color in your image, the Materials box can help. (Press F6 to display it if it's not already visible.) Click the Dropper tool on the Tools toolbar and then click your chosen color on the image. The Foreground and Stroke Properties box inside the Materials box changes to match that color; click that box. Select the Color tab in the Material Properties dialog box that appears. Use the HTML code shown at the bottom of the dialog box in your Web page authoring software to set the color of your text.

If you're creating an image and want to match a color in your image to a text color, the solution is similar: Click the Material box to bring up the Materials palette. In the HTML code value box on the Color tab, enter the HTML code you obtained from your Web page authoring tool. Click OK and your chosen color swatch now matches the HTML document's text color.

Part V
The Part of Tens

The 5th Wave   By Rich Tennant

"That's a lovely photo of your sister.
Now take her head off the body of
that pit viper before she comes in
the room."

In this part . . .

Perplexed? Annoyed? Both? Hey, join the club. But we *Dummies* authors have long been channeling the spirit of David Letterman, and in that spirit we offer The Part of Tens: the ten top things that perplex and annoy us, and some solutions. Among them are ten things that we are annoyed about because they're too advanced to include in a *Dummies* book.

Chapter 16

Ten Perplexing Problems

*I*n real life, your paint brush doesn't suddenly start painting in plaid, your canvas doesn't double in size, and (unless you have kids) your tools don't suddenly become unavailable. In software, however, all the laws of nature are repealed and then reformulated by people whose idea of a good time is to *make* your brush paint in plaid: software engineers.

When the bright colors you see before you are the result of a migraine and not paint, this chapter is a good place to start. Take a deep breath, get a chocolate chip cookie, and repeat, "I am smart, software is stupid. I am smart, software is stupid." Then read on.

"The Tool or Command Doesn't Do Anything"

If a tool or command doesn't seem to do anything as you apply it to an image, the cause is probably related to selections or layers. Specifically, the problem may be one of the following:

✔ **You have in your image a selected area (called a *selection*) that you're unaware of.** Tools and commands are almost always constrained to working within a selection, if one exists. You're probably either not working on, or not looking at, that selection. If you don't really want to be working within a selection at the moment, simply press Ctrl+D to remove the selection.

One reason you may be unaware of this selection is that you have somehow hidden the selection *marquee,* the moving dashed line that indicates a selection's presence. Choose Selections and examine the square button next to Hide Marquee on the menu that appears. If the button has a black outline around it, the marquee is hidden. Click Hide Marquee to unhide it.

Another reason you may be unaware of the selection is that your image is larger than the window and the selected area isn't visible. Zoom out (right-click with the Zoom tool, the magnifying glass icon on the tool palette) until you can see the whole image, including the selection marquee.

✔ **You're mistakenly working on an image layer that's empty (transparent) in the area you're trying to work in.** Switch to the background layer and try the tool again. If that doesn't work, pause the mouse cursor over the names of the various layers to see tiny, thumbnail images of the contents of each layer. Click the layer that contains the content you're trying to modify. Refer to Chapter 11 for more help with layers.

✔ **You're painting in exactly the same color as the background you're painting on!** Change the foreground color or background color (refer to Chapter 9).

If you have been trying to use a menu command with no apparent effect, you may have been having an effect within your selection, without knowing it! When you find the area, check it. If it has been altered unintentionally, press Ctrl+Z repeatedly until the change goes away.

"Paint Shop Pro Keeps Asking Me Confusing Questions!"

Many tools have requirements that have to be met before you can use them; for example, you can't use any of the tools from the retouch tool group on an image that has fewer than 16 million colors, and the Text, Shape, and Pen tools all require the creation of a new vector layer.

Thankfully, Paint Shop Pro is smart enough to automatically take these actions whenever you use the appropriate tool; for example, try to dodge or burn on an image containing fewer than 16 million colors and Paint Shop Pro automatically increases the number of colors for you.

Sadly, Paint Shop Pro defaults to asking you for confirmation on all these minor changes — which is annoying because not only do these questions sound terrifyingly complex, but you also can't do what you want until you click OK anyway. It's sort of like asking "You can't leave the house until the door is open; is it okay if I open it for you?" If you want to go for a Sunday drive — or *any* drive — chances are that you're going to say yes.

You can stop all these confusing questions by choosing File➪Preferences➪ General Program Preferences and clicking the Auto Action tab. Then click the Always All button and click OK; Paint Shop Pro always takes these actions by default. (If it turns out that you really *don't* want to do whatever it was that Paint Shop Pro did automatically, pressing Ctrl+Z undoes your last action, complete with any changes that Paint Shop Pro made to accomplish it.)

While you're there, we may as well tell you how to disable the annoying *splash screen* that Paint Shop Pro displays when it's starting up; click the Miscellaneous tab and uncheck the box labeled Show Splash Screen When Application Starts.

"The Tool or Palette Just Isn't There!"

You can accidentally close or move one of the toolbars or palettes that holds the tool you need, thus stashing the Paint Brush tool where you can't get at it. If you don't see what you need, choose View➪Toolbars or View➪Palettes and look for a likely candidate that would contain the tool you're looking for. (The main offenders are generally one of these three: View➪Toolbars➪Tools, View➪Palettes➪Layers, or View➪Palettes➪Materials.)

If the toolbar or palette is open but has been dragged somewhere that it's not supposed to be, its icon on the menu has a thin gray box around it; choose it twice from the menu to "flash" it, by turning it off and then on so that you know where it is. If it doesn't have a box around it, you have accidentally closed it; select it to open it again.

"The Image Is the Wrong Size Inside or Outside Paint Shop Pro"

Paint Shop Pro displays an image in different sizes to fit the Paint Shop Pro window. The program doesn't change the size of the image — it just displays it with a different zoom factor. As a result, an image may look much smaller in Paint Shop Pro than it does in some other program. To see an image in its true size in Paint Shop Pro, press Ctrl+Alt+N.

If you need to change the true size of an image — which is the size it usually appears in other programs (in Web browsers, for example) — refer to Chapter 2. If you need to change its size as it's printed on paper, refer to Chapter 14.

"The Paint Doesn't Come Out Right"

Paint Shop Pro has a Stroke Properties box, which can make life complicated if you're not sure what's going on. The usual result is that you end up applying paint that isn't what you had in mind. The best solution is to get a good grip on the Stroke Property boxes' features, so turn to Chapter 9 to see how they're used. In addition, settings on the Tool Options palette can make paint come out in unwanted ways. Here are a few specific things to check:

- ✔ **If the paint is too light and kind of dappled, you may be applying a texture unintentionally.** To paint without a texture, see whether the Texture button (the one in the middle) directly underneath either of the Stroke Property boxes is indented. If one of them is, click them to reset them to No Texture.

- ✔ **If the color you're applying doesn't match the color in either of the Foreground or Background Stroke Property boxes, you're applying a *gradient* or *pattern,* not plain paint.** Click and drag down on the Style button (the one on the left) directly underneath the Stroke Property boxes, and drag it up to the solid circle to resume using plain paint.

✔ **If paint is too thin or too thick, adjust the opacity on the Tool Options palette; higher opacity makes a thicker paint.**

"New Text Appears Whenever I Try to Change Text"

The Text tool, in its normal *vector* mode of operation, lets you click existing text to change it. When you click, the Text dialog box is supposed to appear and display the current text so that you can edit it. You have to click right on the text character, not the space between characters — not even within a character's outline, if that character has no fill! Otherwise, you start creating new text. The cursor displays an *A* in brackets, like this, [A], when it's positioned correctly for editing text.

"The Text or Shape Comes Out the Wrong Color, Texture, or Pattern"

Although you may logically expect your text, drawings, and shapes to appear in the foreground color, sometimes they appear in the background color! Sometimes, too, the colors can be weak or mottled or otherwise weird. Here's what's going on.

Shapes, drawings, and text are made up of outlines in one color and are filled with another color. The Stroke Property box controls those colors. The outlines are done in the foreground color (or gradient or pattern) and in the foreground texture — although outlines can be very thin or even turned off. In that case, nearly all you can see is the fill color. The fill color is the background color (or gradient or pattern) and background texture (if any). If the background Stroke Property is turned off (you see a circle with a slash), you may see very little — just the outline.

If patterns, textures, or gradients are unintentionally turned on in the Foreground or Background Style swatches, the result can be strangely mottled or even nearly invisible.

To get plain text, choose a background stroke property and then click the Transparent button (the one on the right), directly underneath the Foreground Stroke Property box.

"The Magic Wand Tool Doesn't Select Well"

The Magic Wand tool, which selects an area based on color (or other pixel qualities), is sometimes not so magic. What looks like a perfectly uniform color to you — one that the wand should be able to select cleanly without gaps or overlaps into unwanted areas — is apparently not so uniform. You may find that when you increase the Tolerance setting, you close the gaps but get more unwanted areas. Here are a couple of things to try besides fiddling with the tolerance:

✔ Try different match modes on the Tool Options palette, by choosing RGB Value, Color, Hue, or Brightness from the menu.

✔ Don't fuss any more with the Magic Wand tool. Use it to do the basic selection job and then use other selection tools to add or subtract from the selected area. For example, switch to the Freehand tool, set it to Freehand on the Selection Type menu on the Tool Options palette, and with the Shift key depressed, drag a circle around any gaps in the selection. Likewise, hold down the Ctrl key and drag a circle around any unwanted areas.

✔ Choose Selections⇨Modify to fill in gaps, expand or contract your selection, or exclude specific colors. See Chapter 18 for details about advanced selection techniques.

"The Tool Works, but Not Like I Want"

The key to a tool's behavior is its Tool Options palette. For painting tools, it controls brush size, shape, edge fuzziness, paint thickness, how speckly the paint comes off, and how close together the individual dots are that make up a stroke. For other tools, it may also control how the tool chooses which pixels to operate on (by color, hue, or other attribute) and exactly what effect the tool has. Refer to Chapter 1 for details about the Tool Options palette, which you can enable or disable by pressing F4 on the keyboard.

Sometimes, though, the Tool Options palette hides some options from you because it doesn't have enough room; look for a small vertical row of single gray dots on the palette and hover your mouse over it. If the cursor turns into a double-headed arrow, Paint Shop Pro is hiding some options from you! Click and drag the arrow down to reveal all the options this tool has to offer. (Sometimes, Paint Shop Pro hides things with a small rightward arrow; if that's the case, just click it and *then* look for the vertical dotted row.)

"Paint Shop Pro Doesn't Open Images!"

Have you ever been in line at a grocery store when some rude person shoved his way in front of you and took your place? Some programs are equally rude, but rather than brusquely take your place in line, they take over responsibility for opening your JPEG, GIF, and PNG files without asking you.

You see, whenever you double-click a file to open it, Windows knows what kind of file it is and assigns one program to open that file type. Certain poorly designed programs assign *themselves* to be that program when you install them, which can be annoying. To put Paint Shop Pro back in charge, choose File⇨Preferences⇨File Format Associations, click Select All, and click OK. Paint Shop Pro is then your default image handler.

If you're using Windows XP, double-clicking an image may bring up the Windows Viewer instead, which gives you a preview of your image; press Ctrl+E to open it in Paint Shop Pro.

Chapter 17

Ten Fast Fixes for Photo Failures

Despite all attempts by camera makers to make photography foolproof, we all still make less-than-perfect pictures. Sometimes, we're the problem — we're too close or too far away or can't figure out how to use the camera's fool-proofing features. Sometimes, the problem is that reality stubbornly refuses to comply with our expectations: The sky is overcast, Great-Grandma can't be present for the family photo, or management has decided to cancel a product that appears in the product-line photograph.

Fortunately, Paint Shop Pro has a wide range of solutions, which range from quick-and-dirty fixes to professional-level retouching. In this chapter, we give the fastest possible solutions to the most common problems. For more in-depth looks, check out the chapters in Part II, which tell you everything a casual hobbyist needs to know about digital photography.

Rotating Right-Side Up

Photos that lie on their side are a pain in the neck. Don't put up with it! Take these simple steps:

1. **Press Ctrl+R — a fast way to pop up the Rotate dialog box.**

2. **In the Direction area of the dialog box, click either the Right (for clockwise rotation) or Left (for counterclockwise rotation) option boxes.**

   If you have added layers to your photo, click the All Layers check box. You probably haven't done so, however, or else your neck would already be stiff from turning your head sideways!

3. **Click OK or press the Enter key on your keyboard.**

Chances are, all your sideways photos need rotating in the same direction. Fortunately, the Rotate dialog box remembers which rotation you chose in Step 2; for future corrections, all you may need to do is press Ctrl+R and the Enter key!

Getting the Red Out

Suffering from a little too much red-eye? Photo flashes tend to make the normally black pupil of the eye glow red. Here's the fast fix for getting the red out. It works in nine out of ten cases — where only the pupil is red and the iris is unaffected; for tougher cases or more finicky retouching, refer to Chapter 7. Follow these steps:

1. **Choose Adjust⇨Photo Fix⇨Red-eye Removal.**

   The Red-eye Removal dialog box appears.

2. **In the right preview window, drag the image to center the eye.**

3. **Click the Zoom In icon (the magnifier with the + sign) repeatedly until the eye fills the preview windows.**

   Repeat Step 2 as needed to keep the eye centered.

4. **Set the Iris Size option to zero.**

   This setting should be zero unless the red covers any of the iris (the colored part of the eye). If the red does affect the iris, refer to Chapter 5 for help.

5. **In the left window, click the red area.**

   A circle appears in a square frame in the left window. The circle should be centered on the pupil and cover it to some degree. (If not, refer to Chapter 5.) In the right window, the red area is partly or entirely obliterated. (If that isn't true at first, drag the Refine slider a bit to the left.)

6. **Drag the Refine slider left until a bit of red reappears and then to the right just until that red is gone.**

7. **Click OK.**

Repeat these steps for the other eye.

Photos without Enough Flash

If things are looking a bit dim in a photograph, Paint Shop Pro can often brighten your outlook. Follow these steps for a too-dim photo:

1. **Choose Adjust⇨Photo Fix⇨Fill Flash.**

   The Fill Flash dialog box springs into action. The photo may already show sufficient improvement in the sample in the right window. If so, click OK and skip the rest of these steps.

   The preview window on the right shows the result of any changes in this and the following steps.

2. **Choose a Strength.**

   The Strength bar shows you how much virtual light will be shed on your darkened scene. Larger numbers equal more light.

   (Unfortunately, larger numbers also tend to wash out the rest of the image and make it pale; if you can't fix it with the Fill Flash alone, try reading Chapter 7 for more options.)

3. **Click OK.**

If the colors appear a bit too washed out after you're done, see the section "Making Colors Zippier," at the end of this chapter.

If this effect doesn't do the job, check out Chapter 7 for more help with brightness, contrast, and saturation. Nothing can restore image data that just isn't there, however. Things that are way dim will never look natural — unless you do some touch-up brushing.

If you can't see an image well in the right preview window of this dialog box, click the button with the eye icon to see the effect in the main image window. Click the button again whenever you want to see the result of your changes. Refer to Chapter 7 for more help with effect dialog boxes.

Photos with Too Much Flash

If you got a little too close in a flash photo, Paint Shop Pro may be able to help you back off a bit. Try this fast fix:

1. **Choose Adjust⇨Photo Fix⇨Backlighting.**

   The Backlighting Filter dialog box comes to your aid. The photo may already look better in the sample in the right window. If so, click OK and skip the rest of these steps.

2. **To make the picture darker, drag the Strength bar to the right.**

   Larger strength values dim the overall light values of the photo.

3. **Click OK.**

Photos with way too much flash are washed out, which may be harder to fix. If, for example, portions of someone's face are practically white, you need to restore skin tone without affecting the rest of the picture. A little work with the Smudge tool (refer to Chapter 8) can help you push skin color into small white areas. Alternatively, try carefully selecting the entire face area with a feathered edge and then using the Manual Color Correction effect, which we describe in Chapter 6, to change the white area to skin tone. (You may have to disable the Preserve Lightness check box in that effect.)

Revealing Dark Corners

If you need to cast light into the dark corners of your life, Paint Shop Pro can help. Of course, nothing can reveal totally dark details, and — as in life itself — details that are *very* dark are generally not too attractive anyway, when brought to light. But, given those limitations, here's something you can do to reveal dark corners or other dark areas of your photo.

This approach is the computer equivalent of an old darkroom trick known as dodging. *Dodging* requires a little eye-hand coordination because you, in effect, brush lightness and contrast onto just the dark portions of your photo. Follow these steps:

1. **Choose the Dodge tool (the white comet-looking icon) from the retouch tool group.**

2. **Locate or open the Tool Options palette.**

   Press F4 on your keyboard to toggle the palette on or off.

3. **Make these choices:**

   Size: To lighten broad areas, the best setting for this value is about 25 percent of the width or height of the image, whichever is larger. (Image dimensions appear on the status bar, in the lower-right corner of the Paint Shop Pro window.)

   Hardness: Set this option very low, or at zero, unless the dark area has well-defined edges and you have a steady hand.

   Opacity: A good typical setting is about 20. A higher number gives you a stronger effect per stroke. A lower number gives you a weaker effect.

   Step: A good typical setting is about 25. If you set it too high, you may see a dotty effect.

   Density: 100.

4. **Drag over the dark areas of the image to lighten those areas.**

   Keep the mouse button down and do a first pass over the area. Then release the mouse button and drag again over areas that need more lightening. Return to Step 3 and adjust any settings that you think may be necessary, especially Opacity (strength of effect) or Size. Press Ctrl+Z to undo your most recent pass at the image, if necessary.

As you brush the image, objects in the dark become brighter and the contrast against any black or very dark background is increased. The improvement can be dramatic!

Removing Unwanted Relatives

Removing unwanted relatives is much easier in Paint Shop Pro than in real life. You're not limited to relatives, though. You can use the same Paint Shop Pro tricks to remove other unwanted features, like power lines or passing automobiles.

Like removing unwanted relatives in real life, this task requires some skill. It also requires some sort of continuous or repeated background, like the clapboarded side of a building, a grassy field, a rail fence, some water, or some shrubbery. If the unwanted relative is blocking more than half of some unique feature (like a fireplace, chair, or china cabinet), the job gets nearly impossible.

The main tool for the job is the Clone Brush tool, which you use to extend the background over the unwanted feature. For example, you can brush out junk on a lawn by brushing lawn taken from just below or alongside the junk.

Refer to Chapter 8 for a full-fledged example (we removed a mat, but the principle is the same). Here's the general idea:

1. **Click the Clone Brush tool (the 2-headed icon) on the Tools toolbar.**

2. **Right-click the background that you want to brush over your object, in an area that has no unique features.**

   For example, if you're removing a pile of junk from your lawn, right-click the lawn, not the junk. Don't click too near the object you want to remove, either. Because backgrounds tend to have horizontal strips of stuff, like grass at the bottom, trees in the middle, and sky at the top, clicking to the left or right of the object you want to remove usually works best.

3. **Drag carefully across the object you want removed.**

   If, in Step 2, you right-clicked to the left or right of that object, move the cursor only horizontally before you drag. That precaution ensures that you extend the correct strip of background and don't paint grass, for example, where you want trees. As you brush, the Clone Brush tool picks up pixels from under an X that starts where you right-clicked and follows your motion. Keep an eye on the X to make sure that it doesn't pick up pixels you don't want. You may need to reset the X in a new location periodically; return to Step 2 to do so.

You probably need some trial and error to get a feel for the process. Press Ctrl+Z to undo any errors.

One problem with removing relatives and other objects is that if they were initially blocking a unique object, that object now has a hole in it. For example, the relative may well be blocking one arm of a person or half of a piano (if that relative is fairly wide). Fortunately, many objects are symmetrical; if Aunt Katy's left arm is now missing, you may be able to copy her right arm and paste it in place of the left one. (You can even mirror half a face to make a whole one in some instances. Your results may be unsatisfactory.)

Use any selection tool (the Freehand tool, for example) to select the object you need to copy (refer to Chapter 3). Press Ctrl+F to float the selection, press Ctrl+M to mirror it, drag it to the correct position, and then press Ctrl+Shift+F to defloat it. Press Ctrl+D to remove the selection marquee. You may need to do a little painting and retouching because any light striking the object is now coming from the wrong direction.

Adding Absent Relatives

If Great-Grandma just couldn't make the wedding, boost her spirits (or seriously confuse other missing relatives) by creating a picture that includes her with the happy couple. The same trick works for adding anyone or anything.

Have a new product to add to your product line? Just add it to the product family photo. Here are the basic steps, with references to other parts of the book that provide more detail:

1. **Open the original photo (the one *without* Great-Grandma) in a window.**

2. **Press Ctrl+B or choose File⇨Browse to open the image browser.**

   The browser window opens. Arrange the browser and image windows so that you can see both. (For example, choose Window⇨Tile Vertically.)

3. **Drag the thumbnail of the new image (Great-Grandma) from the browser to the main image window.**

   The new image becomes a new layer of the original photo. You can close the browser window now, if you like. (Click the X in its upper-right corner.)

4. **With the Eraser tool (refer to Chapter 9), erase everything except the part of the new image that you want (leave Great-Grandma).**

5. **Click the Deformation tool on the Tools toolbar (second from the top) and drag the new image (Great-Grandma) to the place where you want it.**

   Refer to Chapter 4 for help with the Deformation tool.

6. **If the image isn't the correct size or rotation, drag the handles (squares) that appear around the new image to make adjustments.**

   The image may need some repositioning; if so, drag it from any place *except* on one of the handles.

7. **Double-click the image, when you're done sizing and positioning, to apply the deformation.**

Repeat Step 4 to make any additional erasures that you discover are necessary at this point. For example, if Great-Grandma's head and shoulders are to appear behind the wedding couple, erase her from the shoulders down. You're done! Note that you now have an image with layers, so if you save it, Paint Shop Pro asks whether you want to merge layers. Reply Yes.

Zapping Zits

One noticeable difference between professionally done portraits and the ones you (and we) take is that the pros retouch their photos to get rid of unsightly blemishes. Throughout this book, we describe lots of tools that are useful for retouching and even devote one whole chapter (Chapter 8) to removing or adding elements to your photo.

To get rid of a simple blemish, however, is a matter of a few steps. Zoom in on the blemish and then try these steps:

1. **Choose the Smudge tool (the comet streaking to the upper left) from the retouch tool group on the Tools toolbar.**

   (Refer to Chapter 8 for more information about this tool.)

2. **Open the Tool Options palette, if it's not already open.**

   Press F4 to toggle the window on or off. Refer to Chapter 1 for more information about this palette.

3. **Set the brush size to roughly zit-size on the Tool Options palette.**

   See the discussions of setting tool options in Chapter 1 for help with other options.

4. **Click just to one side of the blemish, on clear skin of similar (but unblemished) color.**

5. **Drag across the blemish.**

   Dragging *along,* rather than *across,* any natural folds or wrinkles is usually a good idea. Also, don't drag from one area of unblemished skin color into a differently colored area.

6. **Repeat Steps 4 and 5 from the opposite direction.**

Making Gray Skies Blue

Don't let an overcast day rain on your parade. You can make the skies blue in a photo, and, even though a snapshot may never look completely natural, it will probably be more attractive. You can't make a gray day look too natural because if it were really taken on a sunny day, the sun would appear to shine on all the subjects in the photo, casting highlights and shadows. Paint Shop Pro has several tools you can use. The following steps, however, outline the simplest approach:

1. **Click the Magic Wand tool from the selection tool group on the Tools toolbar.**

2. **On the Tool Options palette, set the tolerance to about 20 or 30 for a typical gray sky.**

   Press F4 on the keyboard to toggle the Tool Options palette on or off. Refer to Chapters 1 and 4 for more information about this window and its options, like brush size.

3. **Click the overcast area of the image, to select it.**

   If the whole sky isn't selected, press Ctrl+D to clear the selection and then try again with a higher Tolerance value on the Tool Options palette. If more than sky is selected, try again with a lower value. Chapter 3 has more ways to help you select just sky.

4. **Press Shift+U to open the Red/Green/Blue dialog box.**

5. **Increase the number in the Blue value box.**

   As you adjust, keep an eye on the right preview window in the Red/Green/Blue dialog box, which is showing you the new sky color. Stop adjusting whenever you like the color, and click the OK button.

Making Colors Zippier

As we take a photo, we find that our mind's eye makes the colors livelier than they turn out to be in reality, and the photo looks a bit dull. Perhaps it's just that our antidepressant doses need adjusting, but if you have the same problem, try adjusting the saturation (of your image, that is). Take these steps and don't call us in the morning:

1. **Choose Adjust⇨Automatic Saturation Enhancement.**

   The Automatic Saturation Enhancement dialog box springs into action.

2. **Choose the More Colorful option on the left side of the box.**

3. **If the photo contains a significant amount of skin, click the Skintones Present check box.**

4. **Choose the Weak, Normal, or Strong option on the right side of the box, depending on which choice gives better results in the right preview window.**

   Click the button with the eye icon whenever you want to see the effect of your chosen options in the image window.

5. **Click OK.**

If that doesn't brighten up your day, check out Chapter 7 or see your friendly primary care physician.

Chapter 18

Ten Topics a Little Too Advanced for the Rest of This Book

Chris Rock, a famous comedian, has a routine that discusses creepy guys who hang around hip nightclubs. "They're not *old,*" he says. "Just a little too old for the club."

That's what the ten items in this chapter are: just a little too advanced for the rest of the book. Thankfully, none of them is difficult (or creepy) — and, after you have mastered the essentials of Paint Shop Pro, these ten techniques save you lots of time.

Saving Tool and Effect Settings As Presets

Paint Shop Pro has *lots* of options for each of its tools and effects, and setting them all by hand can be tedious. If you painstakingly set the opacity, shape, blend mode, stroke width, and thickness to get a watercolor-style effect from the Brush tool, you can save those settings as a single *preset.* Then, the next time you want to paint in watercolors, you can load all your carefully tweaked tool options with a single click. Then, you don't have to remember each of the controls' settings *and* set each of them individually.

You can find presets in one of two separate places, depending on whether the settings you need to save are in a tool, like the Magic Wand, or in a dialog box that pops up whenever you try to apply an effect or adjustment, like the Mosaic effect or the Automatic Color Balance:

 ✔ In Effects and Adjustments, the preset controls are along the top of the dialog box, as shown in Figure 18-1.

 ✔ For tools, the presets are in the upper-left corner of the Tool Options palette. Click the small arrow next to the tool's icon to display the drop-down Presets list.

Presets menu   Save Preset

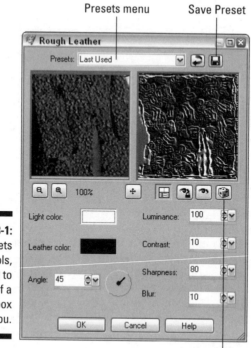

Figure 18-1:
The Presets
controls,
coming to
the top of a
dialog box
near you.

Reset to Default

To save a particular group of settings, set all the dials, slider bars, menus, colors, and other options to the settings you want to remember — and don't do anything else! When you have everything tweaked to perfection, press the Save Preset button (the one with the little floppy disk) and enter a memorable name for the effect. (If you want, you can also add your name, a copyright notice, and a description by clicking the Options button in the Save Presets dialog box.)

Then, the next time you want to call up a group of settings, just choose the appropriate preset from the drop-down list and Paint Shop Pro automatically enters all the numbers you saved. If you feel that you have made too many changes and want things back to the way they were originally, click the Reset to Default button, which sets the controls back to the way they were when you first installed Paint Shop Pro.

To delete a preset, click the Resource Manager button, as shown in Figure 18-1, which pops open the Resource Manager dialog box. Select your preset, click the Delete button, and then confirm the deletion.

The Materials palette has no presets, but you can save textured gradients and colors as *swatches,* which are similar to presets; refer to Chapter 10 for details.

Masking

You have probably used masking tape, or at least you admire those people who do. (They're so tidy!) Masking tape hides certain areas and lets others remain visible.

In Paint Shop Pro, *masking* also hides certain areas while letting others remain visible. A *mask* is a special type of layer that turns parts of an underlying layer transparent, thus allowing a third layer to show through. (Alas, the similarities between masking and masking tape end there.)

You can put any image you like on a mask layer. Where the image on the mask layer is darker, the pixels on the layer underneath it become more transparent and reveal the background (or perhaps another layer). Where the image on the mask layer is lighter, the pixels on the layer underneath are more visible. In fact, you can think of masking as applying a special transparency paint to a layer.

If you don't know what layers are, you have gone too far! Quick — go to Chapter 11 and get the knowledge you so desperately need!

But, what exactly can masking do for you that erasing, selecting, cutting, and pasting can't do? Here are a few instances where masking may work better for you than some alternatives:

- ✔ **Brush rather than cut and paste intricate shapes:** Rather than meticulously select the area of an image you want to combine with another and then cut it and paste it as a layer, do this: Paste the entire image or a roughly selected portion of it as a layer and mask out the portions you don't want. This approach lets you brush an area in or out, which is often easier than trying to carefully select the area.

- ✔ **Create shapes or letters out of an image:** If you put letters or shapes on a mask layer, the background image is blocked *except* for those letters or shapes. This process is much like using a pattern to create nice text (refer to Chapter 12 for details), except that the pattern is a real-life photo.

- ✔ **Gradually feather or fade an image into another image:** If you fill a selected area in an opaque layer with a gradient fill of transparency paint, you fade the overlaid image smoothly into the underlying image.

- ✔ **Brush or spray transparency in a creative way:** You can use any of the painting, drawing, or shape tools on a mask. For example, you can spray (using the Airbrush tool) creative transparent (or opaque) images.

The following section shows you two quick ways to use masks.

Loading a premade mask

Paint Shop Pro comes with several mask layers already built-in, which allows you to create cool effects. To use them effectively, you should have two layers: the primary layer you want up front and the bleed-through image on the background layer.

For this example, we use a simple set of layers, as shown in Figure 18-2: a layer with the text *Paint Shop Pro* and a background layer of a simple gradient.

Figure 18-2:
Two layers,
waiting for
a mask.

To add a pregenerated mask, follow these steps:

1. **Click the layer you want the mask to affect.**

   Remember that the mask blocks out certain parts of the layer underneath, so make sure that you add it to the right layer.

2. **Choose Layers⇨Load/Save Mask⇨Load Mask from Disk.**

   The Load Mask from Disk dialog box pops up, as shown in Figure 18-3, and provides you with several options:

   Mask: Click the down arrow in the Mask area and then choose a category from the drop-down list in the dialog box that appears. Three basic sorts of masks are stored within Paint Shop Pro:

   > **Edge Mask:** Designed to highlight the center of a picture. Think of this type of mask as sort of a fancy frame.

   > If you want a real frame — one that looks like wood — around your image, Paint Shop Pro has a tool to do just that. Check out Chapter 13!

   > **Texture Masks:** Overlay an image with some sort of repeating pattern, like a plaid or brick background.

   > **Masks:** A central image, like a sunburst or a set of boxes. This type of mask isn't terribly useful, but at least it's free.

   In any case, select your pregenerated mask by clicking it. It's that easy!

   Orientation: Here's where you decide how big you want your mask to be (and saved masks tend to be on the small side). You can choose to fit the mask so that it stretches across your selection (that's handy if you're just applying it to a bit of text), have it stretch across the entire canvas, or leave the mask's size as is.

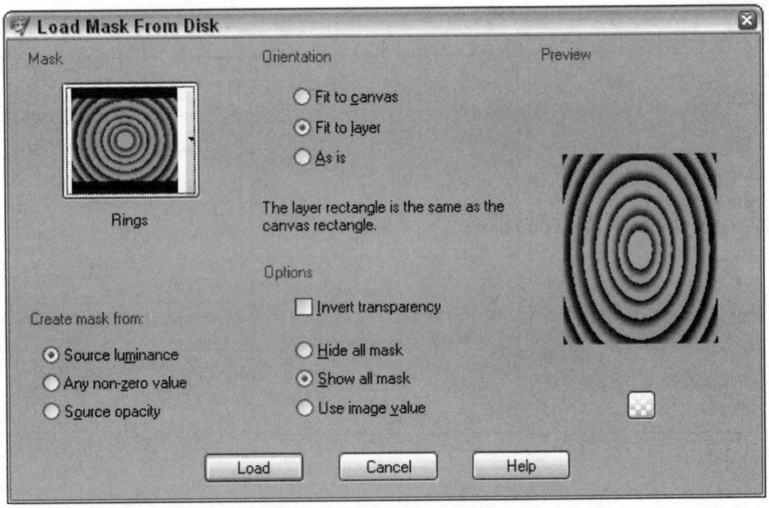

Figure 18-3:
This dialog box allows you to choose from several premade masks.

Create Mask From: This setting controls how the image on your mask blots out the layer underneath it.

Source Luminance: In this default setting, darker pixels produce more of a masking effect and lighter pixels let more of the underlying image show through. (The color of the image on the mask, incidentally, matters not one whit; only the light and dark values count.)

Any Non-Zero Value: There's no subtlety with this setting. Any pixel with a color, no matter how light that color is, blocks out the underlying layer. Only transparent or nonexistent pixels let the layer shine through.

Source Opacity: This setting uses the mask image's opacity, rather than its color, to control how much of the underlying layer gets through. *Opacity,* you may recall, is a fancy word for how dense an area is; areas of low opacity are near-transparent and show almost everything, whereas areas with 100 percent opacity (most pictures by default) block it all out.

Options: You're given a couple of options to work with, just in case you feel like getting kooky:

Invert Transparency: If you check this box, Paint Shop Pro reverses its normal habit of "Dark areas block, light areas show through" and instead switches to a "Light areas block, dark areas show through" mode.

Hide All Mask, Yadda Yadda: This area has advanced stuff, and you really don't need to know about it. (A quick explanation is that determines whether the surrounding pixels are white or black or whether they're taken from previous mask information. We told you that this setting isn't that useful.)

3. **When you have selected everything you need, click OK.**

The mask is now applied, as shown in Figure 18-4. It's a simple spiral mask, but you can see how the spiral mask we have applied to the words *Paint Shop Pro* has rendered parts of the words transparent, which allows the background gradient to show through in a spiral pattern.

Using an image as a mask

If the pregenerated masks don't sound terribly useful (and they're not), you can use any old image as a mask. You need three layers in order to create an effective mask, each containing a separate image:

✔ The image you want to have masked

✔ The background image that you want to show through the masked image

✔ The image you use *as* a mask

Figure 18-4:
The words *Paint Shop Pro* are overlaid with a spiral mask, which allows the background to show through.

That's a little complex — so to show you how it's done, we put text on a mask layer to cut words out of a background. Follow these steps:

1. **Select the image that you want to have masked.**

   This image is blocked out by the mask layer and has the background image show through it.

2. **If the image is on the background layer (as most photos are), choose Layers⇨Promote Background Layer to move it to a separate layer.**

   As we just said, you need three separate layers to create a mask. This step makes sure you don't accidentally swap the background image and the masked image.

3. **Open (or create) the background image, and then paste it into the canvas as a new layer.**

   Move the layer containing the background image so that it's *underneath* the layer containing the image that is masked. (If you don't know how to move layers around, or how to paste images in as layers, Chapter 11 explains it.)

   For this sample masking, we mask a picture of an Amish countryside (as shown in Figure 18-5). The background layer we use is plain white — but it could just as well be another photo, or a gradient, or anything else you can create in Paint Shop Pro. (It could even be transparent, for that matter.) The important thing is that whatever is on that background bleeds through the mask.

Figure 18-5:
A lovely shot of an Amish landscape, which we use as a background image.

4. **On a separate canvas, load (or create) an image to use as a mask.**

You can use any image you want as a mask — words, shapes, even another picture. Just remember that the dark areas on that canvas reveal the background layer when it's used as a mask and that the light areas reveal the masked layer.

In Figure 18-6, you can see the image we have created for our mask; note how it's mostly black, with a fuzzy spotlight effect in the center. That's because we want to block out most of the Amish countryside.

To invert a picture's colors with one click, by turning black into white and vice versa, choose Adjust⇔Color Balance⇔Negative Image.

Figure 18-6:
Our masking image.

5. **Switch back to the canvas that contains the two layers. Select the layer containing the image you want to have masked.**

6. **Choose Layers⇨New Mask Layer⇨From Image.**

    Paint Shop Pro then asks you which canvas you want to use to create your mask and lists all images you have open in Paint Shop Pro. Choose the canvas containing the image you want to use as a mask and click OK. The image is inserted as a new layer, and the image underneath it is masked, as shown in Figure 18-7.

If you don't like the way your mask looks, you can edit the mask directly on the layer. Select the mask layer, and then use the Eraser to remove parts of the mask so that the masked image shows through. Alternatively, you can use the Paint Brush tool to add more blocked-out parts to your mask.

Although your Paint Brush tool keeps whatever colors you have loaded, a mask cannot contain colors. All it has are shades of gray.

Figure 18-7: The Amish countryside, with the mask shown in Figure 18-6 applied.

Drawing Smooth Curves

We show you how to draw single lines and freehand lines over in Chapter 12 — but if you're anything like us, your mouse hand isn't *nearly* steady enough to draw a smooth curve. Fortunately, Paint Shop Pro offers another option for curve lovers: Bezier curves.

Bezier curves are like a high-tech connect-the-dots — you click to create a series of dots, called *nodes,* and Paint Shop Pro draws nice, neat curved lines between the nodes. You can use those nodes to adjust the angle of the curve that connects the two dots, and to change which way the curve turns.

This capability makes it very easy to create professional-looking curves, and they're easily edited, to boot. Is your pretty curlicue absolutely *perfect* except for one curve in the corner? Adjusting the one node that controls that corner section straightens out that segment and leaves the rest of your snaky line untouched!

To play connect-the-dots with Paint Shop Pro, choose the Pen tool on the Tools toolbar, choose your foreground (stroke) and background (fill) material, and then follow these steps:

1. **Select Draw mode on the Tool Options palette, as shown in Figure 18-8. (If you don't see the Tool Options palette, press F5.)**

Figure 18-8:
To create professional Bezier curves, you need the Tool Options palette.

2. **Also on the Tool Options palette, click the Draw Point to Point button, under the word *Mode*.**

   By default, Paint Shop Pro assumes that you want to draw a two-node line — a single curve between two points. If you want to create a multiple-node line, like a spiral or a curve with several bends, click the Connect Segments check box.

3. **Set the Width value, still within the Tool Options palette, to the desired width of your line (in pixels).**

4. **Set the Background and Fill Properties box (on the Materials palette) to transparent if you want just a line or outline, or select a material if you want it filled.**

   To make the line transparent, click the Transparent button on the right side on the Materials palette, just underneath the Background and Fill Properties box.

5. **Click and drag to set the node's properties.**

   Each click you make creates a node, although you still have to tell Paint Shop Pro how steep the curve's angle is and which way it's pointing. Click where you want to place the node — as you drag the mouse, you pull out an arrow by its tip. Here's how that arrow works for you:

- As you drag the arrow farther away from the node and make it longer, the angle of the curve gets sharper as it approaches the node. If you make the arrow shorter again, the curve becomes rounder as it approaches the node.

- As you drag the front end of the arrow around the dot, the curve follows the arrow's direction as best it can while still ending up at the node.

Figure 18-9 shows the effect of dragging the tip of the arrow: Even though the two dots don't move, the curve that connects the dots changes radically. On the left, a curved line is created and the arrow appears for the latest dot. On the right, the arrow's tip is being extended and dragged upward a bit. You can see how the curve broadens and changes its angle to follow the arrow's direction.

As you create this line, if you discover that you have placed a node in the wrong position, you can go back and edit it later. (In fact, we show you how to do that in the following section.) However, Paint Shop Pro doesn't show you all nodes as you're drawing the line — only the one you're working on. If you want to see *all* previous nodes as you drag the mouse, click the Show Nodes check box.

6. **If you want a shape (with a closed line), click the Close Selected Open Contours button when you're done.**

The Close Selected Open Contours feature finishes the Bezier curve by drawing a line between the first and last nodes, which makes it a closed shape. Your line now appears in all its colorful glory.

If you have selected Connect Segments and you don't choose Close Selected Open Contours, you need to tell Paint Shop Pro when you're done drawing this particular curve. Otherwise, when you click a new node into existence, it's added to the end of the preceding curve. To stop drawing when you're in Connect Segments mode, click the Start New Contour button.

Figure 18-9:
Making a curved line. Even though the two dots don't move, dragging the arrow radically changes the curve that connects the dots.

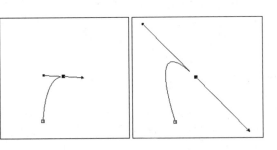

You're done! Hopefully, your curve looks perfect. If it's not, you need to edit your nodes. Read on to the next section!

Editing Bezier curve nodes

Paint Shop Pro users have an old saying: "You can pick your friends and you can pick your nodes, but you can't pick your friend's nodes." It's not true, of course, but that doesn't keep users from saying it. You can freely pick, or pick at, all your nodes — including your friend's nodes, if that person gives you a Paint Shop Pro file with vector lines or shapes in it.

If you want to alter a shape or a line after you have drawn it, you need to get down and dirty and start changing the nodes.

To start fiddling with nodes, you need to select the Pen tool and click the Edit button on the Tool Options palette.

To enter Node Edit mode, follow these steps:

1. **Select the Pen tool.**

2. **From the Tool Options palette, choose Edit Mode, as shown earlier, in Figure 18-8.**

After you're in Node Edit mode, you can manipulate your nodes all you want. Here are some changes you can make:

✔ To select a node for any action (like deleting, dragging, or changing its type), click it. You know that you can select it when a four-headed arrow appears under the cursor; you know that a node is selected when it's solid black.

✔ To move a node, drag it. You can move multiple nodes at one time as long as they're all selected.

✔ To delete a node, press Delete.

✔ To select several nodes, hold down the Shift key while clicking them.

✔ To select several nodes at one time, make sure that you're in Node Edit mode (this action doesn't work if you're in Drawing or Knife mode) and draw a square around the nodes you want to select.

✔ To select *all* nodes, right-click a node and choose Edit⇨Select All from the context menu that pops up.

✔ To join two line segments that are part of the same object (for example, if they were created by cutting a line in half with the Pen tool in Knife mode), select the two ends you want to join by Shift+clicking both of them and then right-click your image and choose Edit⇨Join.

Note that a line has *direction,* based on the order in which you create the line. The control arrow that appears on a node in Node Edit mode points in the line's direction. The word *Start* or *End* that appears when you pause your mouse cursor over the end nodes of a line also tells you the direction. A few things you do may be dependent on direction, such as aligning text to the line or shape.

Slicing shapes in half

The Pen tool is mightier than the Sword tool — or would be, if a Sword tool existed. Ironically, though, Knife mode is a part of the Pen tool, and it's mightier than the *rest* of the Pen tool because it slices in half the lines and shapes you have drawn.

Select Knife mode from the Tool Options palette and drag a line through your vector object. This action separates the object into two separate sets of nodes, cut cleanly where you drew through them with the Knife. Be warned that even if you separate an image in two with the Knife, both still count as one vector object.

Aligning Objects

After you have painstakingly added all the text, shapes, and Bezier curves to an image, quite often you must complete one more step: You want these elements to line up cleanly. The right edge of the text should match up with the end of your Bezier curve, or the elements all should be aligned to the bottom, as shown in Figure 18-10. Fortunately, you can easily align all the objects in your file.

Figure 18-10:
Both images and text are lined up neatly along the bottom in the right-hand box.

Unfortunately, one of the sillier things about Paint Shop Pro is that you have no way (or at least no *easy* way) to convert a layer or selection into an object. And, you can use this technique only to align objects. You can't align, for example, a pasted-in image with a text object in one click; if you need to do that, you have to do it by hand. Sorry!

Simply select all the objects you want lined up (refer to Chapter 12 for details on how to do that) and choose Objects⇨Align. You're presented with a dazzling array of options:

- ✔ **Top, Bottom, Left, Right:** Paint Shop Pro aligns all the selected objects along the margin you have chosen. For example, if you choose Right, the objects are all moved so that their right margins are placed on the same line.

- ✔ **Vertical Center, Horizontal Center:** These items are aligned along their vertical or horizontal axis.

- ✔ **Center in Canvas, Horizontal Center in Canvas, Vertical Center in Canvas:** These options move all selected items (even if it's just one item) so that it's in the appropriate place in the canvas.

Distributing Objects

When you have several objects on a page, you often want to space them in some manner — so that a row of hand-drawn Christmas lights is evenly spread across the page or items are arranged neatly by their center.

Simply select three or more objects (you can't distribute just two items!), and then choose Objects⇨Distribute. You're given a couple of choices:

- ✔ **Vertical Center:** The centers of the objects are spaced out evenly along a vertical axis, as shown in Figure 18-11. Notice that their uneven horizontal positions have been left untouched.

- ✔ **Horizontal Center:** The centers of the objects are spaced out evenly along a horizontal axis.

- ✔ **Vertical Bottom, Horizontal Bottom, Vertical Top, Horizontal Top:** Sometimes, when you have objects of differing sizes, spacing out items by their centers looks funny, as you can see in Figure 18-12. In that case, you can space your objects according to where their bottom or top margins are, which can make things easier.

- ✔ **Space Evenly Horizontal, Space Evenly Vertical:** This option spaces the selected objects evenly across the canvas height or width, depending on whether you choose Horizontal or Vertical.

Figure 18-11:
These circles are a little spaced out, but a little vertical centering neatens them right up. Notice that even though the circles have been distributed evenly along a vertical axis, their uneven horizontal positions have been left untouched.

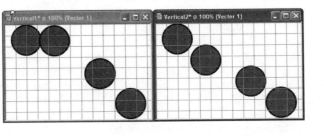

Figure 18-12:
The large circle and small circles here are all spaced out evenly by their centers, but they still look funny. Using Vertical Bottom as an alignment method makes them look a little more natural.

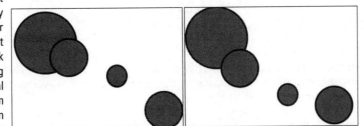

Using the Paint Shop Pro Grids

If you're the sort of person who *really* likes to have your ducks in a row, Paint Shop Pro can display a grid so that you know precisely where your objects are at all times. (As an unexpected bonus, it also makes your image look much like a game of Battleship.) The grid is handy for lining up items.

Furthermore, you can set the grid so that when you drag a selection, object, or layer to within a certain distance of a gridline, the item's edge "snaps" to the grid and moves the edge automatically so that it's aligned with one of the lines.

To see the grid, choose View⇨Grid. A fine tracery of gray lines now overlays your image; you can't draw over or erase the grid lines. If you want to have your selections snap to the grid, choose View⇨Snap to Grid.

To adjust the grid's properties, choose View⇨Change Grid, Guide and Snap Properties, which brings up the not-at-all-interestingly-named Grid, Guide & Snap Properties dialog box, as shown in Figure 18-13.

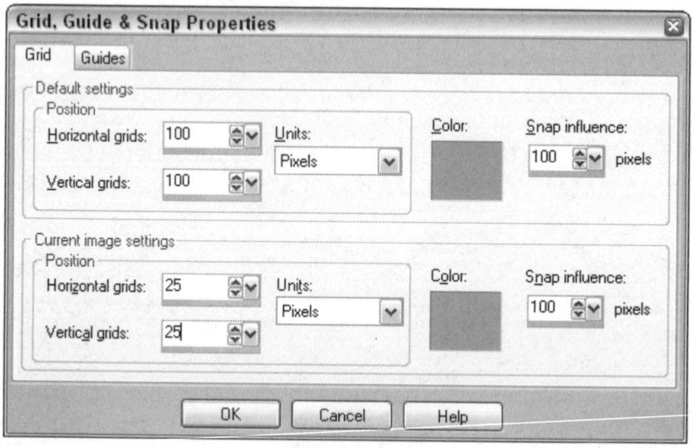

Figure 18-13: The Matrix has you, but the grid merely helps you set things into place.

From there, you can adjust both the default settings for all grids and the settings for the grid in this particular image. In either case, the controls are fairly intuitive as Paint Shop Pro goes:

✔ **Units:** In this area of the dialog box, you can decide which style of measurement Paint Shop Pro should use to set grid lines: pixels, centimeters, or inches.

✔ **Horizontal Grids:** This option controls how far apart your horizontal grid lines should be, as measured in whatever units you choose.

✔ **Vertical Grids:** This option controls how far apart your vertical grid lines should be. (Note that you can set the vertical and horizontal grid lines to different values, though we can't imagine why you would want to do so.)

✔ **Color:** By default, this option is set to a neutral gray, but you can choose a vibrant pink or muted yellow for your grid lines, if you like. Clicking this box brings up a dialog box much like the Color palette, which we explain thoroughly in Chapter 9.

✔ **Snap Influence:** This option controls how strong an influence your grid lines have when you turn on the Snap To option. By default, it's set to 100 pixels, which means that if a selected item's edge comes within 100 pixels of a grid line, the edge is automatically aligned with the line. You can reduce this number, which allows you to move your items about the grid without always having your items snap to an edge.

When you're done, click OK. To stop displaying your grid (which also temporarily disables any snap-to settings), choose View⇨Grid once more.

Advanced Selecting Techniques

Sometimes, you want to select lots of areas that are the same color, scattered throughout your image — for example, you want to select only the sky, as seen through the intersecting branches of a tree. You could Shift+click each spot manually with the Magic Wand tool and painstakingly add area after area. But, fortunately, Paint Shop Pro offers an automatic version of that same task.

First, use any selection tool to select one area. Then, choose Selections⇨Modify⇨Select Similar. Paint Shop Pro selects all pixels similar to the colors within your selection.

How similar? The Select Similar command looks to the Magic Wand tool's Tolerance control to determine how similar to the original color a selected pixel should be. A high tolerance means that a color can be significantly different and still be selected; a low tolerance selects only colors that are very close to those in your original selection.

A difference between the Magic Wand tool and the Select Similar command is that it asks whether you want to select an area contiguously. A *contiguous* Select Similar action adds only the areas that are right next to the current selection; *discontiguous* selections add parts from all over your image, regardless of where they are.

You can also add or remove selections based on how close they are to certain colors. For example, if you're trying to cut and paste The Artist Formerly

Known As Prince Who Is Back to Being Called Prince Again (and who is known for wearing purple outfits), you may want to expand your selection to only lavender areas. Choose Selections⇨Modify⇨Select Color Range, and choose a nice shade of magenta in the color box.

Sometimes, you don't really want *all* the pixels of similar color, just those within a certain region of the image. Fussy, fussy. For example, you may want all the blue sky, including the stuff that peeks through the tree branches, but not the blue pond. No problem. Just draw a freehand selection around the pond while pressing the Ctrl key to subtract that area.

Creating Interactive Web Pages from Graphics

Paint Shop Pro not only creates static Web images (images that just sit there), but can also create the interactive graphical portion of the Web page itself. For example, Paint Shop Pro can help you

- ✔ Slice a single image into a multi-image grid and create the Web page that assembles the pieces into a grid and makes each image a hot link.
- ✔ Create graphical *rollovers* — images that change as you pass your mouse cursor over them — and write the Web page code to make the rollover happen.

To accomplish its Webbish wonders, Paint Shop Pro writes HTML files (Web pages), not just image files. You can then use these HTML files on their own or copy their HTML code (including JavaScript code) into other Web pages.

You probably need to understand how Web pages, hot links, and rollovers work before trying to use Paint Shop Pro to make these features. Check out the Wiley Web site, at `www.wiley.com`, to find various books on Web pages and design.

Creating image slices

Professional Web designers rarely design in HTML; instead, they create an image of how they want their Web page to look, by using multiple layers and futzing with the page until it looks perfect. Then, when they're done, they *slice* that image into multiple images (known as *cells*) and assign a link to each cell. Paint Shop Pro creates the HTML code (a table) that's necessary to hold the images in a grid and also creates a series of new images from your original, single image.

You can use another technique, called *image mapping,* but it has two major disadvantages: The entire image has to be downloaded completely before the viewer can do anything (and haven't we *told* you about the importance of speedy downloads?), and you can't use rollovers effectively. We advise skipping this technique unless you have a pressing need.

To slice an image, follow these steps:

1. **Choose File⇨Export⇨Image Slicer, as shown in Figure 18-14.**

2. **Zoom and position your image in the Image Slicer so that you can see the whole area you intend to slice.**

   To zoom, click either of the magnifier icons below the image: + to zoom in or – to zoom out. To position *(pan)* your image, click and hold the mouse button on the Pan icon and drag in the preview window until you see what you want.

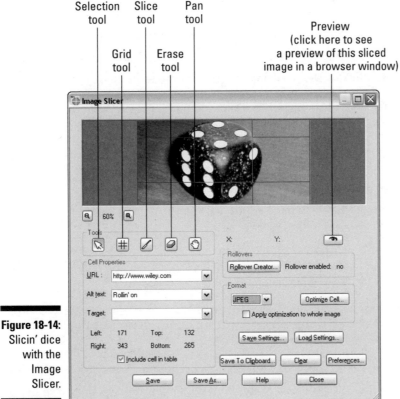

Figure 18-14: Slicin' dice with the Image Slicer.

3. **Click either the Slice tool or the Grid tool.**

The Grid tool divides your image by using a grid of evenly spaced lines. You can adjust the lines and their positions afterward. The Slice tool, although tricky to control, enables you to slice wherever you like.

4. **Slice your image.**

If you use the Grid tool, click anywhere on the image. In the Grid Size dialog box that appears, enter values for the number of rows and columns in your grid.

If you use the Slice tool, click where you want the center of your cut to be and drag either horizontally or vertically; the Slice tool creates a horizontal or vertical cut that expands in both directions from where you originally clicked. You don't need to drag entirely across the image; the line automatically extends to the image edge or to the next line it encounters.

Note that you can use both the Slice tool and the Grid tool to provide extremely fine control; for example, you can create a grid of boxes and then subdivide each of those boxes with the Slice tool.

5. **Use the Delete tool to remove any extra lines.**

Click the Delete tool in the Tools area and click lines you don't want.

6. **Use the Arrow tool to drag any lines that need moving.**

If your image has any solid white cells, you can improve the Web page's downloading speed by not placing an image in that cell. Using the Arrow tool, click the cell and then uncheck the Include Cell in Table check box. This trick also works for other solid-color areas, but you have to edit the resulting HTML file to set the background color to match the image color.

At this point, you're ready to enter the hyperlink (Web address) information that describes what Web page appears when the person viewing your page clicks a cell (see the following section).

Entering links

After you have created your hot spot areas or cells, the next step is to enter the Web address that you want each hot spot or cell to link to when someone clicks it on the Web. Follow these steps:

1. **Choose the Arrow tool (in the Tools area) and click a hot spot or cell.**

2. **Enter the URL (address of the Web page) you want to link to in the URL text box.**

If you intend for the page to appear in a named frame of the current page, enter the frame name in the Target area.

3. **Enter a text description of that new page in the Alt Text text box.**

4. **Select where you want the new page to open on the Target menu.**

   If you want the page to open in the same browser window, you can leave this area blank. Otherwise, you can force the user's browser to display the URL in a new and exciting way.

   The only target that's universally useful is _blank, which opens the URL in an entirely new browser window and leaves the original page untouched. The other three — _top, _self, and _parent, respectively — are useful only if you're using an HTML technique called *frames* to design your page (which is something that's generally considered bad form these days, so we just pretend that they don't exist).

5. **Repeat Steps 1 through 4 for all the cells you have created.**

You may also want to save the work you have done so far, which we describe how to do in the section "Saving and reloading your work," a little later in this chapter.

Optimizing cells

Unless you tell it to do otherwise, Paint Shop Pro saves all your cells as GIF files, which can create grainy images and horribly lengthy download times. A little compression can make all the difference; remember that the JPEG used in Chapter 15 took *four minutes* to download before it was squeezed down. Is your page so cool that you would watch a blank screen for five minutes before you saw it? (Studies have shown that people don't wait for more than 12 seconds.)

To optimize your images, follow these steps:

1. **Select the Arrow tool (in the Tools area) and click a hot spot or cell.**

2. **Choose whether your cell should be a GIF or JPEG image.**

   Refer to Table 15-1 in Chapter 15 for a comparison of formats. (You *can* use PNG, but not all browsers support it.)

3. **If you want to optimize the image — and you should — click the Optimize Cell button.**

   This step brings up the GIF Optimizer or the JPEG Optimizer, as discussed in Chapter 15; pay special attention to the Download Times tab. If you want all your cells to be optimized the same way, click the Apply Optimization to Whole Image check box.

4. **Repeat Steps 1 through 3 for all cells you have created.**

Saving and reloading your work

You may want to go back and change your hot spots, cells, or links later, or perhaps use similar settings on a slightly different image. For those reasons, save your work as a file. (Note that this file isn't the Web page file or an image file; to create those, see the following section.)

Click the Save Settings button. The Save Slice Settings dialog box that appears works just like any other file-saving dialog box. Enter a name and choose a folder for your file, and then click Save.

If you want to use or edit your settings later, open the Image Slicer tool as before and click the Load Settings button. Open your file in the Load Slice Settings dialog box that appears. The hot spots or cells you defined earlier are now set up for the current image.

Saving the result as a Web page

For all this slicing and dicing to be of any use, you need to transform it into a Web file. The Paint Shop Pro Webtools feature produces the two kinds of files you need for your Web page: one or more image files (in GIF, JPEG, or PNG format) and a single HTML file. You create as many image files as you have cells. The Web page (HTML) file that's created incorporates those image files and provides the links, hot spots, and other programming that makes it all work.

Before you produce the final files, you can test your Web page by viewing it in your Web browser. In the Image Slicer, click the Preview button. Your Web browser is launched and displays the result. You can test all the hot spots or other features you have created.

To create your Web files, click the Save or Save As button. If you haven't created any Web files since you launched the Image Slicer, the Save As dialog box appears. As with the Save As dialog box in any program, you enter a filename and choose a folder. The name and folder you choose is the name and location of the HTML, or Web page file, you're creating. (The Save As dialog box doesn't appear if your Web page file already has a name and folder.)

Paint Shop Pro creates a series of cell images in the same folder as the HTML file; although each cell file's name begins with the name of the original image file, Paint Shop Pro appends additional characters to distinguish the cell.

Making rollovers

Rollovers are images (typically, buttons) that change appearance whenever you position your mouse over them or whenever you do various other mouse or keyboard actions. For example, a button may get darker. Rollovers are popular Web page features because they provide immediate feedback to the user's cursor motion.

The basic *mouseover* rollover, which we describe here, simply changes as the mouse passes over it. It requires two images: the original image (a button, for example) and the one that substitutes for the original when a mouse cursor passes over it (a darkened version of the button, for example).

To create a rollover, follow these steps:

1. **Prepare the pair of images for each rollover.**

   For each rollover, you need the image that first appears on the Web page and the image that takes the first image's place. If you like using sliced images, first use the Image Slicer to slice a large image into separate cell images and save your settings. Close the Image Slicer, load into Paint Shop Pro all the cell images created by the slicer, and modify them in some way; for example, you can make them darker. Save each one with a modified filename so that the original cell images remain unchanged.

2. **Open the original image in Paint Shop Pro, if it isn't already open.**

   For example, open the large image you originally sliced in Step 1.

3. **Launch the Image Slicer and load your earlier settings.**

   Load the settings you saved in Step 1 to restore the slicing.

4. **With the Arrow tool, click in the Image Slicer the cell you want to program with a rollover.**

5. **Click the Rollover Creator button.**

   The Rollover Creator dialog box appears.

6. **Click the Mouse Over check box.**

7. **Click the file folder icon on the same line as the Mouse Over check box.**

   The Select Rollover dialog box appears.

8. **Choose the image file that you want to appear when the mouse passes over and click Open.**

   For example, this file is the darkened version of the original file.

9. **Click OK in the Select Rollover dialog box.**

10. **Repeat Steps 4 through 9 for each cell or hot spot.**

Proceed to save your settings and create your Web files as we describe in earlier sections in this chapter.

Advanced Undoing and Redoing

Have you made a mistake? Paint Shop Pro has a classic fix: Choose Edit⇨ Undo. Or, press Ctrl+Z or click the Undo button. Each time, you back up a step and undo the preceding action. If you accidentally undo too far, you can redo the step with Edit⇨Redo. (Or, because Paint Shop Pro never gives you just one way to do something when several will do, you can also press Ctrl+Alt+Z or click the Redo button on the toolbar.)

What if you make lots of mistakes? Or, what if you realize that you made one mistake a while back, but have done several things correctly since then? If you undo all the way back to the point where you made your mistakes, you also undo the valid changes you have made since your mistake.

Fortunately, Paint Shop Pro 9 adds a command history to allow you to see more precisely what commands you're undoing and redoing. Choose View⇨ Palettes⇨History (or press F3) and the History palette appears. It provides enough command of history to finally understand the Peloponnesian War.

Okay, so nobody really understands (or even correctly spells) the Peloponnesian War, but you *can* undo and redo your Paint Shop Pro commands with more insight now. Most (but not all) commands are undoable. Only undoable commands are normally shown on the History palette. To see even the ones you *can't* undo, click the Show Non-Undoable Commands button, second from last at the top of the History palette.

Previous commands are marked with an eyeball to indicate that their effect is currently visible. Click any eyeball to undo a step; it gets crossed out. Click that same eyeball to redo that step. In this way, you can undo a single mistake without annihilating everything you have added since your mistake.

To prepare to undo several steps, Ctrl+click on multiple steps you want to undo. Click the Undo Selected button at the top of the History palette and your highlighted steps are undone.

To undo everything back to a specific step, click on that step. Then click the Undo to Here button at the top of the palette.

Undone steps are now marked with a crossed-out eyeball to indicate that their effect is no longer visible. The History palette Redo buttons (Redo Selected and Redo to Here) are the complements to the Undo buttons. Select the step or steps you want redone and click the Redo Selected button. Or, click one of the X'd-out steps and click Redo to Here. If you're permanently done with undone commands, you "clear" them from History. Click the Clear Selectively Undone Commands button, third from the right at the top of the History palette.

Using Scripts to Automate Repetitive Tasks

William works as a webmaster for an online shop. Three times a year, new products get released and he has to scan in and upload 350 pictures. Of course, the scanned images all have to be the same size, and they all have to have their colors adjusted so that they're clear and vibrant images, and they have to have a black border around their edges.

Doing that by hand 350 times would drive William stark-raving bonkers. Fortunately, Paint Shop Pro 8 debuted a fantastic new scripting feature, which allowed William to save that repetitive series of commands as a single *script.* Now, whenever William scans in an image, he clicks one button — and the script adjusts the image's colors, resizes it, and adds a black border in one go.

The Paint Shop Pro scripting features record a series of commands and then replay those commands as you entered them, which saves you valuable time. If you have ever used macros in Word or Excel, you should be familiar with this concept.

Recording a script

Here's how you record an item:

1. **If you don't see the Script toolbar, as shown in Figure 18-15, choose View➪Toolbars➪Script.**

2. **Click the Start Script Recording button.**

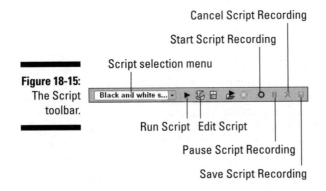

Figure 18-15: The Script toolbar.

3. **Perform the sequence of actions you want recorded, just as you would normally do in Paint Shop Pro.**

   Keep in mind that the settings for the tools you use are saved within the script; for example, if you paint a circle with a 50 percent opacity and 25-pixel brush, that script is always drawn with a 50 percent opacity and 25-pixel brush, regardless of what the Brush tool may be set to.

4. **If you need to pause recording in the middle to do something that you don't want replayed later, click the Pause Script Recording button.**

   Click it again to continue the recording where you left off.

5. **When you're done, click the Save Script Recording button and enter a name, and then click OK. Or, if you have done something wrong and you don't want to save it, click the Cancel Script Recording button.**

You have three options when you're saving:

✔ **Click the Save Materials check box.** This option ensures that the script draws with the material (the color, gradient, or pattern) that was used when you recorded the script, thus ensuring that a red line is always a red line; unchecking this option causes this script to draw with whatever materials are selected when you run it.

✔ **Click the Save Dialog Positions check box.** Choosing this option is a strange business. Normally, Paint Shop Pro doesn't pay attention to where you click — it pays attention to *what you did*. Put another way, if you record an application of the Topography Artistic effect (as shown in Chapter 13), the script isn't paying attention to where you moved the mouse or when you clicked OK — it's paying attention to the settings that were used when the topographical effect was applied.

This capability is A Good Thing. For one thing, it allows Paint Shop Pro to zip through the scripts; it doesn't have to wait two seconds to move the mouse to the OK button, like you did.

If, however, you had a script that needed to place a click at some position in a certain dialog box, you could check this box and ensure those dialog boxes are in the same places. Realistically, though, you can probably ignore this part.

✔ **Click the Remove Undone Commands check box.** We hope that you did everything perfectly when you recorded your script. If you made a mistake, though, all is not lost! You can undo during a script recording. If the Remove Undone Commands option is checked, those commands aren't carried out in the final script. (Why you would want to uncheck it is a complete mystery, but, hey — that's a question that only Jasc can answer.)

You can also, if you're so inclined, select the Description box and enter the author, copyright, and description of your script. This is handy if you expect to pass it on.

> Scripts are saved by default in the My Documents/My PSP Files/
> Restricted-Scripts folder. You can send them to other users, who
> can put them in their folders and run them as though they had been
> recorded on their own PCs.

Running a script

Running Paint Shop Pro scripts is *much* simpler than recording them. Follow
these steps:

1. **Click the arrow on the drop-down list on the Script toolbar, as shown
   in Figure 18-16.**

   By default, you're shown the scripts stored in the Scripts-Restricted category, but you can click other script folders, like Artistic and Photo, to
   see what other exciting scripts Paint Shop Pro has given you for free.

   Note that some scripts are already there. Paint Shop Pro comes bundled
   with several scripts to automate common tasks, like creating thumbnails, and also gives you some artistic transformation scripts that can
   turn a photograph into, for example, a watercolor painting. Feel free to
   experiment.

2. **Click the Run Selected Script button.**

   Certain advanced scripts may have dialog boxes that ask for user input,
   but most just zip through and go about their business in no time.

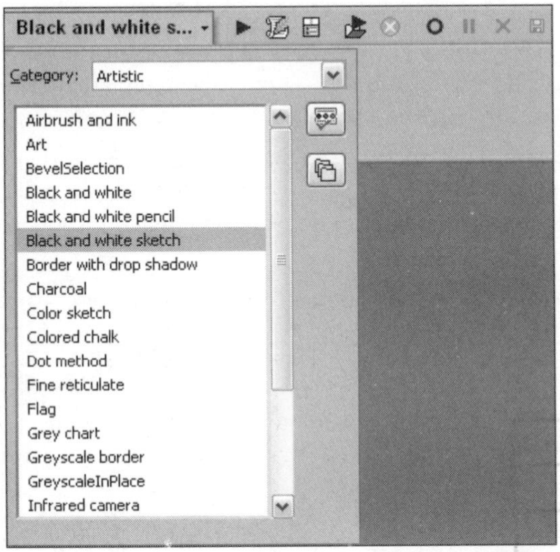

Figure 18-16:
Running
a script
couldn't
be easier;
choose a
script and
click it!

Index